Angel
Watch

G 11/20/01

Angel Watch

Goosebumps, Signs, Dreams and Divine Nudges

Catherine Lanigan

Health Communications, Inc.
Deerfield Beach, Florida

www.bci-online.com

Library of Congress Cataloging-in-Publication Data

Lanigan, Catherine.
    Angel watch : goosebumps, signs, dreams, and divine nudges / Catherine
Lanigan.
        p.   cm.
    Includes bibliographical references.
    ISBN 1-55874-819-9 (tradepaper)
    1. Angels—Miscellanea. I. Title.

BL477.L36 2001
291.2'15—dc21   2001016703

Publisher: Health Communications, Inc.
            3201 S.W. 15th Street
            Deerfield Beach, FL 33442-8190

Cover design by Larissa Hise Henoch
Inside book design by Lawna Patterson Oldfield

This book is dedicated to
my father, Frank J. Lanigan,
who passed through to
The Other Side on Valentine's Day,
1992; on this side of the veil,
to my mother, Dorothy Lanigan.
All the love in my heart
forever.

Contents

Section Two: Dreams

Section Three: Signs

Section Four: Spiritual Visitations

Acknowledgments

*T*hanks to all the angels, human and divine, who have created the wondrous path I tread. In addition to my loving mother, Dorothy Lanigan, my sister, Nancy Porter, my brothers, Robert Lanigan and Ed Lanigan, my son, Ryan Pieszchala, daughter-in-law, Christy Pieszchala, and my best half, Jim Alexander, I send bouquets of appreciation and blessings to: Fortune Alexander, Terry Anzur, Dottie Barrett, Wendy Birkenshaw, Jodee Blanco, Vicki Bushman, Charlotte Breeze, Kimberley Cameron, Jerry Courville, Georgia Durante, Doug Dearth, Deborah Giaratanna, Harvey Gordon, Cherry Hickson, Sabina Khan, Sammi Kirkpatrick, Mary Lanigan, Deborah Hayes Lanigan, Rikki Mayer, Ron Misik, Michelle Mostart, Dr. Evelyn Pagilini, Geneva Pampuro, Lissy Peace, David Porter, Brian Powell, Sharon Reese, Stacy Stoker, and Ed Zabrek.

I would also like to thank the bevy of angels at HCI who have given me the courage to expose my wings: Peter Vegso, Kim Weiss, Matthew Diener, Christine Belleris, Allison

Janse, Randee Feldman, Kimberley Denney, Kelly Maragni, Terry Burke and Tom Sand.

A special blessing to fellow authors and literary trail blazers, Dr. Michael Adamse and David Shapiro.

The gratitude in my heart is not near enough thanks for all that you have endured with and from me over the days of my lifetime. I am honored to have each and every one of you in my past, present and future. God bless you all.

Introduction

Watching for angels is not easy. First of all, most of us don't know what to look for. Too many of us are under the impression that we must be lower than dirt, down and out, at death's door or about to cash it all in before an angel will show up.

The reality is that angels are around us all the time, performing dozens of tiny miracles on a daily basis—the majority of which we take all the credit for.

Think about it. You are in a terrific quandary over how to prepare your monthly report. You're tired, you skipped supper to work. You should be returning a least a dozen calls. The boss has been on your case for weeks. Things aren't going well at all. In fact, if you were honest with yourself, you know this is more than just the regulation monthly report. This report could mean the difference between having a job next month or not.

It's midnight. You're still staring at a blank sheet of paper or a blinking computer cursor. Frustrated and frightened, you give up. You get up from the desk to make a peanut butter sandwich and pour a glass of milk. Before the glass is full, the most brilliant idea of your life simply pops into your head out of nowhere. It repeats itself as if speaking to you. Because your mother told you that if you ever "heard voices" it was a sign you were schizophrenic, you dismiss the voice.

But the idea is sound. It's a new way to attack your entire operational procedure at work. You realize that the faults at work causing you problems are not yours. The system itself, the company's method of handling problems, is antiquated.

You dash to the computer and type out four pages of new procedures. Ideas are coming faster than your fingers can move on the keyboard. Finished, you sit back and are astonished that two hours have passed. Yet you are filled with energy and renewed spirit. Goosebumps squiggle down your back and blanket your arms as you read what you wrote. You can't believe these ideas came from you.

Well, they didn't. They came through you.

This example and others, like the stories in this book, are what I mean by "angel watch." Though there are true accounts of people being visited by winged angels, light beings and thundering voices, the majority of us will go through our lives and never witness such a vision. This does not mean, however, that we have been abandoned or are not blessed with divine intervention.

In this book, we will explore the many methods angels use to contact us. Dreams are one. Signs are another, especially liked for their humor and irony. Goosebumps are validations that we are on the right track—or we need to get on the track now! Actual angelic interventions are rare, but do occur, though often in times of extreme danger or pending death.

Spiritual visitations are the loving spirits of our ancestors, family or friends who come to visit in various manners and methods. Lastly, divine nudges can be the strokes of genius we receive, like the example at the beginning of this introduction. Or the nudge can be so cataclysmic that everything you've known to be your life alters overnight, like winning the lottery or losing your life's savings in a stock market crash. I also call these occurrences "hand of God." If your life has gone from one end to the other in less than a year, you can bet you were picked up by angel's arms off the path you were limping on and moved to a new path.

The worst thing you can do after a "hand of God" trial is to chastise yourself, thinking you did something wrong. What is actually happening is change. You know how human beings despise change. We all wish things would just continue on as they are. We want lives devoid of illness, death, divorce, loss of friends, transfers, financial loss and career change. The fact of the matter is that we are here to learn. And learn we must.

To make the lesson easier, we keep angel watch. If we trust that our angels know more than we do and are wiser than we, and if we pay attention, we just might get through this thing called life with far more ease and greater joy.

Hundreds of millions of miracles happen on this earth every day. Some of those common everyday dilemmas may have disguised pending doom. But an angel or guide stepped in. They were responsible for us misplacing our car keys and leaving thirty minutes late for work. However, due to the timing of our departure, we missed a four-car pileup on the freeway. What about the airplane flight you missed? Though you cursed all during the next flight out, had you taken the booked flight you would have still been sitting on the runway due to mechanical failures—or worse, crashed. Instead of going directly home to your empty apartment, you decide to stop into a restaurant you've heard about. You bump into a friend who invites you to dinner with their friends. You meet the love of your life. Or perhaps, you make a business connection you've prayed for.

Accidents? No way. Angelic intervention is to blame. Our loving guides do all this, I might add, without much thanks from us.

We are too busy running helter-skelter from home to work to kids' soccer games, to parent-teacher meetings, to a movie, to the grocery store or to see our friends. We are too busy surviving to realize the magic of our inter-angelic connection.

The purpose of *Angel Watch* is to lift the blinders from our eyes and reveal the divine ballet performed between humans and angels. From the instant we are born, to the moments of our crossing from the earth plane to the other side, we are not alone. There are no accidents with God.

Skeptics are those who would deny our uniqueness. Experience has taught me that most times you run up against a bona fide, jaded skeptic, you can bet you're staring at someone who is scared senseless of life. They figure if they make you as frightened as they are, as insecure as they are, then they won't be alone. These are the folks who don't need convincing as much as a good stiff angel lesson. Sooner or later, they'll get theirs, because God is wondrous like that. In the meantime, don't let them steal your soul from you. Don't let them create fear in you when your angels and guides are struggling so hard to be heard by you in the first place. The only thing that disconnects us from our protective angelic armor is fear.

When we fear, love cannot abide. And love is what this whole human experience is about. In *Angel Watch,* you will read stories of near-death experiences. The bottom-line word from the top on the subject of life, straight from the mouths of angels, is that life is love. It's the only lesson we are here to learn.

Once you figure that much out, you've got half of this human struggle licked. It's the rest of the experience we need help with.

For better than thirty years, I have read and reread books on angelic visitations, visions of holy saints, near-death experiences, astral travel and "Psi" abilities (our innate hard-wirings in our brains that enable us to "remote view," interact telepathically and envision future events). Psi qualities are more prevalent today because human beings are evolving to a new awareness of ourselves, our position in this great universe and our purpose in life. I have interviewed and exchanged experiences with other authors, researchers, doctors, theologians and scientists.

Just as I was finishing the last of my stories for this book, a copy of *New Age Magazine,* May/June 2000, arrived.

In the article, "Where Science and Spirituality Meet," it states that psychiatrist Elisabeth Targ, M.D., director of the Complementary Research Institute at California Pacific Medical Center, spent time as a child at the Stanford Research Institute where her father, physicist Russell Targ, conducted top-secret research—now declassified—for the United States Department of Defense in which he studied for almost twenty years the ability of people to "remote view."

The article goes on to explain the impact of our consciousness on our physical reality. Dr. Marilyn Schlitz and researcher William Braud, Ph.D., of the Mind Science Foundation, used a biofeedback-type design to conduct fifteen studies of one person's ability to affect someone in another room using their thoughts to try to calm or excite.

Their conclusion was that the subjects' arousal levels were subtly influenced. "There was a three percent shift from at random. The probability that this shift was caused by chance: 1.4 million to one."

Therefore, one person's intentions, or in my words, our prayers, can affect another person or country. We can pray for people to recover from health issues, we can pray for our loved ones to be delivered from harm, we can pray that our planet be delivered from a nuclear war—and it will work.

Each time we put out love into our universe, it will grow and heal our neighbors, our country and our planet.

According to this same article in *New Age Magazine*, in 1979, Robert Jahn, Ph.D., founded the Princeton Engineering Anomalies Research Laboratory to study psychokinesis, the ability of the mind to influence electronic equipment.

He and lab manager Brenda Dunne, a developmental psychologist, have conducted more than 50 million experimental trials. "The ability to intentionally influence the electronic equipment transcends both time and space," they noted.

Their most surprising finding was that among those who exhibited psychokinetic abilities, the subjects stated they had formed a "bond" with the machine; had a feeling of "falling in love" or having "fun" with it.

Writing in *Alternative Therapies,* Jahn concluded that "even by the most rigorous scientific experimentation and analytical logic, it appears that we have come upon nothing less than the driving force of life and of the physical universe: Love, with a capital L."

For many of us, mired in our physical realities of being day-to-day drones for our bosses or slaves to our mortgages and grocery bills, we need to read that science is finally underscoring and validating what many of us have long ago learned in our churches and synagogues. God is love. We *should* forgive our enemies and wish them well. We *should* do unto others as we would have them do unto us. To hurt another is to hurt ourselves. The world is all connected: one heart, one mind, one soul. The veil between the seen world and unseen world is disintegrating. The time has come for us to be at one with the celestial and angelic beings in the worlds that run parallel to ours.

At-one-ness, atonement, forgiveness allow us to be all that we can be as humans; the caretakers of the earth. And to be human beings, we *should* be caring with loving hearts toward our oceans, forests, rivers, earth, fish, fowl and animals. To hold dominion over the beasts and fowl does not give us license to abuse or torment.

"Do not judge, lest ye be judged." And that goes for any living entity.

The layers of the unexplained in this universe are unfathomable. The chances that we will ever know a fragment of what is truth, what is real, are slight. There is no doubt in my mind that we are on the precipice of a spiritual awakening around the world. Like the gathering of summer fireflies, insights and revelations, visitations and apparitions have sparked, then illuminated the shadows of our fears, easing this new era's birth.

The more we talk about our spiritual experiences with each other, the greater will be our awakening. This is our challenge. For our adult generations, we are the midwives to a new Age of Enlightenment. This is our legacy to our children and grandchildren. This is our destiny's path.

The stories contained within these pages are only ones that actually occurred to me, my family or my closest friends. Some of you may feel they are just too strange or bizarre to be believed. The incidents happened exactly as portrayed here. Your interpretation of the event might vary from mine, but the facts of the occurrence are precise.

But for the reader who is looking for answers and keeps an open mind, perhaps by bringing your own perspective to them, you might strike the flint of your mind against the stone of your soul and spark the illumination that has served in millennia past to elevate mankind to its highest awareness. Only you can be the participant. Only you can be the judge of your own realities.

Understand that in no sense do I consider myself an expert. I doubt any of us are. No answers to the great mysteries have yet been explained by science or religion. We are all still wandering. And wondering.

What I am is a chronicler. I am the journalist for these experiences, and that is all. My mission has been both humbling and a great honor for me to accept. Within these pages there may very well be stories that encourage and inspire, just as there will be situations that will unsettle you. They will make you think. Maybe you will even change your mind about your world.

Every day, I find my perspective of life being tweaked and prodded to expand my faith more than I'd ever thought possible. Some days, those simple beliefs of my childhood settle more solidly in the concrete of the foundations my parents laid. Every day, I realize how blessed I am to have been placed in my parents' loving hands and in this great, caring country of ours.

The greatest human adventure is that of self-discovery. Through examination of our lives, we not only learn about ourselves, but where we are going. Once we take the responsibility for the fact that our future belongs not to us, but to the next generation, our desires become focused to the world around us. We take our imaginations out of the vault where we've locked them up so they don't interfere with our career pursuits and daily living. We broaden our thinking. We think with our hearts. We finally learn the one thing we learned when we were children: Though seeing is believing, believing is seeing.

Goosebumps

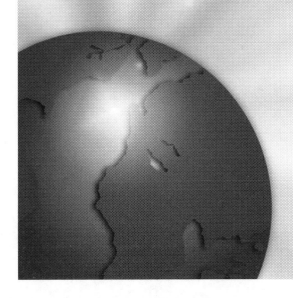

*T*hese are not the kind of goosebumps you get from watching horror movies or from telling ghost stories around a campfire. These are the confirmations of incidents in your life that seem bizarre, that defy deductive, scientific reasoning. When you are in trouble and you've just uttered the words, "God help me," and the fire truck appears. When, lost and alone, you've wondered if there was anyone who cared for you at all, and you literally bump into someone at Starbucks and your life is changed forever. These are the times you get goosebumps.

Goosebumps are, after all, the knowledge that the divine is at hand. I once heard that the Gypsies said goosebumps were angels' breath across your skin. Or maybe the saying was "angels breathing down your neck." For good or ill, to let us know we're safe or to advise us of wrong choices, goosebumps help to move us back onto our divine path. They are instrumental, but only insofar as we pay attention.

Life is meant to be understood. Life is not mysterious. There are explanations for everything that happens in our lives. The problem with divine interventions is that the angels aren't punching a clock. They have no time reference. Sometimes it's hours or days or years before we finally "get it." One of the reasons for our being so slow on the uptake is that we don't explain our actions and efforts in spiritual terms. How easily we pass off the divine as "coincidence" or "mistakes" or "unexplained."

There is always an explanation, if we are willing to look deeply enough for the answer. It takes courage to want to know the future. It takes courage to accept our own pasts. It takes faith to believe that we are all worthy of divine love.

I hope that by sharing these stories with you, enlightenment will fill your eyes and heart. And the next time you feel the hairs on the back of your neck rising to attention, stop and ask yourself if what you're doing is part of your divine path. If someone relates a story to you and goosebumps spring up across your forearms, that is confirmation of the truth. Use those goosebumps, along with your gut feelings, hunches and twinges at your heartstrings, to know when to trust and who to trust. When you've said your prayers and the heavens did not open up and lay the answer out in script for you to read, remember to listen with your inner ear to the words of your loved ones around you. Listen to the suddenly familiar song on the radio whose title might be the answer to your prayer.

You're being contacted every day and every night. But are you watching? Trust that your guardian angels are guiding you, every step of the way.

Grandma Manning's Faith Healer

Crestview, Florida, 1949

My brother Ed was born on January 23, 1949. My parents were thrilled to have a son. Though he looked like a healthy baby, Ed was sick. An inexplicable fever dogged him. He screamed in pain night and day. His belly was so swollen and distended it looked like a tent over his body. Worst of all, his stools were golf-ball sized, white as ash and often bloody. It was a horrible test of wills for my mother caring for him. She rocked him day and night, never complaining about his screaming, though never able to quiet him either. My mother became emaciated living on no sleep and continual fear. Impending death shrouded our home and little family.

My father drove my mother and Ed from one doctor to another looking for a cure, looking for the test result that would calm their fears. The barrage of tests was endless and when they all proved inconclusive, he took Ed to South Bend Children's Clinic, still in search of answers.

The doctor was beating around the bush. Finally, my father could take no more. He stood up and said, "Don't tell me this boy is going to die. I've had five doctors tell me that, and if you say that I'm going to knock you right out of this five-story window! He's not going to die! He's going to live and grow up. And he's going to be great!"

The doctor hung his head. "I don't know what to tell you. All I can do is wish you luck."

My father took my mother and baby Ed and stormed out of the pediatrician's office.

My mother was exhausted and beyond hope.

When my parents got home my mother checked the mail and found a letter from my grandmother.

"What does she say?" my father asked.

"I had asked her to come to Indiana to help me out with Cathy while I take care of Ed. But unfortunately, she doesn't think she would be much help." Mother read on, her eyes getting wider. "Frank, she says she has a housekeeper who is a faith healer and that she truly believes in Mrs. McLaughlin's gift." My mother dropped the letter in her lap and looked expectantly at my father. "Do you think she could really help us?"

"Do I?" My father took my mother's hand. "Let's pack."

My father drove us all from La Porte, Indiana, to Crestview, Florida, in less than twenty-four hours, driving straight through. Because the doctor had prescribed sedatives for Ed, the baby slept. So did my mother and I. We knew we were safe in my father's determined hands.

The following day after our arrival, my mother and Mrs. McLaughlin were in the yard hanging the wash on the clothesline.

From the second Ed woke up, his screams were blood-curdling.

"My God!" Mrs. McLaughlin said, looking at my mother. "Dorothy, what's wrong with your baby?"

Tears filled my mother's eyes. "The doctors tell us he's going to die."

The woman shook her head vehemently. "That baby's not goin' to die."

Mrs. McLaughlin immediately went into the house, took Ed out of his crib and put him on the bed. His belly was so distended he looked as if he'd pop. He was scalding crimson and burning up.

The woman laid her hands on Eddie's belly and began praying. "Lord, deliver the devil out of this child. Lord, Lord, deliver this child."

She began chanting. Squeezing her eyes shut, she knelt on the floor next to the bed, never taking her hands off the baby's belly. She prayed aloud and as she did, she shook her head. Hairpins flew out of her gray hair until it came tumbling down past her waist, but she didn't seem to notice. She just kept praying and chanting. "Lord, Lord, deliver this child."

My mother didn't know what to think. She'd prayed so much herself, she couldn't imagine this woman's prayers being any different or stronger than her own. Still my mother prayed along. As did my grandmother. My father knelt in the doorway, crying and praying.

"Lord, Lord, deliver this child," we all prayed.

Miracles are such tiny things when they are occurring. Sometimes people don't see them at all. Sometimes they deny they ever happened in the first place. It makes them more comfortable to tell themselves that some things just can't be explained.

But no one has to explain to me that while Mrs. McLaughlin prayed over my baby brother, his distended belly went down, inch upon inch, until it was flat as a pancake. His fever broke. The heat dissipated. The trickles of perspiration on his body evaporated. His screams were silenced. He was calm. He was healed.

No one has to tell me there is any other explanation than the one that is. "The Lord has today delivered unto us a child."

Sometimes it is in retrospect that we realize all miracles are large, indeed.

Today, my brother Ed is the Associate Professor and Chief of Plastic and Reconstructive Surgery and Hand Surgery at Michigan State University. He is making miracles for other people every day.

Dorothy's First Encounter with ESP

AUTHOR'S NOTE: *The next three stories, "Dorothy's First Encounter with ESP," "Dorothy's Premonition" and "Dorothy's Gift" were written by my wonderful mother, Dorothy Lanigan.*

 was raised in Crestview, Florida, a small town of 5,000 people in the panhandle of Florida, fifty miles east of Pensacola.

In the early 1930s when I was a teenager, my mother and I were sitting on the front porch on a hot summer day, snapping green beans for dinner. My mother reached down into the colander for another bean and without warning jumped up from her wicker rocker and screamed, "What happened to Jack?"

Dumbfounded, I froze. Her face was fear-filled. Her hands shook so much, she dropped the bean to the porch floor. "Mother, are you all right? You look like you've seen a ghost."

Her hands flew to her cheeks. Her eyes were round as moon globes. "What's happened to Jack?"

Jack was my brother, younger by fifteen months. He and I were as close as twins. My mother's terror was not registering with me. But from the panic in her voice and actions, I knew something was wrong.

"Mother, please. Calm down. I'm sure Jack is fine."

"He's not, I tell you! Something has happened. I can feel it in my bones. In my blood."

"Jack has always been able to take care of himself, Mother," I said, but I didn't feel the words in my heart. I'd heard my father talk about my mother's ESP, as he called it. Extrasensory perception.

Mother had a "way" of knowing things that the rest of us didn't. Some of my mother's friends always sensed things about their children. That kind of thing was expected of mothers. But the actions my mother was displaying were clearly beyond the realm of a simple sensation.

Mother was beside herself. She was as white as a sheet, as she raced inside the house and grabbed the telephone. She called a neighbor lady to try to locate Jack. But no one had seen him.

About twenty minutes later, a male voice shouted from the backyard. "Mr. Manning! Mr. Manning!"

Mother ran through the house like the wind, with me right behind her. At the back gate stood a young man, several years older than Jack.

"What happened to Jack?" Mother demanded, still fighting hysteria.

"Please ma'am. I need to talk to Mr. Manning! Where is he?"

Mother crossed the yard to the young man, grabbed him by the shoulders and kept demanding, "What's happened to Jack?"

"We . . . we were swimming down at the river. Jack dove off the bridge and hit his head on a big rock. He's at the hospital."

"My God! I knew it!" Mother screamed.

I ran into the house and grabbed the car keys. Mother and I drove to the hospital and after inquiries and what seemed like endless, frightening moments finding the right room, we finally found Jack. His head was heavily bandaged.

Mother's eyes flew to the physician. "What's happened to Jack?"

"He had a very long gash in his skull," the doctor said, putting up his instruments. "I've already sutured it. Bring him back in a week and we'll take out the stitches."

Mother finally looked at Jack, as if seeing him for the first time. "Jack," she said with a sigh of relief.

Curiously, I watched her. For the first time, I realized that Mother was now herself. It was as if until that very second, she'd been in a trance. The adrenaline in her body must have been surging. I felt as if she'd tear the hospital apart brick by brick until she found Jack and made certain he was safe.

I could remember thinking to myself, what an awesome and incredible mind power we humans had been given. Of all the things I inherited from her, I hoped I would be given this gift.

The older I got, the more I became aware I'd been given a double dose.

Dorothy's Gift

I was not aware that I had received my mother's "gift" until I was about twenty-four years old. I guess I was just not listening.

I had gone through my college years at Florida State College for Women in Tallahassee, which later became Florida State after World War II. Then I went for my internship in hospital dietetics at the University of Georgia School of Medicine at Augusta. After that came three years of working at Pinebluff Sanitarium in North Carolina, where I met my future husband, Frank Lanigan.

Frank had been sent from Fort George Mead, Maryland, as a Cadre Officer to set up a new base for the 11th Airborne Division. Some of the officers' wives, with whom I played bridge, wanted me to meet him.

About six months after meeting Frank, I received a call from Chandler Hospital in Savannah, Georgia, which needed a dietician. Rumors were that the 11th would be shipping out soon, so I took the job in Savannah.

All these years since I had left home for college were very

busy with work and a great deal of fun. So I really wasn't listening to all those little "signs," small and large coincidences that show us our angels are around us, guiding us and leading us to where we are meant to be in life.

Savannah was different in every way from my former, nearly carefree life. I had a tremendous amount of responsibility in a much larger hospital. I was not going out much at all with my friends anymore, especially since I was new to the city. To be honest, my mind and heart were concentrating on Frank. All I thought about and prayed about was his coming home safely.

I started studying to be a Catholic at Our Lady of Victory Church. I had known since my freshman year in college that I wanted to be a Catholic, but my parents were extremely opposed to my leaving the Presbyterian Church.

I worked long hours and went home to my room to write letters to Frank, telling him about my day, my work and my hope that he was safe and well. Oh, I was occasionally asked to join friends and coworkers for dinner, a movie or game of cards, but always I would go home afterward and write to Frank.

One night as I was writing, I became aware that Frank was in great danger. The room around me seemed to move in on me. I had a suppressed feeling. My adrenaline rushed. It was as if I were living his terror with him. I could tell our minds were connected. His fears rushed over me.

I turned on all the lights. But I kept writing.

Tears came to my eyes, my breath felt hot in my lungs and I remember expelling heavy sighs as if to ward off the danger. Then I was freezing with chills—not the kind from the cold, but the kind that you feel when you say things like, "I felt as if someone just walked over my grave."

I double-checked the locks on my door and windows. It was a calm night outside, beautiful in fact. No, the fear was inside me. And my mind and heart were with Frank.

I knew then I could not fight this thing, whatever it was, alone. I needed God's help.

For hours on end, I would write for awhile and then I would read from the Bible. I read silently. I read aloud. I put some of the words down on paper. I cried. I prayed. I read some more.

This went on all night long. At dawn, I finally breathed freely. It was as if my body sensed the end of the danger before my mind did.

I looked down at the letter and realized I had written twenty-seven pages!

I quickly mailed the letter the first thing in the morning on my way to work. I didn't dare tell anyone about my horrid experience. I went to church and prayed that Frank was all right. I can remember thinking that I didn't think he was dead. Somehow I felt that if he were dead, I would know it. My soul would know it.

The next few weeks were an eternity for me, not hearing from Frank. In my life before Frank, before the torture of war, I didn't know time could move so slowly.

Finally, the blessed letter from Frank arrived. In the letter he told me that on that very night I'd written the twenty-seven pages, he had been in mortal danger. The Japanese had landed on the American airstrip in Leyte. Frank had no place to hide from them. He dug a foxhole and laid in it, then covered himself with brush, dirt and leaves.

The Japanese combed the area, bayoneting the ground inch by inch, looking for men like Frank who had buried themselves, since there was no place to run to or hide. Three times, the deadly bayonet came down in Frank's foxhole. One grazed his cheek, but he held his breath and kept silent. One lanced his shoulder; still he no more than winced. The third actually struck his shoulder.

Frank prepared himself mentally for death. But all the while he prayed. He prayed while I was praying.

"I knew then," he said, "that God was holding my right hand and you were holding the other."

Dorothy's Premonition

When Germany surrendered in 1945, I knew that the war in Japan would end soon.

My parents had told me they would disinherit me if I married a Catholic. My father went so far as to threaten to tear up his will should I do so.

I told him that was the greatest insult he could hand me, for him to think that any amount of money could make me decide to give up the man I wanted to marry, or the religion I had chosen, of my own free accord.

So, believing that I would never see my family again once Frank and I were married, I decided I owed them a visit a few months before the wedding. I resigned my job at Savannah and went home.

In June 1945, I wrote to Frank and told him that I "knew" he would be landing in the states in Seattle, Washington, on November 20.

In his return letter, he wrote that my "prediction" would be impossible. He'd been told he would ship back into San Francisco. Further, he said it would be nearly a year before he got back, certainly not before the Christmas holidays.

On the night of November 20, I told my parents I would stay up all night until the phone rang, which I was still convinced it would. Clearly, they thought I was nuts.

Sure enough, at three in the morning the phone rang. Frank sounded wonderful. "I can't believe I'm really here!" he said.

"But I told you that you'd come into Seattle on this night."

"I know, but . . ."

"You didn't believe me." I frowned, looking at my bedroom door. "But that's okay, nobody here believes me when I say these kinds of things, either."

"Well, no more. That's it, Dot. I'll never doubt your intuitions or predictions again."

"Is that a promise?" I asked.

"You bet," he said.

"Well, I may be good at predicting things, but what I don't know is why," I said.

"This whole thing has been an incredible twist of fate," Frank said. "I was still stationed on the northwest coast of Japan, still believing the reports that we were ordered to stay put for many months until the entire division would be sent home. However, the American Division was leaving for the States and their financial officer had gone AWOL. They needed a replacement. I took his place."

"But you aren't a financial officer."

"I know, but for some reason they thought I was. So, what would you call that?"

"A mystery, Frank."

"I have to agree. So, anyway, our ship sailed into Seattle on

November 19, but they wouldn't allow us to dock that day because there was some big parade being held for General Wainwright and his division."

I was shaking my head at this point. "This is bizarre even for me to believe. It's as if everything was being manipulated just to make my prediction come true!"

"Don't I know it! That's why I said I'll never doubt your intuitions again."

The next morning, around ten o'clock, a florist delivered twenty-two yellow roses.

Once we were on our honeymoon I asked Frank, "Why did you have the florist deliver twenty-two roses and not a dozen and a half or two dozen?"

"Oh, is that how many you got? I just emptied my pockets on the counter and told the man to deliver whatever that amount of money would buy."

For the rest of our lives together, twenty-two roses was our hallmark. When Frank died, I had twenty-two roses put on his casket.

Many years later, on the day of my father's funeral, the family attorney came to the house to read the will. Frank and I took the children into the backyard to wait until he left.

My brother Jack came out and asked, "What are you all doing out here?"

I looked at him. "I'm not included in there."

"Do you mean that all these years you've believed that Dad left you out of his will?"

"Of course. He told me he had torn up the will."

"But, Dot. He wrote a new one after he got to know Frank. He always talked about the happy visits he and mother had when they went to see you and the children. He came to love and have a deep respect for Frank and your marriage. Please, come inside, Dot. You were always part of this family first."

With tears in my eyes, I walked with Jack and Frank and the children back into my family's home.

I Want to Hold Your Hand

Mother was at home when she got a call from my brother Bob that he wasn't feeling well. Mother's instincts went on full alert. Bob had been diagnosed with Crohn's disease when he was a teenager, so anything, even a sneeze from him brought the whole family running. She asked him what he thought as to the severity of his illness.

"I think I need to go to the hospital. I don't feel good at all. In fact, it's getting worse."

"You check in and I'm on my way!" Mother said.

My father was in Indianapolis at a fair board meeting. He was staying at the Claypool Hotel, or so Mother thought. But when she called the hotel, she was told there was no Frank Lanigan registered.

Just as she'd hung up the phone, it rang again. It was Bob's doctor. "Dot, I thought I should tell you that Bob's condition is critical. His colon has burst."

Panic riddled Mother. Cradling the receiver with an icy, trembling hand, she asked, "Can you save his colon?"

"Dot, I pray I save your son."

Nearly paralyzed with fear, Mother dialed my sister Nancy's number. Nancy and her husband were in Indianapolis at the time. "Nan," Mother said between tears, "I'm leaving it to you to find your father. He's there somewhere in Indianapolis at the fair board meeting. I've called nearly all the hotels and he's not registered. I don't know what to do."

"Don't worry, Mom, I'll find him. I just know I will." Nancy breathed a silent prayer. "You just get to Chicago and be with Bob before the surgery."

Nan slammed down the phone and took off in her car. Intuition told her to start at the Claypool Hotel. As she sped up to the front of the hotel, there was Daddy standing on the corner with his friends, heading out for lunch.

Rolling down the window, she hailed my father. "Daddy! Come with me! It's Bob!"

My father's face turned ashen. Without a thought to his belongings or his schedule, he jumped into the car. "Go!" he said, urging her to step on the gas.

They raced out of town with no mind to their speed. Traffic was unusually light that day, cutting their time in half.

Nan looked at Daddy. "They told Mother you weren't registered at the Claypool."

"I was registered under John Davies' name, the other attorney with me. We're sharing a suite. Still, I haven't been in the suite all day," he said. "Nancy, how bad is it?"

"They said his colon burst. He has to have surgery."

This was the worst news. Bob had undergone many surgeries, each one cutting away his colon, bit by bit. However, he had avoided a full colostomy. Every one of us knew the next surgery was the one we'd all feared for him. Bob would no longer have a colon.

Mother got to Northwestern University Hospital in just over an hour. She called me from the hospital once she arrived. I started calling my friends and my pastor to get a prayer line going. She called the pastor at St. Peter's Church in La Porte, who called more friends. The prayer line that day shooting to the heavens must have looked like lasers into outer space.

Racing down the hall toward Bob's room, Mother ran into Dr. Block. "How is he?" she asked tentatively.

"Dot, we have to hurry."

"I understand. Can I see him?"

"Yes. He's been prepped. We're waiting for an operating room to come available."

Mother rushed to see Bob. She clutched his hand. "Oh, Bob," she began, but tears blocked her voice.

"Mom, before I go . . . there's this girl I met. Debbie. Remember I told you about her?"

"Yes. I remember. But what . . . ?"

"Mom, I think she's the one. Here's her number. Call her. Tell her what's happened. Ask her to come."

Mother took the scrap of paper on which he'd scribbled Debbie Hayes' number. "I'll do it. But just you concentrate on getting well, getting through this."

They took Bob into surgery. By the time Nancy and Daddy arrived, the surgery was underway.

During those grueling hours, my family prayed. From coast to coast friends prayed with us.

When Dr. Block approached my parents in the waiting room, he had the best of all news. "We saved him."

"And his colon?" my father asked.

Dr. Block shook his head. "We couldn't save it. It had ruptured the worst I've ever seen. Frankly, it's a miracle he survived long enough to get to surgery, much less make it through that. Still, the worst is not over yet. The next twenty-four hours are critical."

"We understand," Mother said. "When can we see him?"

"He's in recovery. The nurse will take you down."

A few moments later, Mother, Daddy and Nancy were allowed into the recovery room to see Bob, who was still semiconscious.

Shortly thereafter, Debbie arrived to see Bob. She held his hand as Dr. Block came walking in. Debbie looked at the doctor.

"He said you had to take his colon."

"Yes, we did."

Debbie looked down at Bob, who smiled wanly at her. Mother said she knew then. Debbie looked at Bob as if he were her knight in shining armor.

"Doctor," Debbie said, "I just have one question. Bob told me that he had always wanted to climb a mountain. Can he still climb a mountain?"

"Wearing the bag, you mean?"

"Yes," Debbie replied.

"Yes, he can still climb a mountain."

Debbie's smile started in her heart. "Then he'll be just fine."

"That's my girl," Bob said.

"Yes, I am," Debbie agreed. She kissed Bob and left.

Mother, Daddy and Nancy said goodbye to Debbie as a male nurse came in with a hypodermic syringe. Nancy looked up just as the man was about to slip the needle into Bob's IV.

"What's that?" she happened to ask.

"Penicillin," he replied, lifting his hand to the IV tube.

"What?" she screamed, "you'll kill him!

Mother and Daddy bolted to attention. "What's going on?"

"What are you talking about?" the nurse asked.

"Look at his chart!" Nancy pointed to the chart hanging on the end of the bed. "It says in big fat letters 'Do Not Administer Penicillin'!"

"She's right!" Mother blurted. "It's lethal to Bob!"

"How could you make such a mistake?" Daddy asked.

The nurse cowered. "The doctor ordered it."

"The hell he did!" my father blasted. "Go check."

"Thank God you were here, Nan." Mother hugged her.

"Yes, thank God," Nancy replied, her heart hammering adrenaline through her veins.

That nurse never returned, though a bevy of concerned nurses and Doctor Block came running.

"I'll stay with him," Nancy volunteered.

"Good," Dr. Block replied, "because your parents need rest."

"There's no hotel space," Mother said. "I've been calling everywhere to find something. There must be a convention or something in town."

"Don't worry. I'll get you a room at my club. Come with me."

Dr. Block took care of Mother and Daddy, arranging for a hot supper to be sent to their room and making certain they had everything they needed.

Nancy stayed with Bob all night. She discovered she had become, for that time, the guardian of his spirit and body.

He slipped in and out of consciousness, mumbling, then talking, then sleeping again. But always, he held her hand.

At one point, though clearly asleep, he said, "Hold my hand, Nancy. They've come for me. Don't want to go. Don't want to go."

"Who, Bob? Who has come for you?"

"The angels. They're here," he mumbled in his semi-consciousness. Then he slipped back into the netherworld.

In his dream state, Bob was in an ocean, sinking down, down. Floating, drowning, he was aware he was slipping away from the world. From his life.

Out of nowhere, a hand reached for him and he grabbed it. He held on. He didn't know whose hand it was, only that the hand kept him from sinking farther from the world, farther down into the sea—into death.

On this side of the veil that separates this life from the afterlife, Nancy held Bob's hand for nine hours that night. Sensing something was happening to him on the other side, she urged, "Bob, don't leave me. You have to stay with me!"

Bob said nothing. He did not come around. Still, his fingers dug so deeply into her flesh that they broke through; her palms bled. "I'm not letting you go, Bob."

Finally, morning came. Bob awakened and found Nancy still by his side, still holding his hand.

"You're here," he said. "You saved me." He looked at her palms. "Did I do that?"

"It's okay. It doesn't hurt. Losing you would have hurt more."

"Nancy, I saw this hand holding me. It kept me from sliding all the way down. Was that you? Or was it an angel?"

Tears welling in her eyes, she answered, "Maybe it was both."

"I'm sure it was both." Bob smiled and slipped into healing sleep.

Epilogue

I visited with my brother Bob in late May 1998, shortly after his release from the hospital after yet another colon operation. Still the eternal Irish optimist like the rest of his siblings, on the day of his release Bob moved his family into a new house with his wife Debbie, daughters Meghan, Maureen and Cathleen and their dog, Shannon. Bob is still in glowingly perfect health and for our family, the world has been made perfect for us once again.

I Am the Angel

I n mid-January 2000, my husband Jim had the opportunity to go to a Rockets basketball game with a friend. Because Jim never does anything like this, we all looked upon the evening as a novelty. With him gone for the evening, I planned a quiet night of watching and studying my DVD movies, maybe giving myself a facial and just spending time petting our golden retrievers, Beau and Bebe and playing with their eight puppies. It was my kind of quiet night alone with my dogs.

Our kitchen and family room is all one room. It's surrounded by glass on two sides, one south-facing wall being four French doors that all open onto a tiny patio and garden. I like to think of it as "New Orleansesque," rather than the minuscule plot of land that it is. The south side of the patio is guarded by an eight-foot-high, black, wrought-iron fence and gate, the design with the arrows pointing heavenward. The east wall is a nine-foot slab of gray concrete, and the house itself borders it on the west and north.

I say all this to give an exact description of the surroundings, which make my unbelievable story even more bizarre.

At approximately 7:45, the French doors began shaking wildly under the impact of someone banging on them. "Help me! Let me in! Help me!" a woman screamed at the top of her lungs.

My dogs never bark unless there is danger. They sensed it in aces. Beau, the 125-pound male, began barking that sounded like the hounds of heaven roaring down from the sky. Bebe joined in, her bark shrill and maddening more than frightening. Once the eight puppies in their nursery in the garage heard their mother, they all began barking. The cacophony was enough to frighten the devil himself.

The woman outside my French doors was undeterred.

"They're going to kill me!" she yelled, banging even more loudly on the doors.

I bolted from the sofa and shot to the door, but didn't open it. "Who is going to kill you?"

She was hysterical. "Two men. Two men kidnapped me and they're going to kill me. You have to save me."

The woman was in her early thirties, pretty and tiny as a bird. She looked Hispanic, but her English was impeccable. She was dressed in a nice blouse, skirt, jacket and heels. Her long dark hair framed a beautiful face with perfectly applied subtle makeup.

"Get down!" I shouted through the glass. "Stay in the shadows."

"Please, for God's sake, let me in. Save me!"

The dogs were still barking and making a racket. I couldn't think. I was terrified. My postage stamp-sized backyard was not lit. The interior of the house looked like I had a party going on. Instantly, I doused the lights. "Stay low," I begged her.

She was crying and trembling as she crouched in the shadow. "Please, let me in."

I was a mass of confusion. My rational, well-experienced mind told me I was being set up. Her accomplice was no doubt on the other side of my fence, lurking in the dark to spring around the corner and dash into the house once I unlocked the doors.

Visions of myself at gunpoint, the dogs being gunned down in a spray of bullets and blood everywhere terrified me.

Yet my heart told me this was a woman in trouble. She was terror-stricken. Tears streamed down her face. She could hardly breathe.

But in those shadows awaited death for all of us, I believed.

From inside or outside myself, I will never really know, I heard my conscience or my guardian angel say, "But what if I am her only chance? What if it's up to me to save her life?"

I said a prayer, "Please, God. Let me be right. Let us save this woman."

Without another thought in my head, I unlocked the door, eased it open only a crack and reached my hand through. "Give me your hand."

She reached for me. I was struck at how soft and smooth her skin was and the fear I felt flowing beneath it.

Quickly, I yanked her into the house and locked the door.

"Stay down . . . on the floor," I said, envisioning the bullets smashing the glass and killing us all.

At this instant, I discovered something else about myself I had never known.

I placed my body in front of Beau and Bebe so they would be protected from the bullets. I never realized how little value

I place on my own life. When I believed that any second we were going to die, my soul sought to save my dogs and this stranger rather than save itself.

I haven't a clue what this means. I don't think it was courage, exactly, only that I must feel more a part of heaven than this earth. The stuff of heaven must mean more to me than anything here. Or maybe it means I love my dogs more than I want to stay on earth. I don't know. Who answers questions like that? Metaphysicians? Psychologists?

At that point, I did quiet the dogs down. Once Bebe quit barking, the puppies calmed down as well.

The woman's panic increased. "I have to call my husband. They are going to my house to kill my children."

My God, I thought, what is this woman's story and how could a sweet thing like her get mixed up in something so awful? Is she a drug dealer?

"I'll call 911," I said.

"No, the man outside. He called 911."

"What man?" I looked down my front hall to the leaded glass door. I saw my neighbor Chuck sitting in his car outside his house with his lights on.

"That man." She pointed to Chuck.

"Stay down!" I said, crawling nearly on my belly, still expecting the spray of bullets to come flying at any second.

I got to the front door, crouched and opened it a crack. I stuck my head out. "Chuck!"

He got out of his car, but kept watching the gate to our gated community. "Catherine, stay down and stay inside. Where is she? Have you seen her?"

"She's in here with me."

"She's in your house?"

"Yes! Did you call 911?"

"Yes," Chuck replied. "They're on their way. Just stay inside and stay safe."

"I will!"

Chuck was a criminal attorney, so I figured he would know what to do in this situation if anyone would.

What I didn't know was that Chuck was staying in his car for two reasons. One was he wanted to watch the gates for the cops and for any sign of the kidnappers and would-be murderers. Number two was that his wife, Pam, was supposedly following him home from their club where they'd been. He was terrified that Pam could come driving through the gate and the kidnappers would grab Pam just as easily as they'd taken this woman hostage.

I closed the door and turned to the woman. "How did you get here?"

"Those men, they were going to rape me. They said they would kill me."

"Where were you? How did you get here?"

"In the empty apartments over there." She pointed to the west.

"That's crazy, there are no apartments anywhere near here."

"Yes," she cried through huge racking sobs, "the ones right there!"

Her story sounded fishy. We live in an area where there just are not any apartments around. Now I was more terrified than ever. She surely had an accomplice who just hadn't figured out how to break into my house yet.

I feared I'd made the wrong decision letting her in.

"They were going to rape me."

"Who are they?" I asked.

"Two men. They had ski masks. They came into my work. I work at a check cashing place. I'm the manager. They know I know the combination to the vault. They followed me home from work tonight. They jumped me when I got out of my car at home. They said they were taking me back to my work and that I had to give them the combination to the vault. I said no. They took me to the empty apartments. The one, he bent me over and pulled up my skirt. He said they would rape me and kill me. The other one stuck the gun in my head."

She was sobbing so hard I could barely understand her.

"But how did you get away from him?"

"I shoved the one with the gun and I kicked the other in the balls. I ran out of the apartment. Then I ran to the corner and then I saw that man out there in his car, the one who called the police. I saw him driving by. I ran after his car and when he opened the gate, I ran into his garage behind his car. I banged on the car windows, but he wouldn't let me in. He backed his car out of the garage. I ran over here to your house. I climbed your fence and banged your windows. You are an angel—you let me in."

I was stunned. Chills racked my body. "You climbed my fence?" I was thinking that I was five foot ten inches tall. This woman was not even five foot. Yet she scaled that fence that I couldn't possibly climb. I was shocked.

"Yes." She sank to her knees in the small alcove by our front door.

"I'm not an angel," I said.

She was sobbing and she looked at the floor. Suddenly, she was quite calm. "How very strange. I just thought of it."

"What?"

"Just last week, I went back to church for the first time in years and years. I don't know why. I just felt I had to."

My scalp was alive with chills. "You were saved by your angels. They protected you."

She burst into tears again. "My kids!" She reached toward me. "Please, let me call my husband! I have three children. They're going back for them."

I handed her the phone and she dialed. Someone answered. "Get out of the house, quick!" She screamed at the top of her lungs. "Get OUT!"

She was crying so hard she could hardly talk. My heart went out to her as I clutched Beau's neck and held Bebe close to me. I didn't realize I was crying myself.

"Get your daddy! Get out of the house! There's no time!"

Finally, I could tell her husband came to the phone.

"Two men, they kidnapped me from our house. They followed me home from work. They know where we live! Get out!" Then she broke down into sobs and couldn't speak.

I took the phone from her.

Her husband was panicked and befuddled. "Where are you, so I can come get my wife?"

"I'm in the Galleria area."

"That's impossible! We live on the far south side. She doesn't even work around there."

"The police have already been called. I just want to know that you are out of that house."

"We're leaving. Tell her we're safe."

"I will."

"Give me your number and the address."

Warning bells went off in my head. "I won't do that," I said, remembering lectures I'd attended at writers' conferences on how to deal with potential thieves and assassins. What if this woman was the greatest actress in the world? What if she made this all up just to get into our complex? I still wasn't buying the empty apartments story. And how could a little bird of a woman like her get away from two armed men? There was only so far my imagination would let me go, angels or not.

"As soon as the police get here, they will call you and tell you where they are taking her so you can come get her. Just stay by your phone. Just know that she is inside my house. She is safe with me. The police will be here in seconds."

"Okay, but take care of her for me."

"I promise," I said.

Though I finished speaking with the woman's husband, she never stopped crying. She repeated herself over and over. How the men were going to rape her, that the car they had used was a small red foreign car.

During this time, I repeatedly tried to get a message to Jim on his cellular, but he had turned off his phone since he was at the basketball game. All I could do was leave a voice-mail message.

We all hung low to the floor, and rather than walk around the house for phone numbers, I dialed information to get Chuck and Pam's home phone. I didn't know that Pam was not home. My message went to their recorder.

Where were the police and what was taking so long? It had been over ten minutes.

Finally I got brave enough to open the front door and call to Chuck. "Where are the police?"

"I've called three times. They say they can't find our new street."

The incredible became ridiculous. It took the police forty minutes to come one mile from one of their stations to our house.

The woman was just as terrified when the police arrived as she was when she first banged on my doors.

The police took her statement and mine. I told them that her story didn't jive, because she kept saying they took her to the empty apartments and there weren't any apartments in the vicinity of where she was pointing.

Finally the truth hit me. The men had taken her to the townhomes being built just next door to our gated community. There is no electricity there, so of course it was black as pitch on a winter night.

The policeman who came inside took my statement and then wanted to see my garden. He looked out the French door and then back at me incredulously. "That little girl climbed that fence?"

"Yes, sir."

He shook his head.

"Gives new meaning to what a human will do when terror-filled, doesn't it?" I asked.

"She's one damn lucky woman," he said. "By all rights, there is no way she could have gotten away from those two men."

"I know," I replied. "She told me the story three times, and it didn't make any sense."

"No sense at all," he said, writing on his clipboard full of papers. "Unless . . ."

"She was more than lucky? Unless she was blessed?" I offered.

He pursed his lips. "Yep. Someone was looking out for her."

"Good thing he had a strong kick," I smiled to myself.

"Kick?"

"She said she kicked the rapist. I kept thinking, she's too short to have gotten any leverage. Maybe an angel did it."

The policeman laughed. "I can't put that in my report."

"You don't have to," I said. "She knows who saved her and that's all that matters."

He turned his top page down and let the clipboard rest against his leg. "We all do . . . now."

He thanked me again, turned and walked out.

I watched from the front door as the woman sat in the back of the squad car, using a cellular phone. I could tell by the way she cradled the phone in her hand she was speaking to her husband. I expelled a sigh of relief. Her children were safe.

The squad car's lights flashed as they drove out of the gate.

I thought to myself that I would always remember this night and this terrified woman's angel story.

I wanted to remember that the most significant point of the story was that only a week ago she had returned to church; found her prayer.

I was used by God that night to save a woman's life. And I never even learned her name.

Epílogue

Two weeks after this incident, *The Houston Chronicle* ran a story about two men who were involved in a series of robberies, rapes and stabbings of women on the south side, very near the woman's home. At the time of the article, the police had composite drawings of the men, but had made no arrests. The men had stabbed one of the women dozens of times. She was still in intensive care. A second woman they had murdered.

All of the women testified that the men kidnapped them, threatened their families, wanted money either from their purses or their workplaces. Always they were threatened with or were actually raped. Always they were told they would die.

The policeman was right. The woman in my house was more than lucky. She was blessed. If only we all made a practice of asking for protection every day upon waking and every night upon dreaming. Who knows how those statistics above might have been altered?

Cherry Follows the Stars

AUTHOR'S NOTE: *The following story was written by my friend Cherry Hickson. She's told this story to many of our friends, and it still give us all goosebumps to this day.*

thought I was losing my mind. My life was in turmoil. I didn't know how I was going to pay my bills, find a new job or support my three sons. I spent my days wondering why God had put me on earth and my nights crying alone in despair. I was desperate for answers.

A friend told me about an incredible astrologer who lived in Memphis, Tennessee. At first I scoffed. "An astrologer? How could she help me?"

"Geneva is wonderful. She saved my life," my friend said. "Besides, what have you got to lose but the tank of gas it would take to get you there?"

I conjured up visions of a middle-aged woman with dyed black hair, Gypsy earrings and a cone hat with stars and moons appliquéd on black satin. "I can't do it," I said flatly.

"Cherry, she's not a witch. And you just might learn something."

That did it. The challenge of new knowledge was always a beacon to me. "Okay, I'll go."

When I met Geneva, I couldn't have been more stunned. Standing before me was a tiny, blonde sprite of a woman whose face and blue eyes radiated with happiness. She welcomed me to her home with a hug and immediately wanted to cook me breakfast. She flitted around her kitchen, asking me questions and calling me "sugar" and "sweetness" as if she meant it. I sat in that kitchen, smelling the coffee, hearing the caring in her voice as she tended to my needs as if I were a princess. Or better still, her daughter. I wanted to cry, my heart felt so warmed.

"You're nothing like what I expected," I said.

Geneva patted my shoulder and quipped, "You were expecting a pointy nose?"

"Yes."

"Warts and all?"

"Yes," I replied guiltily. "You're so vibrant and chipper and pretty . . ."

"I was a cheerleader. It's in the genes," she said, pointing to the refrigerator where family snapshots were magnetized to the door. "So is my daughter. Isn't she beautiful?"

"She is," I said, looking back from the refrigerator to Geneva who had pulled out my chart to read for me.

"I took down all your information and worked on this for the past two days to have it ready for you when you got here."

Geneva then went on to explain all manner of things about my innermost self, things that only I could know, things about my personality faults and strengths that would have been impossible to know. What riveted my attention was her accuracy and how specific each point was.

In this first session she told me that my middle son, "the Sagittarius son," she said, "is going to fall and hurt his right leg. I want you to make certain that boy gets medical help immediately, because this fall could affect him for the rest of his life."

Staring at the horoscope "wheel," which looked like so much mumbo jumbo to me, I said, "Where does it say that?"

"Why, it's right here, dear. See?" She pointed to a section of what looked like pie with hieroglyphics on it.

Still, there was something so unsettling about her voice and her concern that I agreed to take my son to the doctor should he fall. However, I believed her statement to be a bit on the ridiculous side. My son was not going to fall.

I let the warning slip from my mind as I continued to listen to her concerns about my own physical problems and what she termed my "lessons in this incarnation."

I returned the next day to my home and discovered that Carson, my middle Sagittarius son, had fallen from a grapevine into a barbed wire fence and cut his right groin and scrotum. He had not told either of his brothers or my friend who was staying with the boys until I got home.

Geneva's warning came blasting back into my brain.

"Carson, get dressed! I have to take you to the hospital immediately!"

Frantically, I rushed out of the house with Carson and sped off to the hospital. We were at the hospital all evening while he was examined and sewn up.

Carson is now nearly thirty years old, and the scar on his groin has not affected his athletic abilities or caused a single problem.

And yes, I now believe that astrology is a science, and an accurate one, when performed by a talented and pure-hearted astrologer. God sent me to Geneva that day, and in the ensuing years, I have wisely taken her counsel. I believe there are many signs along the pathways of our lives, but even I found myself being a skeptic too many times and not keeping my mind open to the wonders around me. Fortunately for me and others like me, even when I'm not listening, my angels are still calling, still talking to me. Ever guiding.

Fly Me to the Moon

*I*t was a time in my life when my career was in need of more than a kick in the pants; anything short of a thrust of rocket power would have been insufficient. I needed to hire a publicist, but all I'd heard from the majority of my published friends were horror stories about publicists. The bottom line was that finding a good one was tough. I'd have to fly to the moon to find such a miracle.

I prayed about the situation, but really did nothing more.

At this time, I power-walked every day with a friend I'll call Karen. Her husband, Bob, treated himself every year on his birthday to a reading with Houston psychic Kim O'Neill, author of *How to Talk with Your Angels*. This was ostensibly to keep his business on the "right track."

While I was walking with Karen, she told me that the previous day her husband had gone to see Kim and that the strangest thing had happened.

Right in the middle of his reading, Kim looked at Bob and said, "I know this is off the subject, but does your wife walk every day?"

"Yes," Bob answered.

"Does she walk with a tall, brunette woman?"

"Yes."

"Is that woman a writer, by chance?"

Curious, Bob affirmed she was right again.

"Is that woman's name Catherine Lanigan?"

Stunned, Bob answered, "Yes, it is. How did you know that?"

"Well," Kim said, "this is about the sixth time Catherine's name has come up in my clients' readings. My angels are telling me that I must speak with her and give her the name of my publicist. Would you ask your wife to have Catherine call me?"

"Certainly," Bob answered.

You can imagine how flabbergasted I was. This bizarre encounter was so far removed from my everyday life at the time, I almost laughed it off.

Kim O'Neill is quite famous around Houston and in the Southwest. I'd heard of her extraordinary reputation for accuracy, though I had never met the woman or even seen a photograph of her. I had no connection to this woman.

In addition, to make matters even more far-fetched, I had not been in Houston for three years. Few people, other than my family, knew I had just moved back. I had not been "out and about" doing signings, PR or media. For this woman to have any information about me, to have seen my name in print or on television was impossible. I was in hiding.

Still, because of the bizarre circumstances of her request, I decided to give Kim a call.

Kim was gracious and sweet, and her upbeat energy absolutely radiated over the telephone wires.

"I'm so happy my angels have finally been able to connect with your angels!"

"You do this all the time?" I asked incredulously.

"Of course!"

I suddenly felt deflated, realizing that I was not making enough connections with my angels. Silently, I vowed to start paying more attention. "So now what?"

"It's terribly important for you to call my publicist, Jodee Blanco, in Chicago. You need her and she needs you. I'm being told that you have important work to do together."

"You can't be serious. Just like that?"

"Yes, just like that. This is how it's done."

I felt as if I'd been out of step all my life and Kim O'Neill had been chosen to put me back on track. The fact that my angels were guiding me in such an overt, blatant fashion was convincing. "What's Jodee's number?"

When I telephoned, Jodee was swamped with a billion and one projects and, finally, was on her way out the door for a much needed and overdue vacation. She told me later that when I explained the circumstances surrounding my call, all she could think was, "Another flake with a manuscript." Still, she requested I send her a sampling of my writing and a press kit.

I packaged up what I thought was a small representation of my work and my very homemade press kit and over-nighted it to her so she received it before boarding her plane.

The way she tells the story, "a box the size of a case of wine" arrived. She tore it open, whisked off the top copy of one of my books, *The Way of the Wicked*, grabbed my unimpressive press kit and went to the airport.

In Jodee's words, she says: "Never in my life did I ever experience such a wakeup call from a novel. Not only did the writing itself keep me captivated for ten days on a beach—so much so that I don't even remember what the sand felt like beneath my feet—but there was a soul to Catherine's work that made me believe psychic Kim O'Neill. I thought for sure I had to have been in the *Twilight Zone* and was waiting for Rod Serling to come walking through the walls to tell me I was being featured on an episode. Instead, I got another phone call from Catherine, and this time I was the one who sounded off the wall. Looking back, I know she must have thought I was nuts, I was gushing with such abandon. But I knew there was something there, and we both understood we had a mission.

"Soon after, Catherine's publisher, MIRA, hired my firm to mount a comprehensive PR campaign for Catherine's next three novels, which they were publishing. I immediately flew to Houston in search of the key that would open the floodgates of public interest in Catherine's career. I interviewed her for three hours, although if you ask her, she might use the term 'interrogate.'

Then the real work began.

"After reading all her books, after examining the contents of her soul, I realized there was a quiet message in all of Catherine's work; one that even she didn't realize the brilliance of.

"That message was The Evolving Woman. Every one of her characters, no matter what the plot, evolved from self-sacrificing to self-empowering."

The moment Jodee said those words to me, I realized the magnitude of my mission on earth.

Each of my stories did involve women and men who taught themselves self-empowerment. No matter how much life beat them down, they bounced back. Despite all the odds, they always won.

It was and is the core belief in my heart. It's what my mother taught me. Expect a miracle and you'll get it. Expect failure and you'll get it.

Kim's words that Jodee and I had "important work to do" rang though my mind and soul like an ancient echo.

Jodee had said to me, "The heroines in your books are shadows of real women all across this nation. Let's start a nationwide search called "The Evolving Woman," where we find courageous females who have shaken off the shackles of loving Mr. Wrong."

Little did we know that we'd laid our hands on the heartbeat of a movement. Letters poured in from across the country.

This year, Jodee and I have published, with the help of Health Communications, Inc., our *Evolving Woman* book. We even have a web site: www.evolvingwoman.net for women to visit and post their stories.

Jodee and I have worked together for five long years. There's no doubt in my mind that we have just begun.

Being human, I must admit there are times when I tire of the battle. When I do, I reflect on how divinely Jodee and I were brought together. Somewhere between the earth and the moon, an angel voice had found Kim O'Neill and spoken out loud.

Georgia on My Mind

It was a cold, rainy October night when the jangling telephone startled me out of chapter thirty of *The Legend Makers*. Because Jim was in South America, I expected it to be him. Instead, I heard the voice of a bookseller friend of mine from Barnes and Noble.

"Catherine, it's Rikki. You have to drop whatever you're doing and come down to the store immediately."

I blinked at my computer screen. The cursor blinked back, beckoning. "I'm at a really good part . . ."

She interrupted. "The most amazing woman is here. You simply have to meet her. Her name is Georgia Durante and she's here signing her book. Catherine, her life is like something out of your books. She was married to this mobster who abused her. I instantly thought of your *Evolving Woman*. She's a stunt car driver for the movies and commercials. She said when she left her husband and escaped with her daughter from New York and drove to Hollywood, she had to think of a job where her husband couldn't find her and kill her. She saw a commercial with a woman stunt driver and decided she could do that. That was twenty years ago and now hers is the largest stunt car company in Hollywood. Now that's surviving!"

Mentally, I was in another dimension, producing the final action-packed scenes of my story in a subterranean river. My hero was hanging on for dear life. "I'm not dressed." I was wearing a pair of sixteen-year-old jeans, a gray turtleneck sweater and tennis shoes.

I looked out the window as a bolt of lightening shot across the sky. For most people this dangerous kind of night would be a sign to hunker down with a bag of Oreos and watch a movie. I thought of my deadline. I thought of my heroine still trying to decide between two men.

"She's only here for forty-five more minutes," Rikki urged. "Then she's flying to Washington, D.C., and then New York. Catherine, I have this *feeling* about you and her. I can't explain it . . . chills, really."

That did it! I could practically hear the angel trumpets helping to blast my bottom up out of that chair.

"I'm on my way! I look like hell, but I'll be there in fifteen minutes."

"Hurry!" Rikki said.

Without stopping to change clothes, I bolted down the stairs and kissed Beau and Bebe goodbye, explaining as I always do that Mommy would only be gone one hour. This is meant to assuage their hurt feelings that they are not allowed along and, also, to warn them not to go berserk and dig through the wallboard in frustration over my departure.

I made the trip in ten minutes. Everyone else in Houston had obviously decided to opt for the Oreos and movie.

Rikki met me at the door. "She's over here. You're just going to love her. I know it."

I walked up to a table where an angelic-looking blonde woman dressed chicly in black smiled at me as Rikki introduced us.

It was dark as pitch outside, but Georgia's eyes beamed like midday. "It's nice to meet you," she said, taking my hand.

It was too wet for static electricity, the only physical explanation for that mystical occurrence, when you know you've met a soul-sister; a connection that is not only meant to be, but could possibly last the rest of your life.

I sat down, or rather sank into a chair, awed by what was happening. I was meeting a person who was going to profoundly influence my life and I knew it. I felt it.

I remember my mind being a jumble, not knowing what to ask her or what to say. It was one of those rare meetings, as when I met Jodee Blanco, that I knew God was connecting us to each other to do his work.

I asked her a few questions, but not many, as I purchased two copies of her book—one for myself and one for Jodee, my other soul-sister. Georgia asked me a few questions about my *Evolving Women;* who they were and what my book was trying to accomplish.

"I'm hoping to save lives. I'm hoping to change the entire world, but that's naive and not very adult. At the least, if Jodee and I—through our book of letters from real women who were once abused, physically, mentally or verbally, and who escaped and then prospered—if we change one life, then our lives will have mattered."

Georgia had tears in her eyes. So did I. "That's what I'm trying to do," she said.

"Then we'll do it together," I said.

"But how?" she asked as her publicist urged her to wrap it up; the limo was waiting to whisk her to the airport.

We exchanged cards and she left.

I was emotionally supercharged as I turned to Rikki. "You have to know that you are the angel in all this. You remember that."

"I didn't do anything," Rikki protested.

"Yes, you did. You were listening."

She smiled back knowingly. "Yes. I was."

I went home that night and left my hero near death and my heroine dangling in a dark abyss of indecision. I stayed up all night reading Georgia's book.

I e-mailed her the next day and then called Jodee.

"She's incredible, Jodee. I just have this feeling we'll work with her. I bought her book for you, a Halloween present."

Jodee promised to read it and did. She called me back less than a week later. "Ask her if she'll give us a quote for *Evolving Woman*."

Georgia went further than that. She gave us a synopsis version of her story for our book. It's now the opening story in *The Evolving Woman: Intimate Confessions of Surviving Mr. Wrong.*

Georgia and I continued to call and e-mail each other, getting to know one another by long distance.

In May 1999, Georgia went to the Cannes Film Festival and I thought of how much fun I had when I went to the Italian Film Festival in Taormina, Sicily, fifteen years earlier. I wished her well, getting her story made into a movie.

That summer was the release of my first hardcover, *Wings of Destiny*. In August, Georgia called and said she was giving a fundraiser for Haven House, a woman's shelter in Los Angeles. "I can't possibly expect you to drop everything and spend all that money to come out here for my charity party."

"I'll do it," I said.

"What?"

"Georgia, if I'm supposed to be there, then it will just happen."

"I don't know, Catherine. It's in two days and you need clothes. What if there aren't any flights?"

"I'll be there."

I discussed the trip with Jim and he didn't hesitate. "Go!"

Already I started having cold feet. I was doing a lot of contract work for Jim, as well as preparing for my book tour. The dogs needed me.

"Go," Jim said. "If it's meant to be, you'll make it happen."

The miracles fell into place. I had just enough frequent-flyer miles to not only get a ticket out, but a first-class ticket at that. My friend, Terry Anzur, just happened to be in town over the weekend and said I could stay with her and her family. She had an extra car I could borrow. I needed cash for incidentals. Not a lot, but enough. Miraculously, an odd royalty check for $350 appeared in the mailbox. I needed a haircut for the gala. Terry's hairdresser had an opening the hour before the limo was to pick me up.

Everything on that trip was magic. I gave Georgia's introduction to the 400 people at the Hollywood Roosevelt Hotel. The party was fabulous and Georgia and I felt that "sense of greater purpose" whirling around us.

In November, Georgia called and stated she was coming to Texas for a film shoot, but intended to take two weeks to do promotional book signings. Could she stay with Jim and me while she went in and out of Houston over two weeks?

Of course she could, and she did.

I introduced her to my good friend and public relations genius, Scott Arthur, who booked Georgia all over the south half of Texas. She even spoke to the women at The Star of Hope Mission, the women's shelter I had featured seven years earlier in my novel, *Becoming*.

I say all this in order to give a sense of the weaving of the tapestry that was and is taking place. Each step we take in a positive direction may or may not bear fruit at first, but if we are patient and continue to believe, it most surely will.

While Georgia was in Texas, she asked me if I'd gotten my film deal for *Wings of Destiny*.

"Not yet. I've taken it to three places in Los Angeles, but I haven't heard yet."

"You know, I met this guy from Austin at Cannes. He's a producer. I liked him. He's salt of the earth, good heart. Good people. He's like us!" Without a pause, she picked up her cellular phone and called Dwight Adair.

After speaking with Dwight, I booked an appointment and went to see him in Austin. I viewed the facilities at Granite House. Then we shared lunch and I listened as he spoke of his approach to the Internet. Dwight was not the filmmaker for an epic like *Wings of Destiny*, but he was perfect for my thrillers which could be shot chapter by chapter and streamed digitally into computers. His idea was already ten months ahead of the conventional market, but right on the button with all the techie-insiders I was hearing about via my new venture of e-publishing with Fatbrain.com and Mightywords.com.

The problem was, Dwight said, he didn't have any money.

The forkful of taco salad did not make it to my lips. I was hit with that angel thunderbolt I'd felt so many times before. It's at these times when I realize that my life is not my own. I'm placed with people or in situations where I am the messenger or the connector. I'm the facilitator, the conduit to change lives. I'm not here on this earth for me. I'm here about my Father's work.

It's a humbling and awesome realization. It takes me over and guides my words and actions. I have no choice but to let it flow through me.

"You don't need me, Dwight. You need Jim."

"Who is Jim?"

"My husband. He'll find your money. What do you need? Fifty million?"

Now it was Dwight's turn to drop his fork. "How could you know that?"

I smiled. I didn't know it. But the angels did. "It doesn't matter. Here's Jim's card so you have it. Let's call him."

I called Jim and explained the situation. I told him about Dwight's idea with the Internet, and Jim agreed to go to Austin the following week for a meeting.

After several weeks, Jim put Dwight in touch with the kind of people who can help him out. Plans are being laid to film my books in short five-minute formats called "Webisodes" to be streamed over the Internet. It is exciting to be a part of the new technology that is changing how the world will be entertained.

Only the future will tell me how far this path will take me, but I do know one thing—it all started on a stormy October night and a not-so-chance meeting with an angel named Georgia.

My Holistic Medical Miracle

I'll never know if my experiences into the worlds of prayerful meditations would have been different had I known someone who could lovingly guide me. When I began serious meditation, most everything I learned was through reading.

I was working six or seven days a week in our retail swimming pool store, writing my novels at night and on the weekends, taking care of my son, looking after a house, struggling in a difficult marriage and flopping around indiscriminately on my divine path in life. Frankly, I was just trying to make ends meet and get through the day. I was searching for validation of what I believed was the meaning of life. Aren't we all?

Oddly, more times than not, I got exactly the answer I needed when I needed it. I have an incredible track record of praying intensely for something and getting it. I used to joke to my son that I didn't have just a "connection" to God, but an eight-inch-wide, main-drain-sized pipeline.

In the mid-1980s, I started using visualization techniques to further intensify my prayers. Each one of those stories will be dealt with in this book, because each in its own way is extraordinary.

But this one is probably my most bizarre experience of all. And every bit of it is true.

I awoke in the middle of the night one night with incredible pain in my lower back where my kidneys were. I'd had kidney infections since the age of three, and by the time I was in my mid-thirties, I could usually feel an infection coming on long before it manifested.

This particular "infection" was so strikingly dissimilar from previous occurrences, I didn't know what to think. The pain, rather than being dull, was jabbing, stabbing, even searing, as if I'd been lanced in the back.

I tried to get up, but could hardly breathe because of the pain. I knew I had to get to the bathroom, but the walk across the room seemed an interminable length. Somehow, holding onto furniture and the walls, I made it without fainting.

I remember looking at the clock. It was 2:22 A.M. I was just beginning to learn about the significance of "master numbers" and I knew that 22, like 11, are master numbers.

Once in the bathroom, I realized I was bleeding heavily. This was not menstrual blood because I'd already had a hysterectomy.

I remember having tremendous chills and cold sweats. I was shaking and then burning up with fever.

My urologist had prescribed Bactrim for me and I always kept some on hand in the house for emergencies such as this. I stumbled to the kitchen and after rifling the medicine cabinet,

I discovered the bottle I thought had contained my wonder-drug pills was totally empty.

Now I panicked. I knew to drink plenty of water and that cranberry juice helped to kill the burning during urination. When I went to the pantry, the cranberry juice I normally kept stocked was not there. At the time I thought this very unusual, but I was getting weak standing in the kitchen. This also was a strange sensation for me, because I am by nature the very embodiment of high energy and stamina. The reason I can accomplish so much in a given day is that I literally get bored if I'm not doing five things at once. For me to feel "weak" was just not part of my physicality.

Then I realized blood was running down my leg. I was fearful I was hemorrhaging. The only answer to that was to get back to bed.

I drank a huge tumbler of water, believing I would start feeling better in an hour or so. But as time passed, the pain grew more intense.

I tried to rouse my then-husband, Rod, and told him I needed to go to the emergency room.

"You're waking me up because of another kidney infection?" he grumbled dispassionately. "Go back to sleep. I'll deal with it in the morning." He was instantly asleep again.

I couldn't sleep. The exertion of breathing out and in was crushing. Tears slid down my cheeks. I thought I was dying. I didn't know what to do and so I prayed.

In less than ten minutes, I heard a voice. This was not a voice from "inside my head," such as I hear when I have a story I'm writing and I'm creating something the characters say. This came from without. To this day, I don't know if the disembodied spirit was a ghost, an angel or an alien, but who-ever it was, it was a male voice. It was deep, powerful, not car-ing per se, though I had the sensation to trust the voice and that it was accurate in its caring for my health.

"Do as we tell you," the voice said. "Imagine peach-colored light coming in streams from heaven down to the top of your head and into your body. Visualize sparkling peach/salmon-colored light forming into spinning plates with an axis going through the center. These plates, dozens of them, spin and skim the sides of your kidneys and bladder. See them scraping the infection from the walls of your kidneys. See them clean-ing out the insides of your organs with their light. As the infection is cleared away, the light will then fill up your organs and rid you of this infection."

The voice was so adamant and specific about what I should do and how I should do it, and I felt so weak, that I didn't question the process. I'd never read about anything like this, but I had read a book about colors and their healing powers. However, I'd read that green was supposed to be the healing color. This peach/salmon light experiment was not some-thing about which I'd had prior knowledge.

At first, it took all my strength to visualize the spinning plates, but then they came into "being" quite easily. I imag-ined them cleaning my body, over and over. I lost track of time. All I did was concentrate with all my might on those spinning plates.

The tension in my chest eased. My breathing came more easily to me. I felt my muscles start to relax. I had not real-ized it, but I'd lain perfectly still all that time. Even when my husband rolled over in his sleep, I was barely aware of his presence. I felt as if I were suspended in the air.

The hours passed as I kept meditating. I was surprised when dawn peeked over the horizon. Though I'd kept my eyes shut during the night, the sun threatened to break my concentration. Still, even with dawn, I kept praying and visualizing those spinning plates.

Finally, around seven, I was strong enough to get to the bathroom without stumbling. However, when I did, I realized that my nightgown was soaked with blood. So was the towel I'd put between my legs, as was the bedding.

I cleaned myself up, put on a new nightgown and again tried to rouse my husband.

"If you're sick, go see a doctor and don't wake me up again!" he snapped.

The week prior, Rod had been in a car accident and our car was being repaired. We had borrowed an old clunker from one of our salesmen to get us through the week and half while the body work was being performed on our car.

"I can't drive myself, I'm too weak," I said.

"I told you to leave me alone," he shouted and pulled the covers over his head.

It took me an hour to get dressed, I was so disoriented. It was as if I were moving in slow motion. My muscles didn't want to perform even the smallest task. I remember sitting on the closet floor to put my shoes on.

I got into the car without even calling my urologist's office. I wanted to beat the rush-hour traffic to the medical center, which was nearly thirty miles from our house.

The old clunker was hard to handle, not having power steering, and it sputtered so much I was certain it would never make the trip. For the car and myself, I prayed.

After nearly a one-hour grueling drive, I finally made it to the medical center. My doctor was located in one of those huge high-rise towers with a massive parking garage. Up to the eighth level I went before I found a parking place. I was weak in the knees as I crossed the garage, went down the elevator to the crosswalk to the office building and then up another elevator to my doctor's office.

I knew office hours weren't for another half hour, but I was hoping luck was on my side.

Miraculously, the door was open. I walked in and Sharon, the nurse, greeted me with, "Catherine! What are you doing here? I mean," she gasped, looking at my ashen face, "you look terrible. What's the matter?"

"The usual," I replied, making a stab at a joke.

"Oh, no, it's not." Sharon instantly opened the door for me. "Come in right away. He's not here yet, but he's on his way in."

"Thanks."

Sharon led me to the bathroom, showed me the plastic cup for the urine sample and then told me to go to room number one when I finished. Since I was the only person in the office, she was able to get my records and send the sample to the lab for an immediate culture.

I only waited on the examining table for ten minutes until my doctor came into the room. Without even saying "good morning," he sat down on that little rolling stool all doctors have, peered at me and said, "Catherine, I want to know what you took before you came here."

"Took?"

"What medication?" he asked with an intensity edged with sharp curiosity I'd never seen in him before.

"Harvey, if I'd had any medication, do you think I would have practically risked my life driving here? I told Sharon, there was nothing in the house. That's why I'm here. I knew you wouldn't just phone in the Bactrim, because there were no refills available on my prescription."

He gaped at me. "You had to have taken something."

"No. Nothing. Not even an aspirin substitute," I protested. "Why are you looking at me like I'm some kind of amoeba or something? I'm telling you the truth."

"Okay," he said with a sigh. "I believe you."

"What is it? You look more frightened than I feel. Did the test show I have some kind of disease and you don't want to tell me?"

Shaking his head, he looked back at me. "This is impossible. At least in medical science it's impossible."

I shook with chills, but not the kind that come from being sick. These were goosebumps. "Go on."

"Catherine, we ran the culture. There is nothing but pus and blood. A lot of blood and not much urine."

"Oh, you have no idea," I said, thinking how much blood I passed that night.

He continued. "The results show that there is no bacteria present. That's impossible to have blood and pus and no bacteria. It just can't be. Catherine, you have to tell me what you took."

Suddenly, I felt as if I'd crossed into some zone or dimension that medicine and man had never experienced or, at least, had not revealed. My mouth went dry, but I summoned up the courage to tell him the truth. "It wasn't what I took. It was what I did."

"And that was?"

I told him about the voice I'd heard. I explained every detail I could about the salmon lights and the spinning plates I imagined to scrape off the pus from the walls of my kidneys.

He listened patiently and finally said, "Catherine, I'm a firm believer in holistic healing. I've seen miraculous cures before. People making themselves well. I've even seen cancer cures when there had been no hope of remission. But this . . . this is entirely different. To my knowledge there's never been a case like this."

"I guess there has to be a first time, huh?" I joked.

We spoke a bit longer about the intricacies of my "meditation cure." He took explicit notes, so he would remember everything I'd said. He then gave me a very large single dose of Keflex to take before driving home. I remember having a difficult time getting that huge pill down my throat. It seemed odd to me, because I'd always been able to swallow a handful of vitamins all at once.

I left his office with my newly written prescription for Bactrim and a promise to return in a week for another culture.

On the drive home I was feeling stronger, able to manage the car, when all of a sudden I was overwhelmed with a severe wave of nausea. The urge to vomit was so intense, I pulled the car off the freeway onto the shoulder, opened the car door and threw up the Keflex.

I remember thinking I needed to telephone my doctor the minute I got home.

Just as I closed the car door and leaned my head against the headrest, I heard the voice again. "Do not take this medication."

I was getting a bit fed up with this voice who came and went without my permission. Angrily, I snapped back, "Why not?" I didn't expect an answer, but I got one.

"We gave you this illness and performed the cure in order that you could bear witness to this fact. One day, you will be strong enough and courageous enough to write this down for other humans to read. That is the purpose of our mission and yours."

I drove home and climbed into bed, resting for the remainder of the day. I drank my water and did not take the Bactrim.

By the next day, I was back at work at seven in the morning lining out my construction crews for the day's work.

I went back to the doctor's office the next week and of course, the tests proved negative, just as they had the day I'd come in.

I have never heard that voice again, though there were times when I wished it would have come to my rescue. But who knows, maybe those ghosts or angels are still there, but just don't have anything further to say.

Sports Klutz Meets Jerry Angel

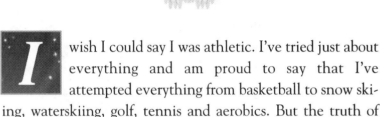

I wish I could say I was athletic. I've tried just about everything and am proud to say that I've attempted everything from basketball to snow skiing, waterskiing, golf, tennis and aerobics. But the truth of the matter is that at half a century, I've never grown into my body. I still feel like a colt trying to figure out what all these arms and legs are about. Given this personal insight, you will more easily understand my story.

Jim and I were out walking our two golden retrievers around the bend of our heavily treed street one hot summer afternoon. The storm clouds around Houston were mounting, and we were anxious to get the dogs out for their walk and back into the house before the clouds opened up.

Our plan went awry. The rain started in those giant drops that feel like stinging pellets against the skin. My little girl golden, Bebe, was only two years old and thought she was two weeks. This is why I love her. She's as klutzy as I am.

I began running with her to get back to the house. Jim and Beau were running behind us. All of a sudden, Bebe simply decided to stop and she halted dead still. Instead of stopping at my side, she blocked my path.

Well, she might as well have been a hurdle in a race.

I went sailing over the top of her and landed "like a sack of potatoes" as Jim said, facedown on the pavement. The "drop and roll" method had never been one of my strong points.

As I saw the pavement coming toward me, all I could think about was the fact that I had a television interview the next day and that I didn't need to have my face scraped or bloodied. So I did what every intelligent klutz would do: I tried to break my fall with my arm.

My arm went sliding along the asphalt, ripping the skin off, and my shoulder took the brunt of the fall. I sprawled there facedown, the wind knocked out of me and in pain. Lots of it.

Jim's first concern was that a construction truck, common in our newly built area, would come careening around the corner and drive over me.

Struggling with two dogs, the rain and my painful cries was a handful. However, he managed to get me onto my feet, and I hobbled home in the rain leaning on Jim, the penitent Bebe lagging behind.

Once home, we doctored the very unattractive scrape up the inside of my arm and the "hole" I'd created in my palm. But my shoulder was a mess. We applied ice and I called my ace chiropractor who has helped me over the past year.

I made an appointment with Scott for the next morning and followed his instructions for the rest of the night.

Upon examination and tests, I discovered that I'd partially dislocated my shoulder and had a torn and damaged tendon. Recovery was going to be a slow process. Unfortunately, I had to get on a plane and go on a book tour for a week. This left me without treatments during a critical time of healing.

I went on my trip and conducted business as usual, letting my sense of humor see me through the worst of it. Upon my return, I then saw Scott twice a week for three weeks and though I healed, it was a terribly slow process. Just when I was seeing some relief, Scott got transferred.

I continued with my exercises, but I was still in pain. Some days were better than others. The nights were tough. I didn't sleep, sometimes for four or five nights at a stretch.

I was at my wit's end. I had other stresses at the time as well, which didn't help my healing process. Finally, one night during my prayers I simply said, "I can't do this anymore, angels. You have to cure this shoulder. I won't live like this any longer. I have too much work to do on this earth and this is slowing me down."

The next morning on my e-mail, I found a message from my publisher. She told me about this amazing young poet who had dropped out of the sky. She had told the poet, Jerry, about me and she wanted to know if he could have my phone number to call me. He wanted to meet me over the phone.

I responded that I would be honored to meet Jerry.

"By the way, Jerry is a healer," Kim said and signed off.

I froze at my desk staring at the blank computer screen, hearing the dial tone. "He's a healer? How good is this?"

Jerry called me not long after that.

Wouldn't you know that each time we started discussing his poetry or something interesting, my other phone rang? His phone had a call coming in. It was one interruption after another. Finally, I said, "Jerry, someone doesn't want us to talk right now. So, how about we make a date for two hours from now? I'll fix lunch for Jim and then we can talk."

"Sounds great," he said.

At our arranged time, Jerry explained to me how he does remote viewing. Not that I'm a skeptic, because I have friends who can remote view, and I once met a woman who remote views for the United States military.

"Your hair is pulled back and you're wearing a pink top. Not bright pink. Soft pink," Jerry said.

"It's peach. Soft peach," I said. "You're dead-on."

We talked a bit more and I asked him if he could help me with my shoulder.

"Of course. What I want you to do is connect with the trees. Maybe around your house there is a special tree you like. Why do I see a tree on your roof?" he asked.

"Not the roof. I have a skylight in my bathroom and there is a huge pine tree out front. In the reflection of my mirror, I see that tree every day and while I'm in the tub, I can look up and see that tree. It makes me smile."

"That's your tree," he said. "I have a huge oak at my grandmother's house I connect with and then I use the tree to heal you. Trees are so amazing. Even the tiniest sapling has enough energy stored within to split the planet apart. After you finish this call, try to find a place to meditate for fifteen minutes if you can. Connect with your tree, I'll connect mentally with mine. Imagine light and energy from the tree going into the top of your head and down to your shoulder, healing it."

I was in so much pain that particular day, after pulling the tendon when fixing dinner the night before, that I was truly a willing participant in this exercise.

In the afternoons our house is like Grand Central Station. Jim works at home when he's in the country, just as I do. The dogs were racing around, the FedEx man came, phones were ringing, the fax was going off and the maid was here running the vacuum.

All I could think was, "I'm supposed to meditate with all this going on?"

However, I went to the bathroom, looked at my tree and imagined white energy and light coming from the tree into my head and to my shoulder. I went to the bed and laid down for five minutes. Though I'd never met Jerry, I tried to see him in my mind's eye connecting with his tree. Mind you, the only thing that came into my head was a diffused vision of light in the shape of a man.

In less than five minutes, that throbbing pain ceased. Just vanished. My eyes popped open. I couldn't believe it.

"This is my imagination."

I stood up. Rotated my arm very, very slowly. No pain.

One of the things I wanted so badly to do was to lift something. Anything. I had no strength in my arm at all. Opening the car door was difficult.

I instantly went downstairs and thought to give myself the test of all tests. I would unload the dishwasher.

Miracle of miracles, I easily put the dishes away. I was even able to lift a heavy pot to the overhead pot rack.

I didn't say a word to Jim. I thought this was too good to be true. I figured I would see how I was through the night, since I hadn't been able to sleep for so very long.

I slept like a rock for the first time in a month. The next day, Jim and I went for our four-mile fast walk. Normally, I carry two-pound barbells on our walk. Because of my shoulder, I'd had to give up the weights. This morning, I thought I'd give this miracle the acid test. I took the weights.

My shoulder made it through like a trooper. I did four miles and didn't feel even a twinge of pain.

Jim was incredibly impressed and asked why all of a sudden I felt like carrying weights.

Finally, I told him the story about Jerry and the tree.

The next day, Jim and I walked five miles and I carried my weights. I was stronger than ever.

That night as we were walking our dogs around the bend for their usual after-dinner stroll, Jim said, "I've been thinking about your story about Jerry. I know our yard is the size of half a postage stamp, but I think he's right about the trees. They have incredible energy and I've figured out where we can plant at least five more trees!"

It's been over a week now since my healing and my arm is doing great.

This past week, I have even managed to go to the gym and work out on the arm machines. Yesterday I increased my dumbbells to five pounds each. Tomorrow I'm going back to my usual eight pounds for my bicep curls and tricep lifts.

Now, when I go into my bathroom and look up at my favorite pine tree, I thank it for healing me and I say one prayer for Jerry and another for Kim, the angel messenger who connected us.

God's Little Urchin, Me

*I*t was a blistering summer in Houston, and my husband Rod and I had been laid off from the swimming pool and spa company for whom we worked. It was right after the 1986 oil crash, and retail business had come to a screeching halt. We did the only thing we knew how to do: we opened our own swimming pool and spa business.

With very little capital, we rented an abandoned building, cleaned it ourselves, found loyal and out-of-work carpenters, plumbers, laborers and anyone who wanted to work for very little pay and a lot of hope.

My son Ryan was only eleven at the time and even he worked every afternoon and all weekend with us. Child labor was not out of the question when we didn't know how to pay for groceries.

We had no money for advertising. We made the sign ourselves, rented a helium tank and ran outside with a lot of balloons to attract attention. Fortunately, we'd made a reputation for ourselves at the other business and old customers came to us for their chemicals and upkeep. When their friends were thinking about repairs or a new pool or an addition to their backyard, they thought of us. Bottom line: we were surviving, but barely.

During those days, I was writing furiously all night long and scrounging for more publishing work to finance the payroll at our company and keep us all alive. Somehow, each month we made it.

Then we got a big break. A friend of ours was an advertiser in radio and he agreed that if we put in a new driveway at his house, he would give us free advertising on the radio. My husband and I came up with a catchy spa sale, and the advertising blitz we planned succeeded beyond all our expectations.

We had more work than we could fill, but we tackled it with joy. And fourteen-hour days. That summer, it was not uncommon for me to send out a truck loaded with pipe, glue, pumps and fittings and have my men laying pipe from ten at night until one in the morning. Our customers were so glad to see us finally show up that they agreed. The men liked it because it was cool late at night and the work went twice as fast.

Finally, we landed three swimming pool jobs we'd been designing and contracting. We felt as if we'd moved into the big leagues. We were ecstatic.

We'd hired a pool crew who were reputed to be excellent workers. In a matter of days, we discovered the opposite to be true. If it could go wrong on a job site, these guys made certain they were the cause of the foul-ups. I felt like tearing my hair out by the roots, these men gave me so many headaches.

Just when I would get things corrected, they would do something stupid, like drinking beer on the job, not showing up for work for two or three days on end or worse, digging the square pool on the lot where the round pool was supposed to be.

Finally, one man on the crew cursed out a homeowner. She threw them off her property, and he declared he was going to come after me with his gun and shoot me for sending him to the job in the first place!

I called the police and they rushed over to our store to protect me. The employee came into the store waving the gun and shouting, and the police hauled him away.

My secretary, my assistant and two of the salesmen were shocked and afraid. Now what were we going to do with no pool crew to put the pools into the ground?

I looked at their faces as they stared at me. I was their link to that paycheck on Friday that fed their children and kept them all solvent. They needed me. And I was speechless.

I didn't know what to do or how to rectify the situation. By this time, the oil crash was debilitating. Construction crews, carpenters and plumbers had left the state of Texas in droves. Tens of thousands of Houstonians just walked out of their houses, abandoning their mortgages, and declared bankruptcy. We all knew there was no one to hire.

The situation was hopeless.

With my employees looking to me for guidance and a solution, I dropped my head to the counter and cried. I felt as if all hope was dead. I lifted my eyes upward and said aloud, "God, this is your little urchin, Catherine. I need help. My company needs help. I need a pool crew. Right now. Today. Thanks for helping, God."

I looked at my employees. Not a smile among them.

"That's it? That's all you're going to do?" my secretary asked.

"It's all I know how to do. I've been calling around town for weeks trying to replace these guys as it was. There's no one."

Just then, the front door to the store opened and in walked three men, dressed in jeans and tee shirts and wearing construction boots.

"Say, lady!" the tallest, burliest one said. "We were just riding by and saw your balloons out front. We didn't know there was a pool company out here. We just moved here from out of town. You wouldn't happen to have work for three pool installers, would you?"

Chills raked my back. Angelic chills.

My secretary screamed and covered her mouth.

"I'll be!" one of the salesmen said, aghast, and plunked down in his chair as if his legs had turned to rubber.

My assistant rushed up to me, grabbed my elbow and said, "That's the fastest answer to a prayer I've ever seen."

I smiled. "You think he liked the 'little urchin' part?"

"Keep using it. It works."

I hired the men on the spot and sent them out to our customer's house. That was, and still is, the prettiest pool we ever built. Must be that angelic cloud that seems to hover above it, blessing it every day.

All that summer, my employees talked about that group of installers and how they came to us that day. They stayed on working for us for years. Therefore, it wasn't that they were apparitions or anything of that sort. They had been praying for work. I had been praying for them.

We came together on our divine paths not by mystery, but by plan. And in its simplicity, it reveals itself to be a most wondrous plan, indeed.

Money Angels

I t was the worst of times for our pool business. We had expanded to a second store, albeit on a shoestring, in order to be where the customers were. However, the oil crash had really settled in by this time and people were walking away from their homes in droves. Houston lost over 350,000 residents that fall. Strip malls were vacant. Office building space was rent-free for the first year, in hopes the occupant could make the rent for the next three years. Automobile sales were the lowest in twenty years. Layoffs from big corporations had trickled down to where now there were no jobs left even at fast-food restaurants. My lawn man was an ex-Shell geologist. We personally knew three men who had committed suicide by that winter once the dust had settled on their bankruptcy papers.

Downtown Houston looked like the cavernous ghost town it was. Two years prior, I'd thought that starting our business in those first days of the oil crash was the worst it could be. I was wrong. It got much, much worse.

We were facing closing down the store itself, selling our home and moving to heaven only knew where.

My husband had no answers. He did the one thing he knew how to do. He left to go on a trail ride with his friends and left me in charge of the sales. I think he believed that it was over and he was giving up. He probably thought he might as well have one last ride, because we'd have to sell the horse, too.

To make matters worse, it was winter when no one is thinking about starting a pool in the first place, so the retail traffic through the store was nonexistent. My salesmen were sitting around pitching cards into their ball caps on their breaks, which lasted five or six hours a day. The feeling of gloom was pervasive. Crew members were either moving on to other companies or other cities. We were down to a handful of men and if we didn't make payroll that Friday, I was going to have to lay off two more. Without those valuable men, we virtually had no business. In all honesty, closing the store was our only option.

Three days before my husband left for his ten-day trail ride for the Houston Livestock and Rodeo, he devised a series of newspaper ads for a sale while he was gone. It was a clever gimmick and probably would only have worked during those bleak days of massive bankruptcies and retail store closings. The ad read: Going out for business.

Read that again. It doesn't say, "Going out of business." It says, "Going out FOR business."

The first day of the sale, I had coffee and cookies in both stores. I had put helium tanks in both stores and decorated the spas and shelves with half the towels, wine glasses and silk flower arrangements from our own home. The stores looked great. But it wasn't enough.

I went to our warehouse and gathered all our remaining employees. I explained that our bookkeeper stated we needed $150,000 worth of sales to get us over the crunch. Back then, that number was astronomical. It might as well have been a million. It seemed like a mountain we could never climb without help.

I knew what we had to do. We formed a prayer circle, got down on our knees and in unison we begged God to save our company, our jobs, our livelihood that kept our children fed. I then went to our largest store and did the same thing with my salesmen. I told everyone in the company that this was our last shot. If this sale didn't work, we were going to have to close.

Throughout the day, every day, I would call the other stores and remind everyone to pray. If there was a single second of spare time, I told everyone to keep praying. I even lit a candle on my desk in our store on the north side of town.

The miracle of that ten days started the first thing Saturday morning. The first customer who came through the door said, "I saw your going out of business ad." I smiled and told him that he misread the article. We were still very much in business, God willing, but that we had one heck of a sale going on. I even told him that if we didn't sell a certain number of pools and spas in that ten days, we would be out of business. He bought a spa, deck and gazebo.

Before this man even finished signing his papers, another couple came in with the newspaper ad in their hands. They had misread the ad as well. However, our sale was legitimate, we had drastic markdowns and great financing. They bought a spa and deck as well.

That day and the following one were two of the most incredible days I've ever witnessed. My salesmen were swamped with customers. The phones rang off the hooks with requests for bookings for deck designs, pool designs and landscaping.

For ten days exactly, the stores were filled to overflowing with customers. People whom my salesmen had called on for a full year previously, suddenly appeared and put down deposits on pools we'd thought we would never build. Chemicals flew off the shelves. Accessories and parts were ordered by the dozens. At one point I had so many people in our north-side store, I had to give a lecture to everyone at one time. I kept the coffee pot going and baked those cookies at night for the customers.

By the time my husband returned from his trail ride, we had cash in hand of $159,000. My salesmen had bids booked up every night for the following three weeks.

When it was over, I was jubilant and in tears. With the staff, we all went to our knees and said a prayer of thanks-giving to God for saving our company. That winter moved to spring, and though things were never quite that hectic again, we were able to maintain our crew and staff through the win-ter until business picked up in the spring and summer, as it always does.

But for those of us who were there and bear witness to the testimony of those miracle days, our experience was a real sign of the power of prayer.

Many years ago I read the lectures of Napoleon Hill, the financial advisor to the Carnegies and Vanderbilts in the previous century. His theory was called the Mastermind. What he believed was that when two minds or more are focused on the same goal, that goal becomes attainable at an increased rate of speed according to the number of minds concentrating on that single goal. Because I enlisted all the office staff, all the crews and all the sales staff, I had a great many minds focused on saving our company.

Even still, I am wise enough to know that it took more than that. Prayer is the rocket-fuel of miracles.

That pool business is still going strong today, providing a career for my son, Ryan, and putting the food on the table that feeds my only granddaughter, Caylin. I would like to think that even today, had I not turned our lives over to God at that critical life-turning time, perhaps our destiny might be otherwise.

Then again, only God knows.

Dreams

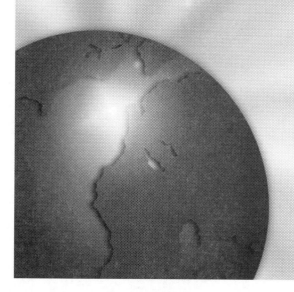

From Calpurnia's precognitive dream about Julius Caesar's death to Freud's interpretation of the Id, Ego and Superego or Carl Jung's "archetypes," dreams and their interpretations are a fact of human existence.

Man cannot live without dreaming. Psychiatrists and psychologists tell us that though we spend one-third of our life sleeping, we are not idle. Dreaming is as necessary to sanity and mental well-being, as diet and exercise are to our bodies.

We all dream. It's the remembering of those dreams that makes the difference in our lives.

History relates how Croesus saw his son killed in a dream. Joseph saved Egypt from famine by interpreting the Pharaoh's dreams accurately. Out of a dream came Coleridge's "Kubla Khan." Joan of Arc predicted her own death in a dream. Shakespeare was inspired to write from his dreams.

These are people who utilized their dreams to shape their own lives and the world around them.

Edgar Cayce, the "Sleeping Prophet" of Virginia Beach, defined dreams most accurately:

Visions or dreams, in whatever character they may come, are the reflection of:

1. *Physical conditions.*
2. *The Subconscious. (Here) the conditions relating to the physical body and its actions (manifest) either through the mind or through the elements of the spiritual entity.*
3. *A projection from the spiritual forces (superconscious) to the subconscious of the individual.*

> *Happy may he be who is able to say that he has been spoken to through dream or vision.*
>
> —Edgar Cayce

The stories in this chapter are of life-changing dreams. Some changed the world forever, as in my grandfather's dream. Some are premonition dreams, much like Plutarch's account of the dream in which Augustus was told to leave his tent immediately and after he did, his enemies came and pierced that very bed with their swords.

I have defined these dreams as nocturnal dreams only. I purposefully did not include stories here that involved the kind of dream-like state one advances to in meditation or prayer.

The dreams described here were influenced by interventions from the angelic and spiritual realms. The element of the divine is present and filters through the telling so that when you encounter such a dream, one that you can't shake no matter how many years have passed or how many thousands more dreams you've enjoyed, you will know the next time when the angels are speaking to you. Hopefully, the next time you will be ready. You will be watching.

Grandpa Manning's Rocket Dream

Crestview, Florida, 1931

My grandfather, Clyde Foshe Manning, awoke one morning, saying to my grandmother, "Ethel, wake up! I had the strangest dream. I saw planes and jets, even rockets, landing at Postal's Point!"

"You've lost your mind, Clyde. There's nothing at Postal's Point but swamps."

"Right now, yes," he said, getting up. "I'm talking about the future. And I could see it."

"See what?"

"The future. And it wasn't anything like a dream. I smelled the fuel. Heard the sounds. They nearly broke my eardrums they were so loud. As if they . . . well . . . broke the sound barrier."

"Don't be ridiculous."

Wistfully, he continued. "It *was* real. Those planes *were* breaking the sound barrier. This place was huge. Hangars. Barracks. That's what it was! It was a flight base."

Grandma grumbled, "You're always having fool notions, Clyde. Forget about it."

As the day and the week went on, Grandpa couldn't forget. He met a friend of his, James E. Plugh, who invented the bicycle spring seat and who started Chicago Linen Supply after his father died to help pay his tuition at the University of Chicago. Even today, every linen supply company in the world pays a royalty to Chicago Linen Supply.

James thought Grandpa's idea was a good one and so they went to talk to James' son-in-law Chuck Ruckle, who also thought Grandpa's dream was viable.

All three of them went to Maxwell Field in Montgomery, Alabama, and spoke to Lieutenant Rich. He not only liked the idea, he lined up a crew of officers and trainers to fly down to Postal's Point to investigate the lay of the land.

They decided that Postal's Point could easily house the necessary barracks, offices and officer's club. They would place targets in the middle of Choctahatchee Bay for flight and bombing training. The flat, arid land was perfect for airstrips and landing fields.

Lieutenant Rich went to Washington, D.C., and told the generals there about Clyde Manning's dream of an air base at Postal's Point in Florida.

My mother remembers those days, because she was in high school and the Army Air Corps planes would zoom over the Crestview High School announcing their arrival. Since my grandfather was tied up in bank meetings most times, my mother would race out of class, run two blocks to her house, get the family car and drive out to the small airstrip in Crestview, then pick up Lieutenant Rich and his superiors and take them home where my grandmother was making dinner for everyone. My mother remembers Florida congressmen, like John Yon from Mayo, being entertained during those exciting years. During this same time, Grandpa was responsible for putting in all the electricity for the southern half of Okaloosa County, which had none.

By the time my mother graduated high school in 1936, the landscape for that portion of northwestern Florida would never be the same. By the time I was in high school, when I visited my cousins Barb and Beth who lived overlooking Choctahatchee Bay, I had to cover my ears to soften the sound of one "sonic boom" after another, as jets broke the sound barrier, just as Grandpa had predicted thirty years before.

Often I conjure the vision of Grandpa and Grandma sitting at their dining-room table with Lieutenant Rich and others, as the United States Army Air Corps laid out its plans to construct what today is Eglin Air Force Base.

It all came into being because my Grandpa Manning believed in his dream and he went after it.

Elusive Love

*T*he Florida beaches of Destin and Fort Walton always played prominently in my dreams of my soul mate, undoubtedly because my mother's parents lived in Florida and owned property in and around these areas. My memories of Destin go back to my very early childhood and then later as I got older, when I visited my cousins Barb and Beth, we spent many summer days shoving our feet through the singing sands.

I was thirteen or fourteen, about the age when all girls start dreaming about the boy they will marry, when I first "saw" my soul mate. In my dream, I was standing in the mist, toes in the Destin sands, when out of the waves a man, not a boy, walked toward me. I couldn't tell anything about him, except that he was tall. He only took my hand, but I remembered thinking his fingers were long and almost poetic, sensitive.

Though it was a dream, the meeting was quite real and for days I couldn't shake the memory of it. When he touched my hand, I swore I'd touched flesh, not a specter.

I didn't dream about him again until I was sixteen. The dream this time was even more vivid, and upon awakening I was shocked it was still the same person. It really didn't make sense to me. I sensed he was extremely intelligent, but I couldn't make out his features and he never spoke.

On my eighteenth birthday, I was driving to work with my father, an attorney, and he said to me, "You've reached the age of consent. You can run away and get married without asking, but I hope that you would."

Though he was joking, I remember looking out at the falling snow from the car window and saying, "Dad, I'll be fifty before I meet the right one."

He laughed. "Don't be ridiculous. You have lots of dates. You'll meet someone before that."

I replied, "I'm having a problem with this dating thing. No one can carry on an intelligent conversation."

He nodded seriously and said, "Unfortunately, you were gifted with my brains. I've had the same problem most of my life."

I gaped at him. "You do?" His admission did not give me much comfort. "So what's the answer?"

"Wait," he smiled.

I threw my hands up. "See! That's what I said! I'll be ancient!"

"Fifty is hardly ancient," he mused.

"It is to me," I grumbled, thinking no one has kids at fifty. Life will pass me by.

As the years passed and I went off to college, I decided not to wait around until I was fifty. My dreams of my "sea-king" were only dreams. I gave up on him. After all, he was a fantasy and I had to go on with my life.

So I put my childhood behind me, got married to Andy, bought a tiny bungalow, planted a garden and experienced the joy of giving birth to my son. I was putting down roots and was quite happy with my sweet, though small life.

Then the incredible happened. On the night before my twenty-fifth birthday, I was dressing to go to a party. I had taken an old television cabinet I'd bought at a yard sale for five dollars, draped the yawning cavity with some cheap blue cotton and created a vanity table for myself. I had one of those lighted makeup mirrors left over from my freshman year in high school. For ten years, I'd gazed into that mirror to apply my makeup. There was nothing new or unusual about my routine.

While putting on my makeup, it was as if my own reflection faded away in the mirror. Instead, in the mirror I saw the face of my forgotten "sea-king." I blinked hard twice, wishing him away. But he remained.

I'd never thought about crystal balls or scrying (the act of looking into the future) until that moment. I remember thinking to myself, "This is my future."

In clips, vignettes and scenes, I saw the majority of my adult life roll out in front of me like a scroll already written. I saw myself many years in the future. At the age of thirty-two, my entire life would change. I saw myself clearly. I was older, I was accomplished, I was on my own and my husband was no longer at my side. Shocked, I put my hands over my mouth. I felt tears in my eyes, because of all the things, I didn't want Andy to die. The idea of divorce was so repugnant to me, I believed the only answer was that he would have to be dead for this vision to come true.

Though at the time of this incident my baby son was only four months old, in the mirror he was nearly seven. Looking deeper, I saw the "sea-king" rising again out of the water as he had in the dream when I was thirteen.

This time, he called to me and I could hear his voice. His accent was strongly Southern. My hands were shaking so much I covered my face, and everything disappeared.

Chalking that scary incident up to my over-the-top imagination, I forced myself to forget it. If I did remember it, I willed those incidents not to happen. I was the master of my fate. I was the captain of my destiny. How many times had my parents told me that? I could forge my future.

A year later, my husband was transferred to New Orleans. We were off on a new adventure and I embraced it wholeheartedly.

Over the next three years, we traveled frequently to Gulfport, Mississippi, to visit my cousin Beth and her family. Every chance we could get out of town for a weekend at the beach with Beth and her sons, we did. My dream about the sea-king returned again and again, until it was nearly a monthly occurrence.

There were times when I felt his presence was quite close. I remember being in a grocery store in Gulfport and feeling as if someone were watching over me. I felt as if he could be in the next aisle. Knowing that was impossible and that I had a life based in reality and not dreams, I forced myself to put things into proper perspective.

We moved to Michigan and a year later I lost a baby, a son, Ethan. I went into a severe depression for six months. I dreamed only of dying. We moved to Texas, but our marriage was ending. I prayed for enough strength to just live through it, because I had to take care of my son.

Fear of the future, guilt, remorse and yet determination to remain sane shadowed my days. When the sea-king showed up this time, it was not in a dream.

It was late afternoon. I was crying on the bed in my bedroom. Suddenly, I had the eerie sensation that someone was in the room with me. I stopped crying and wiped my tears. I looked around the room as chills blanketed my body. Fear gripped me.

My eyes went to the window. Framed by the tie-back draperies was the figure of a man. I could see his dark, straight hair quite clearly. His shoulders were broad and he had a barrel chest like my son and narrow hips. He said, "I'll protect you." Then he vanished.

From that moment, I knew the path I was on may have seemed like the wrong one to my family and friends, but it was the one I was being forced to walk. Even I didn't understand why events were pushing me to divorce and be single, because it is not a lifestyle I embrace. It wouldn't be until much later, from another perspective, that I would have clarification. My only choice then was to continue moving forward.

That year I wrote a book, signed with an agent, sold the book, got my first "real" job in sales, got divorced from Andy, sold my lovely home, rented a townhouse and was on my own for the first time in my life. I was thirty-two.

Not until it was over did I realize that unknowingly or subconsciously, I had fulfilled the dream I'd seen in the mirror on my twenty-fifth birthday.

For fifteen years I worked, wrote, raised my son, moved, got married again to Rod, got divorced, and still never met the "sea-king." Just about the time I convinced myself I had never really seen a vision in the draperies or heard someone's voice, he came back to me again. Big time.

I was at a dinner party with my then-husband Rod and was introduced to Vicki and her husband, Jim. She was polite to me, but I could tell she and I would probably not become friends, because she was very reserved toward me.

A few weeks later, Lisa, our hostess, invited us both to lunch. It was then that Lisa burst out with the fact that Vicki was more than a little psychic and that she, Lisa, had planned the lunch so that Vicki and I could get things straight between us.

"I didn't know there was anything wrong," I said. "I hardly know you."

"I understand. I'm quite up front and honest. And that's just the way it has to be with me."

"I'm fine with that," I answered, not understanding where this conversation was going.

"You see, I'm very moral about things and I don't like being around people who aren't."

I still didn't understand what she was alluding to. Then it hit me. "You think I'm not moral? My nickname in high school and college was 'Miss Goody Two Shoes'! You have to be kidding."

"As Lisa said, I'm psychic. The night we met at her house, I clearly saw the vision of a man standing next to you. From the energy between you, he's certainly not your brother! How do you explain that?"

"What man are you talking about?"

"The one you're having an affair with, that's who!"

I swallowed hard. "You saw a man?"

"Absolutely! You want me to describe him?"

I felt the blood drain out of my body. I wasn't sure I wanted to hear any of this. Yet my curiosity would not be quashed. "Yes."

"He's tall. Barrel chest, narrow hips. Dark hair, thinning on top and turning gray at the temples. He looks like he has wings as it grays toward the back. He has brown eyes and wears glasses. And honey, there is nothing that can keep you two apart. He's from Florida, right? Near Destin or Perdido Key. Someplace like that. He's got a boat, that's for sure."

I knew instantly she was "seeing" my sea-king. "You can see him? Who is he? What's his name? He's been haunting me since I was thirteen."

It was her turn to choke on her tea. "You don't know this guy?"

"Never met him. Only in dreams."

Vicki's eyes were huge as moons. "That's impossible. I've never seen someone who didn't figure into somebody's life already."

I laughed. "Guess there's a first time for everything."

That incident was eleven years before I was formally introduced to my soul mate, Jim, by a mutual friend. The instant I met him, I knew. So did he. His dreams had been haunted by a soul mate with blue eyes, he said.

My stories about the sea-king came out the first night we talked. I wanted him to know right off the bat the nutcase I was.

He didn't blink. We compared times in our lives, places, dates, situations. He'd lived most of his life in Gulfport, where I'd visited my cousin Beth. When I was living in Houston, so was he. He'd been to some of the same functions at the same hotel, knew some of the same people as I. We realized we had continually passed by each other, though only a hair's breath away, for years.

I discovered that his first wife and the mother of his only son was born on the same day and year as my sister, December seventh. She is a Sagittarian. So am I. Is that coincidence or a sign?

When Jim met my son Ryan and his wife Christy, they bonded instantly. It wasn't until a few weeks later when I met Jim's son, Bear, that I received my biggest shock.

"Why didn't you tell me the boys could pass for twins? Even the same likes, intelligence, caring and values?"

He shook his head. "I didn't say anything, because I still don't believe it myself. It's spooky, huh?"

"Spooky or just another sign that we were meant to be."

Still more validation was on the way.

About a year later, I took Bear to see Ryan and Christy's house for the first time. We breezed through the pretty rooms until all of a sudden, Bear stopped dead in his tracks.

His eyes wide, he marched up to the refrigerator where Ryan had a snapshot of me at the age of twenty-four, holding a two-month-old screaming baby Ryan.

Pointing to the photo, he said, "I remember this picture. Ryan, how did you get this snapshot of my mom and me?"

Ryan smiled. "That's not your mom, Bear. She's mine."

"That's not me?" Bear took the photo down.

"No," I replied, rubbing the chills off my arms. "I'm holding Ryan."

"This can't be," Bear replied, then looked at me. He was visibly shaking as he put the photo back. "Well, that's just about the weirdest thing I've ever experienced."

Ryan slapped him on the back. "Better get used to it, pard. That kind of thing always happens around my mom."

If ever I had wanted validation of divine intervention in my life, I'd gotten it that day. It had taken me fifty years to find it.

These vignettes of the ruts and stones of my divine path inspired my novel *Elusive Love*.

The Day Nancy Bit Off Her Tongue

My sister, Nancy, has more energy than I do. It's important to remember that fact throughout my stories about her and myself. When this incident occurred it was October 1957, before Nancy's fourth birthday, which is in December. Since I'm five years older, I would have been eight years old. It's also important for this story to know that this was the height of the Cold War. The end of the Korean War was a bitter pill for Americans to take. Any and all news of our political and social battles with the Communist countries were like living, breathing organisms in our household. My father wanted his children to be raised with an awareness of world events and to be able to conduct meaningful, intelligent conversations at the dinner table.

The fact that we were all eight years and younger (my brother Bob was only a month old at this time) didn't daunt my father's pursuit of imbuing us with a thirst and desire to reach out beyond our small town, to the four corners of the earth for growth experiences. Discussions of my parents' fears and concerns about the Russians and the "Red Chinese," as Communist China was referred to then in the newspapers, were held at dinner ad nauseam.

Personally, I wanted to get excited about pending doom and our country being overrun by some distant warrior nation, if only for the purpose of killing the long boring days of summer. The school classroom and seeing my school friends was more to my liking than doing nothing all summer, except helping my mother with laundry, mowing lawns and changing the new baby's diapers. Fear for me was being told I had to baby-sit all day on a Saturday. Fear, for my parents who had known firsthand the terrors of war, was called China.

We did not own a television up until this time, as my father referred to the invention as "an idiot box." Fortunately for us, we three older children bent him to our collective will by twisting his very words to us back at him. To be aware and politically conscious in the "modern" world, we were being left behind by not owning a television. That, and our promise of foregoing our allowances for the next several decades (we reneged on our promise there) did the trick. It was that October when a brand new Admiral black-and-white television set, complete with rabbit ears, was delivered to our home.

One morning near Halloween, my mother told me after breakfast that she'd had a horrible nightmare the night before and couldn't sleep. "I dreamed that the Red Chinese came to America. They came here to La Porte and they captured Nancy. They took her away and I couldn't find her. I searched everywhere for her and when I finally found their hideout, I saw them through a window as they were cutting out her tongue."

"Mom, that is gruesome!" I gasped in horror. "It's the worst nightmare I ever heard of." My vivid imagination instantly painted a scene in which my sweet little sister was being tortured. Just the thought was more than I could bear.

Mother grabbed me by the shoulders, her eyes earnest and determined. "No matter what happens today, don't you let Nancy out of your sight. I have an awful, awful feeling that something is going to happen to her."

Being only eight my argumentative skills were zilch, but I tried to convince my mother that her reaction was a bit over the top about this dream. "Mom, you always tell me, 'it was just a bad dream,' when I have a nightmare."

Mother's eyes were that piercing gray she gets from time to time when she's looking through me. "This is different. I know this kind of dream. It's a warning." She squeezed my arms a bit tighter. "Promise me you'll watch out for her."

"I promise," I said, thinking to myself, *Geez!*

It was pretty much an ordinary Saturday around the Lanigan house. My brother Ed cleaned out the garage. He was seven and was a he-man already. He told me that daily. He could rip the place apart, if he wanted to, with his bare hands. He was stronger than Davy Crockett. (He told me that, too.)

I helped with laundry and played with newborn baby Bob.

Nancy had the prize, though; she was going to Sherry Parker's birthday party. It wasn't one of the big neighborhood parties with sixteen kids all going. It was a small affair this year, just Sherry and three of her other "same age" friends, including Nancy.

She had a special robin's-egg blue organza and silk dress with a huge sash at the waist and billowing crinolines underneath, making her look like an Irish Dresden doll pirouetting in her brand-new, black patent leather shoes.

I helped Nancy bathe and dress and brushed out her blonde curly hair, which I envied more than was Christian to do. She always had the rosiest cheeks and the pinkest mouth. Truly, I thought she was the prettiest little girl in the county.

Because Nancy couldn't wait to wear her new dress Mother had made, she begged, pleaded and demanded (the last being the loudest) to get dressed two hours before the party. We all gave in. It was easier that way.

Sure enough, true to high-energy Lanigan form, Nancy got bored waiting around for the party.

"I want to go out and play."

"No," I said. "Mom says you have to stay in the house so you won't get dirty."

"I won't get dirty. I just want to play on the monkey bars."

"No. Mom said you can't go outside because it's dangerous."

Nancy's Campbell-kid adorable face screwed up as she shoved her tiny hands on her puffed-out skirt. "It is not."

"It is, too."

Nancy marched indignantly to the draperies that hid the window to the backyard and yanked the side back. "It looks fine to me."

I rolled my eyes. I hated it when she threw common sense back at us.

"Why can't you be like other three-year-olds and just take orders?"

"You're not the boss!" she ranted. "And I want to play outside."

"I tell you what," I said. "Let's watch television. It's Saturday afternoon and we haven't seen half the shows they have on Saturday afternoon."

Then, as now, Saturday afternoons on television hold no lure for a child. Nor for most adults, either. Today we have golf and tennis. Back then, it was bowling.

Nancy held her nose. "It stinks!"

"Look, here's the deal. Mom said you can't go outside until I have to walk you to Sherry's party and that's the end of it."

"Fine!" Nancy spat. "I'll go to my room and play with my dolls until it's time to go."

"All forty-one of them? Good idea. They should keep you busy," I said, suddenly realizing that a movie was coming on WBBM-TV. I sat down on the sofa and was instantly enthralled with the "special showing."

Mother was at the kitchen sink cleaning vegetables and making dinner preparations. Suddenly, she froze mid-motion. She gasped as a chill blanketed her. She dropped the knife. It clattered against the porcelain.

"Nancy!" she screamed and raced out of the kitchen. "Where's Nancy?" Mother demanded frantically, as she rushed into the living room.

"In our room . . ."

Mother's eyes flew to the window.

Then we heard the most bloodcurdling scream I've ever heard.

"Nancy . . ." I said, feeling my own blood turn to ice.

She screamed again. The sound came from the backyard.

Mother and I both turned to the window.

Nancy had evidently fallen from the monkey bars. Her mouth was wide open and blood was spewing down the front of her robin's-egg blue dress.

"I told you to watch out for her!" Mother screamed at me and raced out the back door. "Call your father! Tell him to come with the car!"

I took only one more glance at the river of blood coming from Nancy's mouth and raced to the kitchen and dialed my father's law office. I told the secretary to tell my father to come quick. She said my father had gone on an errand.

I hung up the phone and raced to the door.

"What happened?"

"She bit off her tongue," my Mother shouted back.

Suddenly I felt as if I was moving in slow motion. The scene from earlier that morning came back to me. Mother had dreamed the night before that Nancy was going to be kidnapped, tortured and her tongue would be cut off. Goosebumps devoured me. I started crying. I was more than terrified. I knew for sure God would never forgive me for not watching out for Nancy. He'd sent the angels to warn my mother. And I wasn't listening.

"I'm sorry," I said to both my mother and Nancy, but the words froze in my brain halfway to my mouth. All I could do was cry and shake. *Please don't let her die.*

Mother was halfway up to the house with one arm around Nancy, who was screaming in mortal pain, and the other hand under my sister's mouth.

"Daddy's not there! What'll we do?"

Mother didn't blink. "I'll take her to Fran's next door. I see her car. She can take us to the hospital. Call the office back.

Tell your father what happened and where we've gone. Tell him to come to the hospital."

Terrified at the incredible amount of blood streaming down my baby sister's face and dress, I didn't stop to think. I called the secretary back and she promised to go find my father and tell him about the accident.

The hours it took for the doctor to examine Nancy and sew her tongue back on were the longest, most excruciating in my life. I paced the floor a million times, praying to God not to take my baby sister from me.

I remembered being five years old when my parents told me we were going to have a baby. At the instant I'd heard the news, I knew in my heart it would be a girl. Even though my brother Ed wanted a baby brother, I knew God loved me so much, he'd bring me a sister. It was as if I'd heard her on the other side calling to me before she was born. Curiously, Mother chose the name Nancy Jean before she was born and never chose a boy's name. To me, it was a sign that I would have a baby sister.

For me to have been as negligent as I had been that afternoon, wanting to see a movie on our "idiot box," was inexcusable. I had been given a charge, a responsibility—and I had failed.

I went to my room and prayed on my rosary, but guilt washed over me like a tidal wave. The time had dragged on so long, I knew the news was dire. The phone never rang. I believed I knew why. Nancy was dead.

It was the end of the afternoon and the sun was beginning to glint through the golden autumn leaves of our maple trees. Baby Bob had awakened from his afternoon nap. I changed him, heated his bottle and fed him. Rocking him in my arms, I went to the living room "picture window" and paced with him. Waiting, hoping and praying.

Then I heard the sound of my father's car coming around the corner of our street. My heart stood still. I squinted to see inside the car. There, seated on the front seat between my mother and father, was Nancy.

Not since the day they had brought her home from the hospital when she was born, had I ever felt more joy. I shouted so loud, I upset Bob and he started crying.

Just as Mother and Daddy got out of the car, it was as if the news of Nancy's arrival had been telegraphed across the neighborhood. On bikes, on foot, in wagons and on trikes, every kid in the neighborhood came to see Nancy.

Before I'd even had a chance to hug her, the neighbor kids wanted to see the bloody dress. They wanted to see her monstrously swollen tongue and her stitches. And they all wanted to know the real truth.

"Did you cry when they sewed you up, Nancy?"

"She was a soldier," my father said proudly. "She didn't make a peep. The doctor said he'd never seen anything like it before. She didn't get a pain shot. She just sat perfectly still while the doctor used that black thick thread to put her tongue back on. I'll bet none of you kids could go through what Nancy did."

Mouths fell open in awe.

She could have charged a buck a look and paid off her year's worth of piano lessons I thought, as the kids crowded around her. She was famous!

But it wasn't until the kids heard the story about my mother's prophetic dream that the room fell reverent.

I looked at them all as they pondered the enormity of the day's occurrences. Children are more intuitive and understanding sometimes about the workings of the universe than adults. In that moment, it was if we all could feel the angels hovering around our house. Knowing glances and solemn nods were exchanged.

As they left, one by one congratulating Nancy, hugging her, they all agreed: Nancy was courageous, but Mother was a legend.

Dream a Big Dream

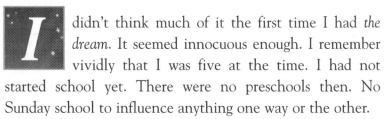

I didn't think much of it the first time I had *the dream*. It seemed innocuous enough. I remember vividly that I was five at the time. I had not started school yet. There were no preschools then. No Sunday school to influence anything one way or the other.

In the dream, I was blonde and five years old. I remember that my hair was braided in thick braids, though in my "real" life I'd never worn braids. I lived in a huge castle, though I don't remember any details about it other than the window. It was winter in the dream, with a thick blanket of snow on the ground. I was not cold, though all I wore was a black wool Tyrolean kind of dress or pinafore over a white long-sleeved blouse. There were lacings on the bodice and embroidered flowers around the neckline of the blouse. Even in the dream I liked this kind of blouse, as I did in real life. My mother made most of my clothes when I was a child and she went to great pains to embroider or ruche the bodices. My sister and I were so proud of our dresses, because my mother made everything special.

In the dream, I heard people laughing and singing. I crept across the snow, hoping no one would see me as I went up to the illuminated window. It was a dark and early winter evening. The window was a lattice pattern of leaded glass, and the stones in the wall were icy as I leaned against the window to peer inside.

Inside were several men and two women. The largest woman was a cook, dressed in a full-skirted dress with a flour-covered apron. She had blonde hair in braids as well. The men were laughing, as well as the women. They all seemed quite happy, sitting near an enormous fireplace with a roaring fire, which was used to boil a cauldron of stew or some food. A trestle table filled the center of the room and on the table were huge loaves of warm bread. The men drank from dull metal tankards.

The most overwhelming aspect of the dream was my awe at how genuinely happy these people were. I thought to myself, "They are poor, but they are happy. I've never known such happiness."

When I awoke, I didn't think much about the dream other than to tell my mother about the story. She thought it a sweet story, but that was all. I didn't think it was me because we always had laughter and happiness in our house, therefore, I would not have expressed curiosity over the fact that this little girl seemed to be stunned by happiness. No doubt at the age of five, I didn't think things through this cogently but, nevertheless, I deduced the girl was not me.

It surprised me how real everything in the dream happened to be. However, in time, I forgot the dream.

The next year, I visited the dream again. This time in the dream, everything was exactly the same except that now I knew my eyes were blue. Nothing changed, however, except that I was a year older.

Again, I told my mother about the dream, but she brushed it off.

For the next eight years until I was fourteen, I dreamed the identical dream over and over. Only now, I visited the dream more than once a year. Sometimes it was as much as six or seven times a year. Nothing ever changed, no more details came to me other than the fact that I grew older.

By this time, everyone in the family was sick of hearing about the dream. To make matters worse, there was no plot or storyline to the dream, only the fact that I kept going there from time to time. I had no one to speak to about this. Psychologists or dream analysts were not heard of, nor did any exist in my small, midwestern town.

Once I entered high school, the dream vanished and so I put it away in my mental archives along with other childish things.

I went off to college, studied psychology and metaphysics, and still didn't think about the dream until at the age of twenty-two, I visited it again. This time the girl was nineteen, and she looked away from the window, as if looking into a camera or at me and said, "Don't you know I'm you?"

Sitting bolt upright in bed, with every cell in my body wide awake, I breathed very heavily, fighting back a scream of terror.

Who was me? The dream was me? I was the dream.

Suddenly, all my existential philosophies began streaming through my head. Was I schizoid? Had I lost it? Maybe I was living an alternate reality. I'd had plenty of hours in front of television watching *Twilight Zone* and *Night Gallery*, not to mention, I was a "trekkie" of the first class.

This time, however, I did have enlightened counsel surrounding me. I could take my pick of all sorts of teachers and professors to help me out with this one. It was at this time, my metaphysical professor introduced me to the concept of reincarnation and past lives. Foreign as it sounded, it was still the only explanation that made sense to me.

My psychology teacher told me that his version of dream analysis is it explains the mental and psychological traumas and problems existing in the mind of the patient at the current moment. Presumably, should one improve or worsen in their mental condition, the dream would change. It would not stay the same. Yes, even he thought this was a *Twilight Zone*-type of situation.

Once I stated all of this to my mother, though she said she wasn't all that sure about such things as past lives, she didn't rule them out. Goodie. Mom is into this, too. It was I who was clueless.

Then, Mother explained that perhaps I was subconsciously tied to our ancestors from Alsace-Lorraine. This made sense to me. I hadn't thought of those roots, high in the Vosges Mountains between France and Germany.

At this time, I was double-majoring in history and English literature. I had minors in about every subject field my college offered. After all, what's there to do at an all-girls school, but study?

Over the period of those four years of college, my ability to tap into the knowledge I gained during that past life came home to roost. I read novels in French class or studied the lives of Germanic philosophers and, without cracking the cover, I "knew" about these people, the places they lived, what it was like 100 or 200 years ago. I could sense their emotions. I knew how they dressed, the kind of foods they ate.

Their cultures and worlds were as alive as if I were living them. The more I studied about them, the more information came to me. I would spend hours on the weekends in the library consuming more biographies, not required reading, or poring over magazines or pictorials about past ages, past castles, past art and architecture.

What drove me was that the more I explored their world, the more I opened the treasure trove of knowledge within my own mind.

Sometimes, I would read about certain lives and have incredible emotional reactions to their joys or tragedies. I couldn't explain any of this to anyone, because I didn't know what it was or what it meant.

What it did do for me was to help me gain a 4.0 grade average nearly every semester of my academic career. There was a high practical side to this dream–memory stuff.

I never shared these experiences with anyone for fear of being tapped crazy or worse, lazy. I worked hard for my grades, but at the same time, I was teaching my brain to "click on" when I needed it.

By no means did I retreat to a fantasy world. What I was doing was better. I was taking fantasy and making it workable in my everyday life. I wasn't Walt Disney, but I was getting closer by the minute. My research papers became delights to write. My reports sparkled with insights that were clearly beyond my meager mind. During my philosophy classes and metaphysics seminars and weekend retreats, I learned more about tapping into the unworked portions of my brain. I didn't have to meditate or pray for hours on end. I simply relaxed, took a couple deep breaths and asked for the information I needed.

Asking is key. I remembered that line in the Bible, "Ask and you shall receive."

These days I think about how we stumble around, grumbling and mumbling about what we don't have. What we need. Why we can't "get it together." The real truth is, few of us just *ask*.

Each day when I sit down to write, I ask my angels to bring me whatever it is I need to make my story the best it can be. If I need research, I can guarantee I can drive over to the bookstore, walk down the aisles and suddenly, I'll just stop, turn and stick out my hand. Voila! There will be exactly the title I need, the information at my fingertips. Now, with the Internet, I don't even have to leave the house. However, I do enjoy the drama of the bookstore scenario. Many is the time I've walked through a row of shelves at a library and the book I've needed has literally fallen off the shelf.

I don't think my story is unique. I think it happens to people every day, but they are too afraid to call it what it is. It's your guardian angel helping you down your path.

I don't know who that girl was in the recurring dream. To this day, she's never told me her name, but I have no doubt she is one of my ancestors, helping me from the other side.

I don't necessarily think she actually was me, or that I was her in the past. I think she was trying to say she is a part of me. Her blood is my blood. Her memory cells are recorded in my DNA, or at least I read that scientists have proven that cell memory from our ancestors is part of our human heritage. That's why each generation builds on the previous generation. Otherwise, it would take us until adulthood to simply learn to speak.

I take comfort in the fact that she's helped me find a way to use more of my brain than I might have without her. She's sent me on decades of investigations. I must say, they have all been interesting and insightful.

What I do wonder, though, is how long I will go before I meet her again. I've read that angels come and go in our lives, serving a purpose for a particular time or crisis. Then they move on.

I wonder. Then I shake my head and say, "Nah. She's still around. I'll bet on it."

Sharon and Josh— Mystical Mother and Son

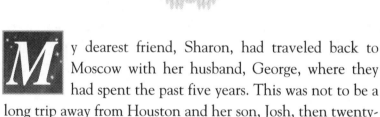

My dearest friend, Sharon, had traveled back to Moscow with her husband, George, where they had spent the past five years. This was not to be a long trip away from Houston and her son, Josh, then twenty-one. She was hoping to return in two weeks.

Working and going to school kept Josh busy enough, but he graciously looked after Sharon's house, the yard, mail, bills and cats for her while she and George had to travel so much. Over the years apart, Sharon and Josh, always close, had formed an even closer, almost telepathic bond. They seemed to know when the other was thinking about them. She would hear a particular song on the radio and think of him at precisely the same time as Josh had heard the same song half a globe away in Houston.

Sharon and George had been in Moscow for over a week and had been staying in a hotel, rather than at the "dacha" where they used to live. In relating this story to me, she told me that the time difference was nine hours between Moscow and Houston.

At three in the morning, Moscow time, Sharon bolted upright in bed, enveloped with chills and the sensation that something was wrong with Josh. Not since he'd been a small child had she felt that kind of fear.

At first she tried to shake off the eerie feeling, but it wouldn't go away. She thought she could hear Josh's voice calling her, but told herself such things were absurd. Still, going back to sleep was out of the question.

The intensity of the fear gripped her even more. This time, she heard his voice as if it were in the next room. Now she knew in her heart something was dreadfully wrong with Josh.

Dashing out of bed, she placed a call to her home. It was 6:00 P.M. Houston time. Josh answered immediately.

"Josh, what's wrong? I just know something is wrong!" Sharon said.

"Mom, I can't believe you called. I'm sick, Mom. So very sick." Normally calm and quite together, this time Josh was crying. He was terrified. "I can't stand. I can't see. I'm sh . . . shaking all over."

Sharon instantly realized that for some reason, Josh was convulsing.

"Josh. You have to call Jim and Catherine. Can you do that? Can you hang up and call them?"

Josh gathered his wits long enough to answer, "Mom, I . . . already did. Jim's on his way over."

Incredulous, Sharon told him to hang up the phone. Sharon dialed Jim's cellular in Houston and got through just as he was walking in the door to find Josh on the floor, convulsing. Jim bundled him up and helped him into the car.

I was out buying groceries when Jim called me on my cellular and told me what was happening. Though I had planned to finish another half dozen errands, something had "told" me to go home immediately. "Jim, you won't believe this, but I'm right around the corner."

When I walked in the door, Jim and Josh were at our house. Josh was nauseous by now, huddled on the bathroom floor wrapped in a blanket. His face was white as a ghost under his tan.

I knew that Josh was working as a lifeguard. It had been incredibly hot that day. I realized instantly what was wrong. "It's heat prostration. Dehydration." Quickly, I got some Gatorade and Josh drank it.

It was amazing. We could almost watch his color returning.

Moments later, Sharon phoned from Moscow, and Jim assured her that Josh was going to be fine.

Within an hour, Josh was truly back to normal. "What are you fixing for dinner?" he asked with a smile.

"Steaks," Jim replied. "How would you like yours?"

"Thick." Josh smiled as he dialed the phone for the last time that night to tell his mother that he was fine and he loved her.

In Sharon's own words, "I have had that 'feeling' from time to time all my life with my son, but never as strong as that one night."

Submitted by:
Mrs. Sharon Reese
August 18, 1998

Bells Are Ringing

*T*he dream was short and sweet. The Voice came to me and said, "Catherine, go see the doctor."

I was forty years old at the time. I knew better than to question The Voice. He and I were practically on speaking terms. I sometimes wondered why Mr. Voice didn't just pick up a phone and call me. I wouldn't have to waste all that time sleeping. But then, perhaps that is what sleep is . . . a cellular phone line to our angels.

First thing in the morning, I got dressed, got in the car and drove over to my doctor's office. I didn't even call ahead.

I walked into the office and said to the new nurse I'd never met, "I have to see Ed. Is he here?"

"No, he's off today," she answered. "He'll be back tomorrow. Is this an emergency? I could call him."

"An emergency?"

"Yes," she said, getting a bit peeved at my inability to be specific.

I was used to the old nurse who knew me, my life and practically my cell structure intimately. Suddenly, I was aware that I had no idea what or if anything was wrong with me. My actions were due to a dream, not any symptoms of illness. I just knew I had to see Ed.

"I, er, that is, I . . ."

She began the litany all gynecological nurses are trained to ask. "Any unusual bleeding?"

"No."

"Cramping? Fever?"

"No."

"Vomiting?"

I held up my hand. "Forget the quiz'em on the air. There's nothing wrong with me that I can tell."

"But you want to see the doctor so badly, you didn't call for an appointment?" She was really blowing her patience quota.

"I know it sounds weird, but I . . ."

Just then, the door flew open and Ed Zabrek came back-end first into the waiting room. He was carrying a small television set. He was wearing jeans, tee shirt and running shoes. He was clearly not intending to see patients.

"Catherine! What are you doing here?"

"I'm not sure. I thought it was your day off."

"It is," he smiled, hoisting up the television set. "I found this in my garage while I was cleaning it out. I wanted to see if I could hook it up to my new computer . . ." He stopped abruptly.

"What do you mean, you're not sure?" he asked, his smile fading.

Glancing at the apprentice nurse sheepishly, I turned back to Ed. "Something told me I should see you today. It's urgent."

"Something?" His eyes widened.

"Okay. Someone. It was in a dream. This voice came to me and said I had to come see Ed immediately."

In a flash, Ed was all business. He took my arm. "Come on."

The nurse was beside herself, bolting off her chair. "Doctor?"

Ed spun around. "You see this woman? Her name is Catherine Lanigan. If she ever calls and says she has a cold, alert the hospital! She underplays everything. Stuff like this happens to her all the time. Get room four ready. I want to do an ultrasound." Then he looked at me with a wink. "Guess I'll be needing this television set today after all."

The nurse gasped. "You *need* that TV? Now?"

"Come on, Cath. You get undressed."

"But doctor, she doesn't have any symptoms . . . of anything."

As I closed the door to change I heard Ed say, "Do you think it was coincidence I just happened to find this television set I'd forgotten about in my garage, the day after I realized we needed a new monitor for the ultrasound? Do you think it's coincidence, she just happened to be here as I was coming in the door? You didn't even know I was on my way up."

"Well, if it's not coincidence, what is it?"

"You'll see."

Ed hooked up the television monitor, while I climbed onto the table. He flipped a switch and in the next second, I was watching a televised version of my post-hysterectomy interior.

Suddenly, a big black spot came into view.

Ed froze.

"What's that?" I swallowed hard.

The nurse gasped and turned ashen.

"Ed?" I felt chills blanket my body.

"It's a tumor. The size of a four-month fetus is what that is."

My world went reeling out of whack. Tumors. Cancer. I'd had a brush with cervical cancer five years earlier. Ed had saved my life back then. Now this.

My career was on hold. The books weren't selling like they once had and, though my writing was better than it had ever been, my publisher was looking for reasons to let me go. Death would be a good reason.

Personally, my son was off to college and didn't really need me any more. The strangest thing was that eighteen months earlier, I had remarried my ex-husband Rod. It was a disastrous mistake. He claimed he wanted the one thing I couldn't give him: children. Ironically, my body had manifested a growth—a tumor, not a child. Even more eerie was the fact that Ed described the tumor not as the size of a fist or a basketball, but "the size of a four-month-old fetus."

Had the entirety of my life not looked so tragic to me, I would have cried. Instead, I laughed. Then I cried.

My intuition told me that I'd come close to death at least a half dozen times in life. Maybe I'd lost count and this was my ninth brush. I was out of chances.

In those seconds, I was trying to decide if I should try to hang onto any of the shreds of what was left of my life. I decided that if it was God's will, I would check out. I was forty-three years old. Maybe it was time to go. I remembered that I'd had a past-life dream that I died in a car accident at the age of forty-three in my last life. Maybe that's all we do: reenact the past. If so, I was prepared to go.

"What do we do about it?" I asked, my tongue sticking to the roof of my mouth.

"We operate. First thing in the morning."

"Okay."

"You know the drill. Nothing by mouth after midnight. I'll have the nurse set up the operating room. They'll call you from the hospital and do a preregistration over the phone."

"I do know the drill," I replied, looking over at the screen. "Can I have a printout of that?"

"Sure," Ed said, printing out the black blurb onto a tiny fax paper.

"Go home and get some rest."

"I need to talk to my son," I said, looking at the photograph of the tumor that would kill me.

My emotions were not angry or bitter. I was resigned to my death. If anything, I was numb, but resolved to make certain I set things straight with my son. I wanted him to know that I loved him and how I wanted my personal items divided up. Things like that. I was shocked at how calm I felt about my life being over.

Ed turned to the dumbfounded nurse. "You see what I mean? Catherine had a dream she should come to see me. Somehow, destiny worked a miracle and I showed up here today, instead of being out somewhere."

My eyes shot to his face. "You think I'm going to live?"

It was his turn to be shocked. "Of course I do. We've always made it together, you and I, to death's door and back. You're going to be fine. I know. Otherwise, why would you have had that dream telling you to come here?"

"Oh, yes. The dream. The Voice."

I walked out of the office in a fog. The day was beautiful and hot. It was the end of July. Children were in the throes of summer vacation. Our pool business was going great guns.

There was activity, life all around me, but I couldn't see it.

I drove home and began the preparations for the surgery the next day. I called my friends Vicki, Stacy and Cherry. I called my mother, who vowed she was coming down to be there for the operation. I begged her not to, then realized that if I was going to die, she needed to be there for Ryan. I agreed she should come.

That night I told Ryan the truth. I knew in my heart I was going to die. I was lucky. I had warning. I gave him the key to my safe-deposit box, which contained my will, some of his baby things and odd sentimental things only a writer would think were valuable.

I told him that if by some fluke I would survive this surgery and live, everything in my life was going to be different. I told him I would be getting divorced again. I was going to have to find a new tack with my writing. Find a new day job. Find a new place to live. Find a new life.

Because Ryan's head was screwed on the right way from birth, I knew he would be a good man, a good husband and father someday. I would help him out from the other side, and I would always love him more than I loved anyone or anything my whole life through.

We held each other and cried a great many tears that evening. I thought it odd that Ryan insisted he didn't think I would die. He wanted me to live, once again, if not for myself, then for him.

My mother arrived on a late-night plane and I went to pick her up. With her arms around me, I was glad she'd insisted upon coming. She talked of how to fight cancer if the tumor was malignant, but I wasn't listening.

"It won't be cancerous," I said. I didn't tell her it didn't make any difference, because I wouldn't be waking up.

The following morning was a blur, driving to the hospital with my very worried mother, my frantic son and my husband pretending to be concerned.

The paperwork was filled out and finished in seconds, it seemed. I was prepped and going into surgery before I took a deep breath. I remember thinking that once one has realized death is imminent, it doesn't come slowly, it comes fast.

I remember counting backward to 99 from 100. Then everything went black.

Imagine my surprise when I woke up in recovery.

I even asked the nurse, "Are there hospitals in heaven?"

She thought I was crazy. But I wasn't. I was alive.

When I was taken to my room, my smiling, loving mother was there to greet me, as was Ryan, who was overjoyed that I decided not to die.

My husband walked up and leaned over the bed. "Cath. Your publisher called and said they read your newest book and they want you back on contract."

"You hear that, Mom?" Ryan's voice was trembling. "See? Nothing has changed."

I held his hand. "No, everything has changed. I've crossed a barrier I didn't believe was possible. I told you, things will not be the same. I saw my future when I was asleep. I saw your first child. I saw so many things."

The nurse came in and told everyone they had to leave. Hugging everyone felt so good. I can't describe the flood of emotions I felt, as the gentle pressure of love against my skin melted down into the marrow of my bones. I was embracing life again. I knew, in that half-conscious state, that Rod and I would say goodbye for the last time and it would be soon. I knew that my mother was healthy and would remain with me for many years to come. I knew that Ryan's life was going to be happy and free of the kind of pain I'd experienced in my own life. I knew that grandbaby's smell was all around me.

Ed came for his rounds that night and, as I'd expected, he told me we got the tumor before it had turned malignant. "You're clean as a whistle."

Smiling, I looked at him and said, "This may come as a surprise to you, Ed, but guess what?"

"What?"

"This is the last surgery I'll ever have."

He squeezed my hand. "You got that message, too?"

Gasping in disbelief, I said, "You . . . you know?"

Nodding, he said, "Sure do. It's the last."

My recovery from that operation was the fastest healing I've ever accomplished. Three months later, I was moving out of the house again and going out on my own. I felt I had a new lease on life.

Physically, I didn't die that day, but there was a death of the old me. No longer was I living for other people. Perhaps there was something to the idea that I had passed a barrier I'd set for myself with my past life when I died at forty-three.

I changed many things about myself during the months and years that followed. I trusted more in God and his mission for me on earth, rather than trying to push and prod my own issues through. I let go of doubts and fears. I let go of anger and I embraced the spiritual, intuitive soul I'd always been.

It was at that time, I vowed never to repress my soul-driven nature ever again. I was given many gifts when I came to this life. I'd tried to downplay them for too many people, for too many years. This new life was about Catherine. I was going to be me.

All of this took place over a decade ago. Other than two bouts with winter colds, illness has not been part of my life. I have somehow managed to keep writing, though the nature of all my writing has been transformed, transmuted to what you are reading on these pages. I'm not certain if I'll ever write fiction again, though I still feel a tug on my heart to put stories down on paper.

However, my soul thrusts me to write about real life. Real matters. And so long as God and the angels keep me on the earth, I have no choice but to say and to write what they dictate.

What a glorious challenge it is!

Snuggle House Dream

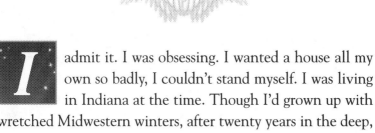

admit it. I was obsessing. I wanted a house all my own so badly, I couldn't stand myself. I was living in Indiana at the time. Though I'd grown up with wretched Midwestern winters, after twenty years in the deep, deep South, I had forgotten that it actually can get to 88 degrees below zero wind chill and a mean/ambient temperature of 49 degrees below. It wasn't my imagination. Life on the prairie is rough.

I missed everything about Texas. I missed planting a garden in the middle of January. I missed Mexican food with too many jalapenos. I missed my friends. I missed my son.

I was miserable.

I wanted to move back, but financial and personal circumstances in my life kept me rooted in Indiana. The flip side of this misery was that I brushed up on my visualization techniques to occupy my mind. I felt like those Vietnam prisoners of war who told stories of building houses in their heads, though they were confined to bamboo cages. I felt trapped physically, but my mind was free as a bird. It could do anything.

Though I was working at my sister's store for more than eight to ten hours a day and writing at night and on the weekends, I still had energy to burn. I would lie awake at night and dream of the kind of house I would build for myself someday. As the winter weeks passed, I began to talk aloud of this house I wanted to my mother and my sister. They would look at me indulgently, but I knew what they were thinking. How will the money for this house appear? Out of thin air?

I pondered this. Thin air wasn't all that bad. Thin air had its good points. But not much else in my life at the time did.

During the corporate turndowns, takeovers and mergers of the early 90s, I had been "released" by my publisher. This is a nice way of saying thrown into a free fall. I didn't have income, only outgo. I wrote synopses and story ideas with incredible profusion and speed. I worked on one novel after another, trying to find the magic formula that scintillates an editor into leaping out of her chair, rushing down the hall to a "board" and saying "This is the great American novel." It didn't happen.

Instead, I kept writing, filling my antiquated hard drive with words. I worked in an unheated converted garage, wrapped in double sweat suits to stay warm. Across the street loomed a water tower. Between the cracking, peeling paint, it wore graffiti. Out of the other corner window, I stared out at a rusting trailer in a neighbor's yard for inspiration. I tried to find something uplifting about this life, but there was nothing. It was as lifeless as the winter snow outside.

The only hope I had was that my words flowed like a river, ancient, constant and endless. I lost track of time for hours, nearly days on end.

My other hope was that somehow, I would find my life again. My new life, I proclaimed to myself, would be spent in my "snuggle house."

Next to my bedside, I kept all matter of old decorating magazines my sister and mother had tossed in the trash. I sent away for free floor plans or clipped them out of the Sunday newspaper. Since I used to be in the swimming pool and room remodeling business, I knew that if one were to cut open my veins, they'd find sawdust. Not from the circus, but from construction. An aphrodisiac to me is fresh-cut pine lumber. I love the hum of hammers and saws as they build. As they create. I am thoroughly convinced that in a previous lifetime or lifetimes, I was an architect. A builder. A carpenter. All of which are worthy skills.

The good thing about winter is that it passes. Once April was around the corner, I had promised myself I would take a few days off and drive to Houston to see my son and daughter-in-law. I was so incredibly proud of them. Not only were they soul mates who had found each other, but at their very young age, they were building a house! They were about to break ground and I wanted to be there to help them christen the site.

The night before I was to leave, I had one of my precognitive dreams. I saw myself walking up to a construction site. I knew instantly that it was not Ryan and Christy's house, but my own. I was spellbound by the size of it. I craned my neck to see the roof. Even in the dream, I was shocked that the house was clearly three stories high.

This, of course, was impossible, since I knew full well that no one built three-story houses—at least not in Indiana and certainly not in Houston, which was where I always hoped to return.

In the dream, I could smell the wood. Smell the pine. I walked atop a long pine plank from the curb to the house. I remembered thinking it was a very small front yard, the distance was so short. The front door was incredibly tall, well over eight feet, and above the door the entrance was curved, not square. To the right was a huge window to the living room. To the left was a garage. The plywood was just being hammered onto the framing. I had the sensation that the house was truly part of my future and that in the present, my house was in the process of being built.

I stopped just short of the front door and I said to my guardian angel, "I know you have given me this dream to give me hope. But I want more. I want you to show me exactly when this house will be built. At what point in the future will I be going through this experience?"

Lo and behold, in the dream, I was suddenly holding a child. It was not Ryan and Christy's child. It was not my granddaughter, that I knew. I knew it was a girl. Then suddenly, there appeared another child of the same age standing next to me. She took my hand, stuck her finger in her mouth and looked at me.

I looked at the child standing next to me. "How old are you?" I asked.

"I am twenty-two months old."

"And what month is this?" I asked the other child.

"It's nearly the end of July."

"And who are you?" I asked them both.

They giggled at each other. "We belong to Rod."

At that moment, I bolted awake.

I was trembling and sweating. I got up and went to the living room and curled up in a wing chair I'd owned since Ryan was four years old.

Rod was my ex-husband. Among a litany of problems we had, one was that Rod wanted children of his own. I'd had a hysterectomy. I couldn't have children. But he could.

Rattled beyond belief, I realized that I'd been given an incredible personal glimpse into the future. My future and that of others.

I left for Houston and had a wonderful, thoughtful trip. When I got to Ryan and Christy's apartment, we all agreed that Mexican food was in order. Over fajitas, I asked Ryan if my ex-husband was remarried or dating anyone seriously.

"No," Ryan replied. "What's up, Mom? You don't usually ask about him."

I told Ryan about the dream, but both he and Christy passed it off, at the time, as nothing more than a dream. I told my friends about the dream. Being older, wiser and having known me for as long as they had, they listened more intently.

My fun time in Houston came to an end and I went back to Indiana.

A year later, circumstances in my life changed enough that I was able to move back to Houston. Ryan and Christy were ensconced in their new home but, having recently graduated from college, had no furniture and few household goods. I gave them the contents of my twenty-four-foot Ryder truck, enough furniture to finish their house and fill the cabinets. I kept my eleven-year-old computer, my desk, my chair, files and clothes and went to live in a rented room with a friend, until the fall when I could move to Boliver Island and rent her beach house for the winter.

On Father's Day, my friend hosted a family brunch to which she had invited Jim. She told me he was everything I couldn't stand, Irish (like me), dark hair, dark eyes and an attorney.

She told Jim I was not his type, since he preferred shapely blondes with no careers to tie them down, as he traveled all over the world and expected companionship.

On our first date, Jim asked me what some of my goals at this latter point in my life were. Among them, I told him, was that I wanted to build my snuggle house.

As our relationship grew and I trusted him more, I told him about my snuggle house dream. Curiously, he asked me if I'd seen it again in any more dreams. I realized that I had not.

That very night I had my second dream. This time, I was standing inside the completed house. I was in the kitchen. Even in the dream, I was aware how important it was that I remember the details of the house. I saw a long counter covered in tortoiseshell. There was a huge Sub-Zero refrigerator, which I remember because a hired woman or caterer was putting something away in it. I remember going to the sink and looking in the sink, then up at the huge window. As I looked out the window, I saw a red brick wall right smack dab up against the window. I turned to the caterer and said, "Why would I build my snuggle house next to a brick wall? Surely, there have to be trees between us. A ravine. Some nature somewhere!"

Just then I heard a man's voice say, "Darling, the people from *People* magazine are here."

I heard a woman's heels against a wood floor, then against marble.

I was very nervous, because I knew they were there to interview me about *Wings of Destiny*. I ran to the sofa and sat down. I was stunned that the sofa was white and all down-filled, and that it was sitting in the middle of the kitchen! My surprise was enough to awaken me.

Three years later, Jim and I built *our* snuggle house. During all the days of planning, moving lines around on blueprints, laying out the structure on the lot and picking colors for the interior, I didn't think too much more about my dream.

We were living half-time in Ecuador. I was writing three and four books a year. I now had two golden retrievers to feed, bathe, walk and care for, as well as a new grand-daughter. My life was so full twenty-four hours a day that reflection was not logged into my scheduler.

At the end of July, I braved the 117-degree afternoon to meet the builder at the construction sight. He was late. The carpenters were applying the plywood to the side of the house, as I walked across a pine plank up to the nine-foot-high front door.

Suddenly, I stopped dead in my tracks. It was the particular scent of hot pine lumber. Unless it had been so incredibly stifling, I never would have experienced that particular smell. The dream came careening back to me.

The most popular house design in our part of Houston near the Galleria in 1998 is a three-story, detached, townhome-looking house. It has a rounded portico for the front door. To the right is a double window into the living room where I hoped to put the biggest Christmas tree I could find. To the left was a two-car garage. It was a short distance indeed across the plank from the curb to the front door.

In the dream, I remembered, I had been holding those "dream babies." They had told me it was the end of July in the dream. The blood in my veins froze. I shivered. "My God, it was all true."

In the ensuing three years, my ex-husband Rod had remarried and became a father to twin girls. Those girls were twenty-two months old that July day, as I stood there on that plank.

I rushed into the kitchen and stood at the window which had just been installed. It rose ten feet to the ceiling. Only five feet from my window was my neighbor's house. A red brick house.

At the end of where the island was to be, Jim and I had planned a Sub-Zero refrigerator. The countertops we'd just selected were not tortoiseshell, which is illegal and impossible, but they were dark cocoa-brown granite that looked like tortoiseshell.

The floors in the living and dining rooms were to be wood, while the foyer and open family room/kitchen area were to be marble.

Three years earlier, Jim had surprised me with a white down-filled sofa which we would put in the family room, close to the island, so that Jim could talk to me while I cooked. My sofa was in the kitchen!

And the people from *People*? That has yet to happen. But I have a feeling, it's all just a matter of due time.

My South American Dream

im had been working diligently for a domestic oil company, selling oil royalties. It was an uphill battle on a good day. The stock market was so strong, virtually no one was going to invest much of anything in domestic drilling. Because he was wise enough to see the handwriting on the wall, Jim began looking for other business opportunities.

Within days, a German aircraft company contacted him about representing them. Jim took meetings over the holidays, and the phone calls to Europe seemed promising.

The Germans wanted Jim to fly overseas and meet with them the first part of January. However, due to his previous commitments, he told them he was not able to get away until the end of January. Everyone agreed that on the last Tuesday of January, Jim would fly over for the meeting he hoped would finalize the deal.

Over the holidays, I began fantasizing what it would be

like to see Germany. I had never been there, but I have to admit that I replayed the scenes of Shirley Temple in *Heidi* a million times in my head. I remembered my grandmother's stories of Munich and Frankfort and how much she loved the German people. I still had a tiny, ivory edelweiss pin she'd brought me from Munich thirty-five years earlier.

Christmas passed, I took the tree down and put the decorations away and began a new book. Life fell into our same routine.

In mid-January, I awoke one morning quite early. Jim was already downstairs doing what he did best: thinking and pacing.

"I had the strangest dream," I said. "I dreamed that we packed a U-Haul and drove to South America. It was so real, I can't get the vision of that packing out of my mind. We even took Beau with us."

Jim patted my hand patronizingly and said, "That's nice, sweetheart. But if there is any moving to be done, it's your German you need to brush up on. Not Spanish."

Shrugging my shoulders, I said, "I don't speak either language, so I guess it's not a problem. Still . . . the last time I had a dream like that, it came true."

Jim harrumphed off the idea. "On Monday I'll be going downtown and they'll be telling me they don't need my services any longer, and that will be that." He went to his office, rummaged around in his briefcase and returned to the breakfast table. "See? Here's my ticket for Tuesday morning to Germany. Everything is set."

"I know," I nodded and removed my dishes from the table. As I started up the stairs to my study, I kept thinking, "He's right. After all, why on earth would we ever go to South America?"

The following week, I had all of Jim's winter wools cleaned and ready to pack. I even stopped at the department store and bought very warm wool gloves for him. Living in Houston, such things are not high priority.

On Monday morning, Jim packed up all his files to hand over to the oil company regarding the contacts he'd made over the fall and winter and reports about the results.

Though he was on time for the meeting, the president and the board of his company were in a closed session. Jim was told to wait in the hall, but that it shouldn't be much longer. Fifteen minutes passed. Then a half hour. Jim waited patiently.

Suddenly, the board room doors opened and the president stepped out. "Jim! You're just the one I wanted to see."

"I am?"

"Who do you know in Ecuador?"

Jim smiled. "Only the ex-Minister of Energy and Mines."

The president's jaw dropped. "Come in, Jim. We need to talk."

I was at home waiting for Jim's call. He'd told me the meeting wouldn't be long and that we would have lunch together.

I waited. Lunchtime passed. One o'clock passed.

I gave up waiting, went back to work and lost myself in the next thrilling chapter of my book.

At a quarter to four my phone rang and it was Jim.

"You won't believe what happened," he said. "I'm leaving tomorrow."

"I know, Jim. You're flying to Germany."

"No, there's been a huge change in plans. I'm going to Ecuador."

"Ecuador? I'm rusty on my geography," I said as the hairs on the back of my neck prickled. "Is that in Africa or is it . . ." I was afraid to say the words as flashes of my dream rolled across my memory, "in South America?"

"Bingo! South America. Is that bizarre? I'm going to South America."

"Just like in the dream," we said in unison.

I was shaking. It was another dream come true. Except I hadn't wished for it. It just happened.

"You need to unpack all those winter things. It's summer in Ecuador now. However, I'll be in Quito where it's like spring all the time. I have to change over my ticket and . . ." He was excitedly going through his litany of chores to do before he left.

"Jim. This is really true?"

"Yes! Believe it! Your dream was accurate."

"All except for the U-Haul part," I said. The words were no more than out of my mouth, when I felt as if my blood had frozen. "We're all going to go, Jim. Even Beau."

"Well, we'll see about that part. First I have to go down there and see about the possibilities."

Suddenly, I could see our future spreading out before us like a picnic. "We'll be there by spring. In a house. It's big and white."

"Sure, Honey," he said. "I'll be home in a few minutes and we'll talk about it then."

We hung up, but my vision of Ecuador wouldn't go away. I could see flashes of rooms of a house. I had no idea where

Quito was. Though I looked up information on the Internet and in my encyclopedia, nothing prepared me for the natural wonders I found during the ensuing two and a half years when we called Quito, Ecuador, our second home.

Dream a Little Dream of Me

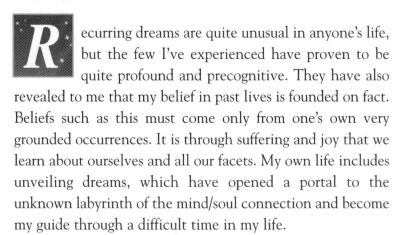

R ecurring dreams are quite unusual in anyone's life, but the few I've experienced have proven to be quite profound and precognitive. They have also revealed to me that my belief in past lives is founded on fact. Beliefs such as this must come only from one's own very grounded occurrences. It is through suffering and joy that we learn about ourselves and all our facets. My own life includes unveiling dreams, which have opened a portal to the unknown labyrinth of the mind/soul connection and become my guide through a difficult time in my life.

My purpose in including this past-life dream in this volume is to perhaps shine a light on your unsolved dreams and musings which appear on the surface to be nonsense, but which are, in fact, guideposts on your divine path.

As human beings, we think of mysteries as dark, shadowy culprits lurking in our psyches or in our episodes of daily life. They confound us and confuse us. They lead us astray. If we were to strip them of their masks, and reveal their truth, wouldn't that be our goal?

One would think so. However, too often, the truth stands out among us, glorious in its essence, but we turn away from it. The truth might force us to change our thinking. We might find it necessary to work a bit harder at our lives, on our soul structure; we might have to pray in earnest, rather than giving lip service. And what, of all those prejudices, must we dispose of?

Acceptance of truth is tough. It's part of our evolution into more spiritual beings. But we can do it, with God's help.

I don't remember having this particular dream before I was in my teens. It came to me in bits and pieces, like a kaleidoscope of colors and shapes. The elements were all there to compose the symphony of a story, but it took maturation and hard-core life experiences, mostly of the painful kind, for the dream to evolve into a cinematic production.

I have always loved those wooden inboard motor boats of the 1920s and 1930s. Their sleek lines, gleaming varnished teakwood and chrome appointments spelled "class act" to me. My parents never owned a boat in their lives, despite the fact that we lived in a town with seven lakes. No, my love of those boats came from clips and shorts in dreams more than any particular hands-on experience I had with such vessels.

Some people dream of sailboats or ocean liners. My dreams were always of speed boats. By the time I was out of my teens, whenever I dreamed of a boat, I now saw myself and friends in the speeding, gleaming boat, all of us dressed in navy and white. The women were in pleated white skirts with navy blazers, the men in white slacks with navy blazers. I remember the boat captain wearing a white hat with a navy patent leather bill. It had an anchor insignia on the front. We laughed and told jokes among ourselves. I remember always waking up and thinking how the people in my dreams had so much fun, when I wasn't having any.

For years, I told myself that my once-a-month dream was simply my mind balancing my workday real life with my fun-loving dream life. I told myself the dream was a mental exercise.

About the time I turned twenty-eight and my son was four years old, the dream began changing. I now saw faces rather clearly. The captain of the boat was blonde. I did not know him in real life. I'd never met anyone who remotely acted like him or sounded like him. On one particular night, he specifically said to me, "Don't you know me yet? This is 1935. It's important that you remember me and the year. Very important."

I awoke shaken. I felt I had been visited by someone who was alive. The voice was not the same angelic voice I'd heard before, but a real man's voice.

Still, I was young. I passed it off as a nightmare and went about making pickles and canning fall vegetables.

Only one month later, the dream was playing again. This time, it was a story. There were five of us, two men and three women. This time, we were wearing bathing suits. I remember that my bathing suit was white and very tight to my body. It was rather long, feeling almost as if I was wearing short shorts. The bodice was gathered and to my current mind, I thought, "Boy, there's a lot of fabric in this bathing suit."

We had been out boating all day. Some of us had gone swimming. I was a good swimmer, despite the fact that the water was icy cold. I knew, somehow, that we were at Lake Louise near Banff, Canada. I have never been to Canada in my life, and certainly never to Lake Louise. My mother had visited that region of Canada when she was a child with her parents, but even at the age of thirty, I'd never been. To this day, I've never gone to Lake Louise, though it's on my list of "must visit" sites around the globe.

The blond captain of the boat was a large man, much older than I. Apparently, I knew him very well and was fond of him, though I sensed he was in love with me. I also knew that I was not married to anyone, nor had I ever been or hadn't been for a very long time. I was exactly the same age as the year. It was 1935.

The captain docked the boat at a pier and we all ran across the soft green grass toward a house. I distinctly remembered commenting on the flagpole in the front yard and the colorful flowers planted in a ring around the flagpole. I got the impression it was the Fourth of July and we were there on holiday.

One couple running behind me were arguing about something between them. I didn't know them very well, but I turned to make note of their faces. She was blond and had interesting yellow-green eyes. She was Jewish and very much in love with the dark-haired, green-eyed man who was her lover. I knew that she was pressing the man to propose to her, but he was having none of it. He was a notorious playboy. I had known him for at least a decade and thought to myself, "He's up to his old tricks."

We rushed into the house, which was a large one, but by no means a mansion. It was large for that era and the fact that it was a second home revealed the captain was quite well-to-do. It was built of washed rounded stones, light stained woods and many paned windows. The floors were wide-planked pine, highly polished or varnished. The furniture was over-stuffed and covered in floral-patterned English chintz. Brightly-colored Navaho rugs hung over the open banister work on the second floor. The main ceiling area of the living room was pitched and beamed. A huge, black wrought-iron chandelier hung in the middle of the room.

The fireplace was massive, made of these particular stones which I've seen in California and Colorado, but not in the north or in Texas. Over the mantle hung a lovely painting of the "Lone Pine" near Carmel, California, depicted in every-thing from postcards to watercolors and oils.

I stopped dead in my tracks as we rushed into the house, chilled by the oncoming night air. The captain grabbed an afghan off the sofa and threw it around my shoulders as I observed the painting.

He came up from behind me, placing the afghan over my shoulders. He pressed his hands into my shoulders.

"This is my favorite painting," I said, gazing at the pine.

"I know," he said.

"You bought this painting for me?"

"I built this house for you," he replied.

I was stunned. I turned around to face him. Gazing into his blue eyes, I saw tears. He was profoundly in love with me.

"But you're married," I said, feeling a blow of sadness strike my soul. I knew he would never leave his wife and children.

I was not yet his lover. At that moment, I knew I loved him in return. I also knew that I was about to become his mistress.

"I have asked her for a divorce."

My sadness turned to elation. I threw my arms around his neck and hugged him. I had waited a very long time to hear those words. I believed him. I loved him. He would, of course, be telling me the truth.

Then he turned me around and with a little urge, moved me to the right. There was an alcove area where the stone turned to wood panels. Hanging in the alcove by a long blue satin ribbon, as was the style in the twenties, and lit by an art lamp was a black-and-white photograph portrait of me.

I looked precisely as I do in this lifetime.

I was brought to tears of gratitude and love for this man who seemingly had poured his heart out to me.

His arms encircled my waist as he leaned his lips down to my ear. "I love you," he whispered.

I took a pace forward and touched the wood frame. As I gazed at the portrait, the strangest thing happened. Suddenly, I was no longer in the dream. I was standing outside the dream and was cognizant of my life in both eras, the past and the present.

I said aloud, "Upon my death, how do I feel about my past life?"

From the depths of my soul or the heights of heaven, The Voice boomed, "Disappointment. You must do it over."

Flooded with incomprehensible shame and self-judgment, I was heartily sorry to God for wasting the precious lifetime I'd been given. I didn't know why at that point I was disappointed in myself, but I was. I felt that my soul knew why

I'd come to earth, but I hadn't lived up to my soul's mission. I hadn't let anyone down, but myself.

I didn't think it was a moral issue over the captain's marital status. It went deeper than that and was profoundly more diminishing. This was a matter of soul-ethics. I'd not done something I should have. That was the crux of my scandalous crime.

Eerily, the photograph began to burn from the right hand corner upward, as if the film had been overexposed. From a small pinprick hole, the burn melted the portrait. My face in the photograph became ugly and mangled.

I awoke with a scream. I was sweating and, yet, trembled with chills. I bolted out of bed and went to the bathroom and doused my face with cold water. I suppose, I thought initially that I was on fire.

I gazed at my reflection in the mirror. I was only thirty years old, not thirty-five. It was 1977, not 1935.

At this time in my life, I shrugged off my recurring dreams, both this one and the ones of the "sea-king." They were not the same man and besides, I was too busy taking care of my family and new home to spend time on esoteric thinking.

Again I told myself this was only a dream. Its memory would fade away, as nightmares should.

Over the next years, the dream did not fade. It was as if once it had put itself into proper order, it liked return engagements.

My life changed. We moved to Texas. I was divorced, going to work and living on my own. Other recurring dreams sprinkled my night moods. More past-life memories intruded into daydreams. It was as if I was being forced to accept or reject the idea of past lives once and for all.

Then one night, after I was married to my second husband Rod, the dream returned and cast glaring illumination on my current life.

I realized that the dark-haired, green-eyed man who was fighting with the blond woman was my now-husband. I'd seen him in a dream four years prior to our marriage. You can imagine my shock when I awoke. The realization that I'd inherited my mother's ability to see the future in dreams hit me between the eyes. Rather than the dreams going away, they were becoming more accurate.

Six years after this, I actually met the yellow-eyed blond woman from the dream. We became friends, yet she departed my life harboring ill feelings toward me. Rod and I divorced after ten years together. Fully fourteen years after the first time I'd experienced this dream in its totality, I met the blond captain who had built the house for me. We were companions for over a year and then, he, too, departed my life.

That dream does not visit me anymore. I believe that in that lifetime, I harbored anger toward other people when I should have learned to release them in love. I believe I didn't pray for them with an open and unconditional heart. My lesson, I was to learn from the dream and this life, is to continue to love all those people who have entered my life and had an influence on me. Through my experiences with each of them, I have been given the opportunity to love. I have charted my own course, down my own divine path. I am solely responsible for the turns I've taken, and I grant that each of them was a beacon for me to light my way.

They were not, nor are they now, the villains in my life. Nor am I the heroine. They are the heroes for returning to give me another chance to set the record straight. For that I bless them and release them to God.

On the day of my death in this lifetime, my goal is to look back and say, "Satisfied."

Dottie's Past Life

I shared with my friend Dottie about my past-life regression with my former companion and though I was expecting a reaction, I wasn't prepared for what I got.

Instead, she said, "I know exactly what you mean. I know the name of my past life. I was John Smith."

My eyes flew open. I know every detail about my most recent past life, but I've never been able to uncover a name. Dottie had never told me anything about her beliefs and when she blurted out this information, I was surprised. "How do you know?"

She explained that she, too, had recurring nightmares about a death scene. Only in her past life, she was a man. She saw herself dressed in a Navy uniform—she was just a seaman—aboard a huge ship.

"I wasn't anyone important. I was a deckhand. For the longest time, I passed over this nightmare, but as I got older and Sonny and I were married, the dream came more often, offering more details."

"Details?"

"In the dream, I realized I was in Hawaii and that my death was at the time of Pearl Harbor. There was a huge explosion. I felt as if I was in hell, there was so much fire and smoke. I was terrified. I knew I was about twenty-two in the dream. I saw myself flying through the air and dying midair from the impact of shrapnel or debris. I felt no impact when I hit the water. In fact, the dreams were so violent, so vivid, that I used to wake Sonny up screaming from terror."

"What did you do to stop them?"

"I didn't do anything, but finally, Sonny had enough of my tales of past lives. He came home one day with two plane tickets to Hawaii. He said, 'we're going to put an end to all this foolishness right now.'"

My mouth dropped open. "He took you to Hawaii to investigate a past-life dream? This is my kind of guy!"

"Sure. He thought he was going to prove I was an idiot, shuttle me off to a shrink and that would be the end of that."

"Don't tell," I said, "it turned out differently."

She smiled broadly. "It was nothing like he'd thought. We got to the hotel and immediately called the director of the historical museum there. We booked a meeting. Then, I also contacted the local library and explained we were searching for newspaper clippings about the Pearl Harbor bombing."

Sonny pulled more strings and, through the military, found a list of the men who died that day. Going down the list, we found a John Smith. We took the list to the library and, from the newspaper articles, discovered a description of the explosion on the ship where John Smith had flown through the air. His body was fished out of the ocean by one of his shipmates.

There was the proof, in black and white, for Sonny to see. For years, he'd scoffed at Dottie's dream, claiming that she could at least be more inventive with the name. John Smith was just far too common.

Dottie said that from that day on, Sonny was a firm believer in reincarnation. He had something many don't have. He had solid evidence.

After that trip to Hawaii, Dottie's recurring dreams of John's death ceased. She slept more soundly, even if Sonny didn't.

Signs

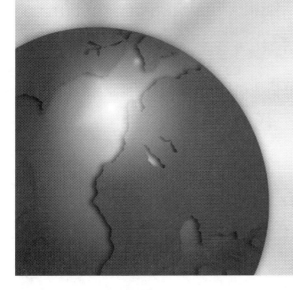

*P*oor signs. Skeptics love to ridicule them. They're so easy to misinterpret. They're usually minuscule and mean little or nothing to anyone but the recipient. The desperate and lonely look for signs in the oddest corners of their lives.

Signs are nobody's pushover. They are tough little guys that keep bouncing back for more each time you knock them away. They are persistent and ever-present. Signs are delicate morsels of reassurance. They are those odd quirks and sparks that give you a reason to smile instead of frown. Signs put a bloom in your cheeks when you're wearing the pallor of hopelessness.

You know what it's like to be stuck in rush-hour traffic wondering what on earth you're doing working for an unappreciative company who is about to give you a pink slip. You feel your life is in shambles. Then the morning drive time deejay plays "Reach Out (I'll be there)."

You think of a best friend. Your child. A departed parent or the sermon you heard on Sunday. That's a sign for you to buck up; that even if you get laid off, it's supposed to happen this way. Better things are in store for you.

Once you open yourself up to this tiny miracle of divine intervention, you'll receive more abundance than you can imagine.

Let's say you brush the incident off as "coincidence."

You go to work, get laid off and it's weeks, maybe months before a job opportunity comes around. Even then, it's a worse situation than what you'd just left. You become despondent, depressed and then desperate. You'll do anything to find the right job for you. You succumb to the only course of action. You pray.

Within days you receive a phone call from one of the very first companies you interviewed with. This time, the job is a step up in responsibility and pay. It's the challenge you've been wanting. But you had to go through an "opening-up process" to achieve your goal.

Let's go back to that day in the traffic when you heard that special song. Now, let's say you recognize that your angels sent you just that song to tell you that your life is changing in the material world, but still you have all your angels listening to your wants and needs. They are looking out for you. You are protected.

You go to work. You get laid off. You still panic. After all, you are human. But the panic lasts only a moment. The butterflies in your stomach settle down and that small inner voice tells you that your life is changing. The answers will come to you and you will know your direction, because you believe in your angels.

You go out to dinner with friends that night. They introduce you to some friends who just happen to stop by your table. You chat. You discover they are starting up a new company and have just received their funding. They're looking for a person with your qualifications. You like their easy smiles and openness. You agree to meet the next day.

You scramble at home to find your resume. Miraculously, it's in the first file you check. Your best business suit is cleaned and pressed and ready at the cleaners; you'd forgotten you'd taken it in two weeks earlier.

You awaken in plenty of time for the formal interview. Traffic is inordinately light going into town, freeing you from freeway stress.

The meeting flows effortlessly. Everyone is more than a well-precisioned work team. You have the sense of a loving family when you converse. Not only is the money exactly what you were wanting and needing, but the projects are exciting, challenging and creative.

When you arrive home, there's a message on your recorder. Your new employers are so happy to have you come on board, they couldn't wait to phone you with the good news.

When you are at a crossroad in your life, signs point away from the fear that will set you back. Signs point toward divine love. Signs show the way to help create an "openness" to receive the joy, happiness and abundance that are yours when you are connected to the divine side of life.

As you read these stories, it is my wish that you will begin to "see" God working in your everyday life; in everything that you do.

Sedona, Stacy and Me

I n the autumn of 1989 my friend Stacy, her boyfriend, my then-husband Rod and I went to Phoenix, Arizona, for a convention. While the men went to workshops and buyers meetings, Stacy and I rented a car and drove up to Sedona. I'd told her so much about the calming, spiritual aura I'd felt there during the time when my father lay at death's door in the Flagstaff hospital. Stacy had always had a particular affinity for anything regarding American Indians, and she couldn't wait to see the rocks and the terrain.

While in Sedona on my first trip with my mother and sister, I'd purchased several books about the Indians, their culture and the history of Sedona. I'd even read the Hopi Indian Bible and found it incredibly fascinating. Though Stacy hadn't read any of my books, we'd had enough time on the trip up for me to relate the bare basics about the beauty and topography. An artist, Stacy brought a camera, lots of film and a sketch pad and pencils.

We'd planned to have lunch in the little town along the river where I'd had lunch with my family previously. The food was good, but the aura of the trees, river and rock was like none other I'd ever experienced. Stacy was accepting of my experiences and was looking forward to a pleasant day of sightseeing and shopping. None of our ordinary tourist mindset prepared us for what actually happened.

After going through the shops to get our bearings, we chatted with shopkeepers and locals about particular sights. We were stunned to discover people talk about UFO sightings and strange visions in the night sky, as if this kind of thing happened every day to everyone. We tried not to smile when we were informed that if we wanted a truly "unique experience," we needed to ride out to Cathedral Rock and meditate awhile.

Intent on embracing as much Indian lore as possible, Stacy inquired about the "prayer wheels" one of the shopkeepers mentioned.

"Oh, yes. There are prayer wheels on most of the higher elevations and cliffs. But you have to climb to get to them. Besides, everyone knows you don't need a prayer wheel," we were told. "Only an open heart."

Intrigued, we bought a local site map and got explicit directions to Cathedral Rock.

The day was incredibly beautiful. Not a cloud in the sky and the clearest, cleanest air either of us had ever experienced. By early morning it was warming up. We'd worn jeans in case we decided to be adventurous and climb one of those cliffs everyone had talked about. We shucked our lightweight jackets and drove on to the rock.

Cathedral Rock was disappointing because, well, I'd expected it to look like a cathedral, I suppose. Upon seeing this enormously elongated high mesa, I fell into a frump. "There's no steeple! How could anyone think this looked like a cathedral?"

Stacy was not at all disappointed. "You've never been to France, but I have several times. It looks exactly like a French cathedral, long and elegant. Those rocks extending from the top downward to the ground resemble flying buttresses, giving it a similar appearance to Notre Dame in Paris."

I have a great imagination. I make my living with it, but clearly I was out of my element with this one. Stacy was better at making rocks into cathedrals than I was.

We pulled the car off the road and parked in a clearing. It was a good quarter mile or better to the rock, but from our vantage point we could take great photos. We snapped a few, breathed that fabulous dry, clean air and filled our vision with the incredible surroundings.

It was amazing to me that rock and earth could be so red and the sky so blue. In fact, the sky was almost a teal color, unlike a blue sky. As I gazed upon the rock, I noticed that the sky around it seemed even darker blue, as if the rock were outlined in navy. Then the sky became a teal color around that band of light and then dissipated into a more normal color of azure blue. Without thinking, I said to Stacy, "I'm not an artist by any stretch, but it looks to me as if there's a navy blue band around Cathedral Rock."

"You see it, too?"

Stunned, I said, "Too? You mean it's not my imagination?"

"No. In fact, it looks to me as if that light is the aura of the rock. Then after that band is a band of green blue. . . like . . ."

"Teal?" we said together.

Instantly we faced each other and stared wide-eyed.

"You think this is a phenomenon or something?" I asked.

Stacy looked back to the rock. "The colors haven't changed."

I was almost afraid to look. This time it looked to me as if the rock was moving, pulsing, like a mirage. Now I knew my eyes were playing tricks on me. Except that with my contacts (which I always wear), I have more than perfect vision.

"Is that rock glowing?" Stacy asked.

"You mean that kind of golden color off the sides?"

"Yeah, that," she gulped.

"This is some weird sideshow," I replied.

We walked a bit closer, crunching wildflowers and weeds under our athletic shoes. Suddenly Stacy stopped. "Let's say a prayer here," she said. On a patch of prickly grasses, she sat Indian-style on the ground.

"Anywhere is a good place to pray," I said.

I stood behind Stacy, my hands on her shoulders, while still staring at the seemingly pulsating Cathedral Rock. I started to say something else when suddenly a wind kicked up.

This was no ordinary wind.

The scraggly pine/cypress trees 50 to 100 paces from us were untouched by the wind, but it was there around us. My long hair was lifted off my shoulders. I could feel the breeze in my face, its dry touch against my skin.

"Are you seeing what I'm seeing?" Stacy asked, pointing to a big round ball of tumbleweed. It moved toward us for about five feet, then began rolling around us in a perfect counter-clockwise circle.

"I'm seeing it, but I don't believe it."

The tumbleweed slowly rolled in two complete and perfect circles around us. It took a matter of five minutes or so for the two circles to be completed. I don't think either of us breathed, at all, as we watched the phenomenon. I could have sworn my heart stopped beating.

Just as the tumbleweed stopped rolling, I looked down at the ground inside the circle with us. (We were in the very center of the circle the tumbleweed had "etched" out for us.)

It was as if the red clay earth had transformed and become transparent. Lying just beneath the now invisible earth's surface was a series of energy grids, much like fine wires with sparkling gold electricity running up and down the lines, crackling and igniting. North to south and east to west they crisscrossed each other, with about a foot between each grid either way.

"What is it?"

"I've heard of ley lines. The energy grids of the earth," I said.

"Well, I never have!" she said. "Why am I seeing the same thing?"

"I think we are both here as witnesses to this. We didn't ask to see this."

"I wanted a prayer wheel, Catherine. Do you realize this is exactly what's happened? Someone or something has created our very own prayer wheel for us."

"Great. Now what do we pray for?"

"I don't know. But I have the feeling we better make it good."

"I say we first pray for the earth, for it to be environmentally pure and always clean enough and abundant enough to support man. Then we pray for the people on the earth."

"Yes," she said. "Both the seen and the unseen."

"Really?"

Stacy nodded. "You know, I've grown up with ghosts all my life. Maybe this is my chance to help them."

"Well, somebody wants us to do something."

Suddenly, we both felt inadequate, underprepared and humbled at the opportunity we'd been given by God, the universe or perhaps the departed Indian spirits of the area. We didn't know if were on or near hallowed ground. But whatever it was, it was a special moment in our lives.

The grids remained visible to us for over fifteen minutes. It was time enough for us to pray for everything and everyone we could. Not a cause or cure wasn't thought about and uttered. When we finished praying, the grids vanished and the red clay earth became dense again. The wind had long since gone. The air was still.

Stacy and I remained there in prayer for another twenty minutes or, perhaps, a half hour without speaking. We wanted to absorb all we'd seen. We thanked whatever forces or spirits had tried to reach us that day.

We didn't know if we'd ever find out the reason for our strange adventure, we were only thankful for the opportunity to use that incredible energy to send it out to the rest of the planet.

Silently, we walked back to the car. As we drove away, we were awestricken over these occurrences.

In all our lives, we agreed, we'd never been so overcome with that much peace and tranquility. We were certain such a bizarre happening would never occur in our lifetimes again. We couldn't have been more wrong.

Stacy's Automatic Pen

After our eerie experience at Cathedral Rock, Stacy and I were not much in the mood for further "sightseeing." We decided to drive back to Phoenix for the dinner party being hosted that night by one of my husband's manufacturers. Actually, we had plenty of time. We wanted an excuse to have time to digest all that had happened to us.

After being in the car only fifteen minutes or so, and both of us yakking so much I don't see how we heard each other's questions, Stacy paused for a moment and said, "What did you say?"

"I didn't say anything."

"Oh," she replied, throwing me a quizzical look. Then she sat bolt upright and said, "Didn't you hear that?"

"What?"

"That voice. That man's voice," she said, her tone rising an octave.

My first thought was to check the radio. It was off.

"I didn't hear anything," I said and at the moment I did, I heard a man's voice in my head. It wasn't one of those voices you hear outside yourself. It was as if it came from within.

"*Tell her to write*," the voice said.

I looked at Stacy. I knew I must have turned white.

"He's telling you that he wants me to write something?" she said, eyes like saucers.

"You got it," I replied, dry-mouthed. This was getting a bit spooky for me. "Where's your sketch pad and pencils?"

"In the backseat."

"Get them and see what happens."

"You mean automatic writing?"

I nodded. "I think that's what is about to happen."

Sure enough, Stacy grabbed pencils and paper and closed her eyes, but only for a fraction of a moment. Instantly, her hand was gliding across the page, words seemingly spilling out of her. Or the distant "beyond."

I kept driving. I almost didn't want to know what was going on. I'd tried my hand at automatic writing from time to time. The only occurrences I'd had of anything of value coming forth were after deep, long meditations, at which time I knew I'd cleared my ego, brain and "restricting thoughts" out of the way to make room for the truth or whatever it was to come in. Let me be clear: at the onset of each of my meditations, I preceded them with an intense blessing, repetitions of the "Our Father" and had surrounded myself, the room, my house and my entire neighborhood with white light. Most times, I entered my meditation holding my Bible or my rosary at the very least.

Obviously, I am a security freak.

Quickly, I cautioned Stacy to stop for a moment while we both prayed the "Our Father" and then surrounded ourselves in white and silver light for added protection. I didn't mind a visit or two from ghosts, but I wanted to make certain the ones who were coming along for the ride were not only "of the light," but that they were intelligent and not just some prankster type. In other words, I wanted Stacy's first experience at automatic writing to be the real McCoy.

As she wrote, she said some things aloud. While still driving, I learned that our visitor was an Indian, old, wise and once the chief of his tribe. He told Stacy that he had been her grandfather in several incarnations. The most important of those lifetimes was one in Egypt. In that same lifetime, Stacy's mother's name was Constance. He told her that she was going to go on a trip to Europe before the year was out.

"That's impossible," she said. "I have to work and have no vacation built up."

The writing revealed that the trip would be a gift to her. That she would be going to England and France. While in England, he would reveal himself to her and that his words were true. He told her she would receive a ring as a gift.

The Indian chief also told us that years in the future, I, Catherine, was to be witness to this experience and that I would write not only this story in a book to tell the world about the existence of living spirits on the "other side of the door," but that it was my mission, my destiny in this life to be the voice of those spirits on the other side. That through me and my novels, I was to explain to people "how it works." That I was put on earth to help dispel fears about dead souls, spirits, former inhabitants of earth.

One of the "jobs" a spirit has on the other side is to be pure enough in their own hearts that they may come through human hearts and speak. There is life after death.

For one to believe that beyond this life there is nothing is erroneous. More so, it is limiting to humans to plan for only the life in the flesh. Humans must realize that they can, and should, take advantage of their ancestors and friends in the spirit world to help them through their daily lives. Our spirit guides can help manipulate meetings, connections and opportunities. They can ease our tensions over careers, financial decisions, love interests and friendships.

All we have to do is ask. Asking is key. It's like talking to a friend on a telephone. Just say, "Please help me." Spirits have work to do in their plane, just as we have work to accomplish. Their job is to make our lives more joy-filled.

The stuff of movies about ghosts being fearful creatures is wrong. The fear is in man. Man creates demons with his mind. If you believe there are demons, you'll create living, breathing entities that will haunt you and hinder you forever.

Get those thoughts out of your mind. Fill your head with love for each other, with desire and passion to make the world a better place—and you'll have dozens of spirits flocking to your corner to make things happen rapidly and in correct order.

There are only certain times of the year when spirits take their "vacations." The most important is when the planet Mercury goes retrograde. It's like the energy grid we were shown. During that time, the grids are vibrating on a different tone. The messages to and fro get garbled and mistakes happen. This occurs three times a year, for three weeks at a time.

However, this is a good time for humans to "go back" and retrace their steps. Get the closets, files and garage cleaned out. Make certain all work is double-checked. It is an excellent time for writing, however. For some reason, even automatic writing does well at this time. It has something to do with the right brain (the creative side) being more energized. It is not overshadowed at this time by the mathematical left brain.

Stacy stopped abruptly and looked up at me.

"I think that's it."

"What? No goodbye? No last words of wisdom? I want closure!" I joked.

Stacy looked exhausted. She wiped beads of perspiration from her forehead as she looked down at the papers. "I wrote all this?"

"You don't remember, do you?"

"Barely any of it," she shook her head. "This is amazing."

"I agree. There sure is a lot in there about what I'm supposed to be doing."

"He was quite clear about your mission in life," she said. "Are you going to do it?"

I scoffed. "Not in a million years. Two million years. Everyone who ever read that would think I was nuts. I'm already accused of being over the top with my imagination. What would people say? I'd be burned at the stake." I cast Stacy a warning look. "Let's make a pact. Nobody ever, ever hears about this day and especially not that garbage you wrote in those papers. In fact, maybe we should tear them up."

"No way!" she replied, protectively folding them and putting them in her purse. "These are mine. I'm keeping them."

"But why? They're evidence that we . . ."

"We what? May have found the truth? May have contacted a disembodied spirit? Or maybe it is just our own brains being able to see the future in some unknown way. Don't worry, I'm not going to alert the media that you were in on this. It's my handwriting. It's my stuff now."

"Okay, have it your way," I relented.

"Besides," she laughed to herself. "It can't possibly be true. Who would ever give me a trip to Europe?"

I laughed with her. "You're right. This is just our imaginations getting the better of us."

In mid-November, Stacy's parents gave her an early Christmas gift. They were planning to go to England and France, and because Stacy had just gone through a divorce, they wanted to do something special for her. They gave her a ticket to London. Since Stacy's father was on business, Stacy could stay with her mother and keep her company. The trip would last a week.

The next day, Stacy went into work and was about to ask her boss for the time off, when he came to her and told her that the firm was so pleased with her work that for a holiday bonus they were giving her a week's paid vacation, which she would be allowed to take before the holidays if she wished. Flabbergasted, Stacy couldn't believe her good "luck."

Stacy flew to London and after landing at Heathrow and then unpacking in the hotel, she went to dinner that night with her mother. Stacy noticed a beautiful ring her mother was wearing that she'd never seen before.

"It looks . . . Egyptian," she said, instantly drawn to the ring.

Her mother was thrilled, because earlier that day she'd gone antique shopping in London and had found the ring.

Though inexpensive, it had caught her eye. "Stacy, darling, look," her mother said, "it was the inscription inside that caught my eye."

Stacy's neck hairs prickled. Suddenly, she remembered the "sign" the Indian chief had told her she would receive. "Inscription?"

"Yes, it says 'To Constance from Mary, 1826.'" Stacy's mother sighed.

Stacy turned pale, remembering the Indian guide's prediction. Dry-mouthed, Stacy stared at her mother, then at the ring. "Could I try it on?"

"Of course. I thought I would give it to you for your Christmas present."

"You did?"

"Yes, it looked like you somehow."

"It looks Egyptian," Stacy said.

"That's right," her mother nodded. "I know how you've always been drawn to Egyptian things, even as a little girl."

"I was? I mean, I was. Am."

Stacy's hands were shaking when she slipped the ring on her finger. It was a perfect fit. "I wonder who Mary was?"

"I don't know, dear. But I had the feeling it was a gift from a grandmother to a grandchild."

Chills blanketed Stacy's body. Her mother was saying precisely what Stacy was thinking.

"I think you're right, Mother."

Night Angel

*T*hough Stacy and I were determined not to ever, ever tell another human being about our eerie experiences at Cathedral Rock, we faltered. Stacy let the cat out of the bag to her boyfriend that very evening. He, in turn, immediately said something to my husband.

Cynical to the nth degree, Rod scoffed at the whole thing. In fact, his ridicule was so great that he challenged us to produce a second spiritual event.

We explained that one doesn't simply command such occurrences. They either happen and you're open-minded to it when it's there, or nothing happens at all. I tossed in the fact that perhaps such things are happening all the time, hundreds of tiny miracles every day, and some of us are just too deaf, blind and dumb to hear, see or receive their wondrousness. This statement, of course, went over his head.

However, right after our dinner, we all changed into jeans and at 11:00 at night, we drove an hour and a half up to Sedona. On the way, Stacy reiterated that we were told in the shops that the best night sky watching was at Bell Rock. If we were going to see something, that would be the place to go.

Both men scoffed at us. They couldn't wait to prove us wrong.

Stacy and I hunkered down for what we knew in our hearts was going to be a disastrous night. It was going to take us years to pull out of this nosedive. Neither of these men would ever believe a thing we told them after this. Our goose was cooked.

There were few cars on the road going up to Sedona. But as we drove away from the polluted city and out of the bowl, my sinuses, which had been draining like a sieve, began to clear as that fresh air surrounded us. Climbing into the mountains felt to me, as if I was being lifted to heaven. There are a great many man-made chemicals in the air in Phoenix and I decided on that trip, I was highly allergic to all of them. I was miserable in the city, blissful in the mountains.

It was nearly one o'clock by the time we found our way to Bell Rock following the maps the shopkeepers had given us. When we pulled up, we were stunned to see at least two dozen cars and pickups around the area.

Looking up, we saw a large group of people sitting in a prayer circle nearly at the top of Bell Rock. They had a campfire burning and what looked like candles and lanterns. Their lights lit the way.

We started climbing up.

Before we were halfway up, the prayer group broke up and began coming down the mountain. As we passed each other, I inquired if our presence had dispelled their prayers. I was assured they had no idea anyone else was in the area. They had realized they'd been hours after their intended stay.

My husband flippantly asked if they'd encountered any aliens. Then he laughed.

A middle-aged man, well dressed in an expensive jog suit, looked down at him and said, "Depends upon what you mean by aliens."

Rod replied, "Aliens. Little green men."

The man looked at him straight-faced. "They're gray." He walked on.

My husband instantly sobered.

We kept climbing until we reached the top. The view of the night sky was unbelievable. Surrounded by that much space and infinity, I felt as if I were floating. I truly found it difficult to keep my balance. The moon was full, giving an inordinate amount of silver luster to the earth, illuminating the mountains, mesas and rocks. It was a sight I'll never forget.

We all commented on the unimaginable beauty. We were all four amazed that over an hour had passed since we'd parked the car.

We watched the sky for another twenty minutes or so, but no UFO's appeared. No green men. No gray ones, either. We started back down.

At the base of the rock, all the other cars were gone now. We were the only ones left. Just as we were about to turn back toward our car, I asked the others if we could just pause and say an "Our Father," if for no other reason than to thank God for our health and the opportunity to see this beauty. All agreed. In unison we said the prayer aloud, holding hands.

We took one last look at the sky when Stacy's boyfriend said, "What's that funny red glow up there?"

"What red glow?" my husband asked. "I only see the green one."

Stacy and I held our breath as we glanced at each other. Our gaze followed to the place in the sky where they were pointing.

I kept my mouth shut. So did Stacy.

I didn't see a red glow or a green glow. I saw both. Stacy later said she saw both.

The glowing lights grew brighter and bigger. Doubling in size. Tripling in size. They seemed to blend together and created two streams of purple light. The colors became brighter and whiter. They spread like wings wide across the sky and from earth looked as if they were a half mile in width.

"Did you see that?" Stacy's boyfriend asked.

"See what?" she said with a trembling voice.

"Those . . . those wings."

"It's a dove," I blurted and then clamped my hand over my mouth. I'd sworn not to say anything.

"That's not a dove," my husband said.

"It's an angel," Stacy interrupted.

The purple long shafts of light had turned to white, creating what looked like a white flowing robe extending out from the wide angel's wings span.

"I see an angel," Stacy's boyfriend said.

"An angel," Rod said.

I was the one who heard a voice. "It's trying to send us a message," I said, forgetting my code of silence. "It's saying, 'Peace on earth to men of good will'."

"I don't hear anything," my husband said.

"I heard it," Stacy said.

"I didn't hear it, but I see it," Stacy's boyfriend said.

I blinked my eyes. The vision was still there. I closed my eyes and opened them again. It was still there. "Everyone," I said. "Close your eyes and then open them. See if you still see it."

Everyone did. We all still saw it. We continued watching the vision for twenty to twenty-five minutes.

"This is nuts. I'm not seeing anything," my husband said.

"Don't worry," I told him. "Your memory is so poor, you'll forget it by morning."

We all laughed, because Rod did have an awful time remembering things. We joked around, but still the vision remained.

"This is an optical illusion," Rod. "I say that when we turn our backs and walk away, it will disappear."

"That's a good idea," Stacy's boyfriend said, and was the first to hightail it away.

I moved to the right, to the left. The vision just kept hanging there in the sky. Stacy did the same. We walked back the fifty yards to the car and even at the car, the angel-shaped vision was still there. Not for just a little bit, but for a solid fifteen minutes.

Then, suddenly, the angel disappeared and turned back into the white dove-looking outline. Slowly, it dissolved into the purple light, which then became the red glow and the green glow. Then it became a huge white glow, like a planet in the sky.

We got in the car and began driving away.

We watched as the planet-looking light diminished into an ordinary-looking star.

"Look, no one could ever tell there was anything unusual there at all," I said.

I noticed that Rod was holding the steering wheel very tensely and he was chewing his bottom lip.

"That is the most amazing experience of my life," Stacy's boyfriend said.

"Mine, too," Rod said.

We all continued talking a bit when suddenly I realized something wasn't quite right.

"That message they or it or whatever it was gave us, they had it wrong. It's supposed to be 'Peace on earth, good will to men.' But that's not the message they gave us. They said 'to men of good will'."

"What does it mean?" Rod asked.

"It means that in order to receive blessings and peace, we have to have pure hearts. We have the responsibility to be of 'good will' first. Then we will receive."

"We are accountable," Stacy added.

All of us fell silent as we pondered these thoughts on the drive back to Phoenix.

In that moment in time, all four of us bore witness to a phenomenon. Each of us saw a different part, but all saw the same thing. Later, in the weeks and months that followed, Stacy and I were the only two who continued to believe that what we saw was real and not a "figment of our imaginations."

I have often thought of that night. Of that message I'd heard. Stacy was right. There is a tremendous accountability in that statement from the "night angel." Ten years later, I realize that the world is sorely lacking in accountability these days.

And I can't help but wonder. Have I been wrong not to write these things down and give them to the world? What about other people who are on "Angel Watch" and don't come forward? Is their silence, also, part and parcel of a nation which forgives its own president for indiscretions that a decade ago none of us would have ever tolerated? And of our "tolerance" toward a Hitler-type neophyte, who massacres entire towns of human beings because of their nationality and their religious beliefs?

What of all our inabilities to be accountable for acts of abuse and discouragement toward each other for the sake of one's own ego? Or the corporate bottom line?

Men of good will.

In the decades to come, I hope that we can become as strong as we are meant to be.

Lissy Meets a Jodee Angel

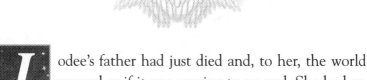

Jodee's father had just died and, to her, the world seemed as if it was coming to an end. She had an apartment on North Lakeshore Drive in Chicago, where she worked her three public relations accounts squeezed in between the time she was helping her mother handle her father's business. She was at her wit's end trying to think of ways to get her own career back on track and let it take off, the way she knew in her heart she was destined to do.

A sudden brainstorm hit Jodee. She remembered Tracy Becktol, a woman she'd worked with in Los Angeles years before. "I need help," Jodee said to Tracy. "You are the best PR agent, besides myself," she said not too humbly. "I've got these huge clients all launching lines and I need to be able to help them grow."

"How can I help you, Jodee? You're in Chicago and I'm in Los Angeles. I can't leave here."

"And I can't leave Chicago," Jodee replied.

"Oh, my God! Jodee!" Tracy exclaimed. "Lissy!"

"What's a Lissy?"

"Only the best PR person besides ourselves on planet Earth. You aren't going to believe this, but Lissy is driving to Chicago this very minute. She just left Los Angeles a couple of days ago."

"This is impossible! She's moving here? Why?"

"She just got married and her new husband, Ron, works there."

"I'm getting that Kismet feeling, Tracy."

"Me, too. I'll find a number for her and let you know."

The next day, Lissy was unpacking her things in her new husband's apartment. She was loaded down with wedding gifts, PR files, client Rolodexes and her computer. She said she'd never forget that moment, because she was wearing her mother's leggings and one of Ron's old shirts.

Ron came in and said, "Sweetie, some girl on the phone says she has to talk to you right away."

Wiping the sweat from her forehead, she said, "Ask her to call me . . ." she looked around at the mountain of boxes, "to call me sometime next week."

"She said you *have* to talk to her."

"Oh, all right," she said, and took the call.

"You don't know me, but my name is Jodee Blanco and I'm a friend of Tracy's and she said you are the best PR person she knows," Jodee said.

"How do you know Tracy?" Lissy asked.

"I worked with her once."

Flabbergasted, she responded, "Tracy is my best friend. If she said I have to meet you, then I will."

Lissy instantly turned to Ron and said, "I gotta go."

"What? Now? You just got here." Ron kissed her good-bye and she was off.

Jodee was stunned when Lissy simply showed up at her apartment.

"You're here?!" she said.

"I am. Tell me what you need."

Jodee showed her in and grabbed a handful of press releases her former assistant had written for her. Lissy read them over and rather than responding to even her first question posed, she began tearing up the releases. "These are crap. Let's get to work."

"God, you are an angel. And one with guts!"

They sat down right away and started working together as if they'd been a public relations team for decades. At the very least, they both instinctively believed they must have done the same work together in another lifetime.

They jabbered away while they worked, and right there on that first day, they knocked out everything that had been causing Jodee concern.

That was the glorious beginning of what one year later officially and legally became their company, Blanco and Peace, with offices in New York, Chicago and Los Angeles.

Jodee and Lissy believe they were brought together by their angels and guides, and those same guides are the spiritual glue that keeps their business growing and expanding. They are also responsible for what they believe is the magical conduit that just "happens" to bring every one of their clients to them. Each client is like family to them. Each has their own particular destiny, of which Jodee and Lissy now know they are an integral part. Their clients' destinies are theirs.

Santa in the Summer Suit

*I*n the summer of 1996, I had traveled to New York City to be a guest on a talk show. I was staying at the Hotel Nikko in the upper thirties near Grand Central Station. This was my first time to experience this section of New York, since I normally stayed in a small hotel in the upper nineties across from Central Park.

The hotel was a welcome surprise for me, being very Japanese and decorated not only in restful colors of beiges and creams, but it was even aromatherapeutically correct. My flight in was uneventful, and knowing that I did not have one of those grueling early morning television air times, I thought I would treat myself to dinner downstairs in the dining room. This is a very unusual thing for me to do. I almost never take my out-of-town meals anywhere but in my room. I'm usually tired, jet-lagged and frankly, I don't like eating out when I'm alone. I like to read while I eat or if there's a good movie on, I'll watch that rather than sit in a restaurant in an unfamiliar part of town by myself. After this many years of knowing myself, I have realized that my over-the-top-imagination causes me to fear kidnappings, bombings, alien space invaders and drive-by shootings. I figure, when out of town, stay in.

That night, I felt different. I chalked it up to the feng shui of my Japanese room.

I bathed, dressed in a comfortable pants outfit and grabbed the novel I was reading. Just as I turned to head out the door, I saw myself in the reflection of the mirror.

Tonight I'm going to meet a movie producer. Something I have written will find its way to film.

I shivered as the impact of the thought gelled in my head. "What a ridiculous thing to think! I'm in New York, not Los Angeles. Why would a film producer be in this hotel of all places?"

Casting the wild idea aside, I headed downstairs. The ambiance of the garden dining room was lush, inviting and just what I could cope with. It was empty.

Other than myself and the maitre d', there was no one in sight. I checked my watch. It was after eight in New York. I asked the maitre d' as he escorted me to my banquette next to a stunning vase of Hawaiian ginger, "Is it always this crowded?"

He laughed.

"Maybe everyone eats later in the evening here," I offered.

"No. It's July. Everyone is out of town."

"All ten million?" I asked, sitting down.

I ordered a chardonnay and opened my book.

Not five minutes later, I heard a cheery, older male voice from across the dining room address the maitre d' by name.

I looked up and what to my wondering eyes should appear, but a man who looked like the spitting image of Santa Claus.

His hair was white as snow, his face round and rosy. His beard was as white as his hair and he laughed merrily, the way a child imagines Santa would. He was dressed in a pale blue and white striped seersucker suit, with white shoes and snazzy suspenders. "Why, it's Santa in a summer suit," I mumbled aloud to myself.

The maitre d' seated the man on the same banquette as myself, but on the opposite side of the planter with the colossal vase of flowers. He ordered his drink and made jokes with the waiters about the absence of clientele in the dining room. I laughed in spite of myself.

We both received our wine, then soup, each eating separately. I pretended to be reading my book; he was incredibly well-acquainted with the staff. Our entrees were brought and the usual repartee was shared with the waiters. Finally, when we'd both finished our meals, he poked his merry face through the wall of flowers and said, "Don't you think this is just silly? We're the only ones in this restaurant. Won't you come share coffee with me at my table?"

"I'd be delighted," I said, wanting to know this friendly man.

"My name is Gregory Peck," he said.

"Like the movie star?" I gasped. Sign number one.

He chuckled. "Far from it. I'm an attorney."

It was my turn to smile. "My father was an attorney."

"He's no longer living?" he surmised.

"No. He passed away four years ago. He's greatly missed."

"I'm sure he is," he replied. "Are you in town on business or pleasure?" he asked.

"Business," I replied quickly, but then thought I should have told him the opposite. I'm not one who likes telling people what I do. One question always leads to five hundred more, it seems, when all I really want to do is be the one asking questions of them. How can I discover the mysteries of human nature, if the only topic is myself?

"What kind of business?"

I figured I'd get on with it as quickly as possible. "I'm here to tape a television show about my new book."

"You're a writer!" he beamed.

"Yes."

"Should I know you?" he asked.

"I write women's fiction, but you might have seen *Romancing the Stone* or *The Jewel of the Nile,* for which I've written the novelizations."

"Ah!" His smile at this point was megawatts. "My son thinks he's a film producer. He's out in Hollywood."

"Don't tell me. He drives a Volkswagen Beetle and has three unfinished manuscripts in the backseat."

"He's not that lucky. He doesn't write."

My ears perked up. "I'm intrigued," I said, thinking of my earlier precognitive thought that tonight I would meet a film producer. "Is he looking for material?" Just as I asked the question, my skin crawled with gooseflesh. I knew this man and I were brought together for a reason. I wasn't sure if the reason was that I was supposed to help this man's son, or if he was to help me, but it was clear, somebody's angels had brought us together.

"Yes, he is, as a matter of fact. He tells me he's got some money now and opening offices. He's a good kid. He'll do well. He's persistent and that's what matters most," he said.

Gregory told me more about his son, Adam, and his daughter. We chatted over a second cup of coffee. It was an incredible evening for me. All the while I listened to this man, I had the sensation that I not only knew him from somewhere, but I trusted what he told me about his son. Slowly I came to realize that I was meant to meet this man and connect with his son.

I gave Gregory my name, address and phone numbers, and I took his card and jotted down Adam's number as well.

"When I get back to Houston, I'll give Adam a call. Perhaps there is something we can work out together."

We shook hands, parted and left.

Once back in Houston, I called Adam. His father had called him and told him to expect my call, though he hadn't thought I would do it. Adam faxed me information about his company. I sent him a bio on myself and gave him a couple of film ideas I had rolling around in my head.

For three years, nothing came to fruition. I was winging back and forth to South America. Things were topsy-turvy in Adam's life, too. He expanded his company, made several films, learned some lessons and yet, we kept in contact.

Finally, I had the wonderful opportunity to meet Adam this year. Not only is his business expanding, it's thriving. After a very long lunch, I found I trusted the son as much as the father. He was energetic and honest, two of my favorite traits. We discovered that we had more than one or two projects that we wanted to join forces to produce. We would have to limit ourselves to less than a dozen!

Even as I write this, I can almost see our future relationship materializing. What fun we will have working on family films and cable programs together! All these possibilities and opportunities for both of us . . . and all because I'd taken the chance to believe in the premonition I'd had that I would meet someone special on a summer night in New York.

Who says there's no Christmas in July?

SECTION
4
FOUR

Spiritual Visitations

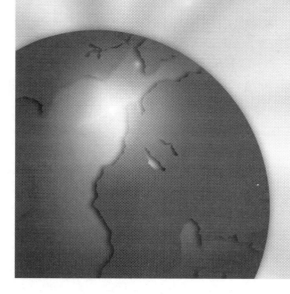

T hese stories are not the visits from creepy, angry, frightening ghosts that make up the bulk of horror books and movies. These are quite the opposite. They are true visits, contacts with spirits, but are loving gestures of people who once lived and knew us. Sometimes we see the essence of deceased persons, but we have no idea who they are or where they are from. We only know they are there. We sense their presence.

From what I have gathered through my own near-death experience, my own "spiritual sightings" and my father's near-death experience, we are all guided and protected every minute of our lives by guardians. Some, I do believe, are guardian angels from the angelic realm. This is a different dimension from the one inhabited by persons who were once mortal.

When I relate in my story that I have "seen" a ghostly persona, I do not mean that I'm seeing a flesh-and-blood human being. That kind of story is covered in my angelic visitation section, where flesh-and-blood figures influence a current event, then vanish from sight.

In the case of spiritual visits, the essence of the person is shadowy or cloudy, or perhaps they don't manifest in a shape at all. Sometimes I have heard a compelling voice, steering me clear of danger. Frankly, whoever this is, I wish they would come around more often, because the three or four times over the past fifty years when this has occurred, this Voice saved my life or, at least, turned the course of my life. Whenever I'm searching for answers, I'd sure like to have that direct line to Mr. Voice again. Those messages came in loud and clear. I have three of those stories in this section, always about Mr. Voice or The Voice.

I'm sure many of you saw the movie *The Sixth Sense*. For the most part, the movie was incredibly accurate. My friends, who are "in touch" with the other side, have related that this child's experience was much like their own. From an early age, most of us who talk to spirits have had to learn the hard way that not everyone we see is alive on this plane. It takes time and experience to learn that some of the people they see around them were alive and some were formerly alive.

My own experience is that spirits do not appear to mediums or psychics or even the general populace in a state of "dishabille" with flesh rotting off their skulls. Our loving spirits are beautiful, young, healthy and whole when they pass over to the other side. Nor would loving people come to call with half the back of their head blown off.

However, it is quite true they may contact us to help them bring justice to bear, as was the case in the movie *The Sixth Sense* with the little girl who had been poisoned by her stepmother and delivered the videotape of that heinous act to the little boy. The boy, in turn, took the video to the deceased little girl's father.

Spirits are not bitter and vengeful; however, they do want to set the record straight. They also know that some mysteries are not quite so mysterious once the truth is brought to light.

Truth, beauty, love. These are the attributes of the spirits I have encountered and my friends and loved ones have experienced. There is nothing in the pages to follow that will frighten you. To date, I have never had an experience to convince me there is a hell. Hell, evil, negativity, loneliness and disease are experiences the soul undertakes in this realm of human life. These situations and forces do not exist on the other side, I have been told by the spirits who "visit" me.

Years ago, I read a medical article stating researchers have discovered that near-death experiences, the tunnel of light, heaven and other such phenomena known as heaven can be activated by sparking a certain center of the human brain with an electrode. Thus, would heaven be a "state of mind," as recently stated by the Pope?

All of this makes sense. If the "kingdom of Heaven is within," it is to our souls we must look for the answers. Neither the body nor the brain lives on after death. The soul, or the energy source we call the soul, is what endures.

Energy is energy. It can be transformed, but it does not evaporate. It metamorphoses into another structure, but scientists have concluded energy endures for eternity.

Many researchers have described, in medical and scientific detail, the mysteries and some explanations for near-death experiences, sighting of spiritual beings at death and other times of crisis or deep need. These include Raymond A. Moody, Jr., M.D., in his books, *Coming Back: A Psychiatrist Explores Past-Life Journeys, Life After Life, The Light Beyond* and *Reflections on Life After Life*; Dr. Brian L. Weiss in his book, *Many Lives, Many Masters*; and Kenneth L. Ring in his book, *From Alpha to Omega: Ancient Mysteries and the Near-Death Experience*.

Angel Watch is not a clinical book. I am not a doctor, not even close. What I am attempting to show in the real stories in this section is that spirits/souls exist beyond this earth. They are part of nearly all we do. They come to us in dreams. They give us signs. They help us through the ordinariness and the extraordinariness of our days. They save our lives. They speak to us innumerable times nightly. What is sad is that we aren't paying attention.

Hopefully, the stories in this section will wake up a few slumbering or just plain lazy humans to the fact that their guides and angels deserve a pat on the back. It's not all that difficult to acknowledge a gift when someone hands you a prettily-wrapped box. That's all they are asking is for you to realize fully, with all your heart, that they exist; that they love you and want only a life of abundance, joy and well-being for you.

Everything you ever dreamed of as the good life for yourself is within reach. All you have to do is ask. Then believe.

Dorothy's Love Cloud

AUTHOR'S NOTE: *This story was told to me by my mother only days after this angelic visitation. I told her then that she had been unbelievably blessed to have experienced this phenomenon, and she agreed. What we both found unusual was the particular manifestation this visitation utilized. We both hope you will glean comfort from her testimony to divine intervention in this earthly realm.*

Not long after Frank died, I was still dealing with legal situations, thank-you notes to friends and the general adjustment to my new life with him gone. I was physically exhausted after nearly a decade of caretaking, the last five being the most difficult and straining. I can honestly say that I was not in any kind of shock over his death. My grieving undertook a different kind of persona than most widows deal with. I was not suffering or angry or even lonely at this time. Frank had been so very ill for such a long time that I had urged him to let go of this life. I wanted him to have peace without pain. However, there was, as there still is, that part of my heart and life that missed him.

I say all this so that you understand I was not taking any kind of medication to deal with death and loss angst. I was handling a myriad of tasks as I always have, with a controllable amount of energy and organization. I was sleeping relatively well, which at my age always brings a measure of insomnia, but that is to be expected.

One night, I awoke from my sleep. I read for a bit, dozed and read again. Finally, I turned off my reading lamp. Again I found myself awakened.

This time, I went out into the hallway that stretches half the length of our one-story ranch home. Off this hallway are three bedrooms, the bathroom and the doorway to the kitchen, which opens onto the family room. During the course of Frank's illness, I moved into the middle bedroom, which once belonged to the girls, in order to let both Frank and myself sleep uninterrupted by the other's nocturnal habits.

This particular night as I walked into the hall, I saw a layer of white cloud coming down from the ceiling. There were no lights per se in this cloud, but it was luminescent enough that I could distinguish it from simply air.

For those of you who live in the South and are used to air-conditioning coming from the ceiling that could, on a very humid day, create a cloud or fog, let me say right off that there is no air-conditioning vent in my ceilings and certainly nothing of the sort in my hallway. My house does not have heat or air-conditioning in any kind of vent structure at all. Frank and I built our house in the early 1950s, when "radiant heat" was popular. Radiant heat is a system of heated water tubing that runs through the ceiling and a gentle heat then warms the house.

This cloud descended from the ceiling over my head. It was followed by a "layering" effect of more clouds, one after the other. I wouldn't describe them as smoke, but rather a clear fog. This cloud slowly moved down over me and covered my shoulders.

In that instant, I knew this was no smoke. No atmospheric anomaly. The cloud enveloped me and I was filled with the most incredible, unearthly sensation of unconditional love I have ever experienced. In fact, I've never experienced it at all. This was beyond the human. I knew I was loved beyond measure, that none of my faults mattered, that no sin, no guilt, no omission of action or thought for which I hold myself in ransom mattered to this being, this divine spirit or this angel.

I heard no voices. I saw no beings. I didn't see Frank. In fact, I do not think this was Frank at all. It didn't have that sensation about it. There was no personality to this phenomenon. My own supposition is that I was experiencing an angel. In my heart and mind, that explanation seems to rest the most comfortably.

However, I did receive the feeling that everything was as it should be about where Frank was at this given time and where I was. I sensed that the world was in order. I suddenly felt reassured that everything would be fine. My apprehensions about the future melted. My anxieties died. I was overwhelmed with a sense of calm and peace, as well as the love.

This entire experience lasted several minutes. It was long enough for me to assess what was happening to me and to make certain I remembered details.

To this day, nearly eight years later, I have not enjoyed a repeat performance, though it would be nice to do so. It is uncanny how distinctly and precisely the details come back to me and in that, I suppose, it is like the angels visiting me again and again.

Epilogue

Upon reading this story, my sister, Nan, called to tell me that she remembers Mother driving to her house the next morning hours after this incident. Nan described the moment:

"I watched Mom getting out of her car. There was something different about her. She looked ethereal. She appeared as if she were floating up the drive to the walkway. She was glowing in a way that people don't glow. I knew instinctively that something had happened to her. Even after she came into the house, before she began relating this experience to me, I sensed an angelic presence about her. Without actually going through the 'visitation' itself, I believe that to this day, I am the only witness to what happened to her that night. She was transformed. I believe she was visited by angels. Often, when I hear of someone in need or searching, I tell this story to give hope and awareness. We are not alone."

March 1, 2000

Mother called to say that she had a painter recently come to the house to do some ceiling patch-up work. He looked around and after getting to his work, he commented: "Aren't you afraid being in this big house all by yourself?"

Mother only smiled and said, "No, I'm not afraid. I know that Frank is here by my side, and the angels fill my rooms. I'm never afraid when I'm here. This is my home, my sanctuary, and I am protected."

Sonny Angel's Airplane

AUTHOR'S NOTE: *The next three stories you are about to read I call the "Sonny Angel Airplane Trilogy." In order to understand the deeper significance of the machinations involved, it is necessary for me to relate some of this history.*

onny Hughes was Jim's best friend in the 1980s, when both men were successful in their businesses. Sonny had bought a Jet Commander airplane and to please his wife, Dottie, a former airline attendant, he'd had a bathroom installed on the plane for her.

They flew this plane back and forth from their home in New Orleans, to their home in the Cayman Islands. It was on this very plane that Jim flew to Cayman Island for the first time in his life. Sonny also used the plane on business trips to Houston and around the country. At the same time, Jim had his own corporate jets and the two friends, among other things, shared their love of aviation with each other.

However, in 1984, Sonny was experiencing a rare financial cash-flow problem in his company. His bank gave him one day to dispose of his assets before they took over. Sonny immedi-ately called Jim and asked him for help. They agreed that Jim would write Sonny a check that day for the plane, buying the plane from him so that Sonny could pay off the bank.

Of course, business being business, times improved and Sonny's business got back on track. Sonny told Jim he'd repay the favor someday and that he would always be grateful for bailing him out of his temporary financial hot water.

These angelic stories take on a more pointed meaning once you have these facts in hand.

The Night Sonny Died

J im and I had last seen Sonny at his home on Cayman Island in October. He was incredibly ill, we all knew that, though Sonny, being Sonny, would never tell anyone he was dying. The only one who knew the real truth was myself.

I'd had a neighbor die of cirrhosis and pancreatic cancer years ago. Sonny had all the same visible symptoms, especially the yellow-orange tint to his eyes. However, it was the intangible elements that gave him away. There were times when he would look at me and I could nearly read his mind. To this day, I believe he realized I was on to him.

Dottie was uninformed about the disease, and with Sonny's continual denial of anything being amiss, she scrambled for every ounce of information she could find about alcoholism, liver disease and cancer. I provided her with a reading list that would daunt the strongest of souls. But Dottie wouldn't rest until she understood the truth and then did something about it. When we were all in Cayman together, Dottie arranged for Sonny to go see a nutritionist, thinking that an alteration in his diet could turn the disease around. Dottie was holding up hope where nothing could be done. Sonny's disease was so far gone that only a transplant could have saved him. That, and a will to live on Sonny's part, which I believe he did not have at this point. Sonny was resigned to dying.

Normally, Sonny would have flatly refused to see a nutritionist. Herbs, holistic healing and balanced nutrition were not part of his makeup. At this stage of the game, he had nothing to gain from this experience, except to make Dottie happy.

Sonny asked Jim to go with him to the nutritionist. With Jim in the patient room, the woman explained to Sonny that it was essential to his life that he cut his sodium intake to zero. He was told he could never have any alcohol the rest of his life and that he needed to increase his intake of proteins and carbohydrates. She gave Jim a list of preferred foods, jars and bottles of cleansing herbs, vitamins and energizing teas. She stuffed their hands with brochures and pamphlets about meditation, a schedule of yoga classes and a list of local masseuses, chiropractors and energy workers.

Sonny walked out of the office with Jim, got in the Suburban and told Jim to drive down by the beach.

"Where are we going?" Jim asked.

Sonny paused, looked out at the clear blue sky and said, "Let's go to the Hyatt. I want to walk in the sand. Sit under a palm tree for a bit."

Jim smiled. "You've got it!" He turned onto the road and headed south.

They turned into the hotel parking lot and had the valet park the car, so that Sonny didn't have far to walk.

Carrying his bag of vitamins and minerals with him, Sonny led the way to the poolside bar. He then proceeded directly to a trash barrel and dumped everything into it.

"What are you doing?" gasped Jim.

Sonny only stared back. "Let's find a table under the palms."

The waitress came up and asked for their order.

Sonny smiled charmingly at her. "I'll have a marguerita with salt."

Jim dropped his jaw. "I'll have a chardonnay," he told the waitress. "Sonny, did I miss something? Didn't that nutritionist just tell you not to have salt or alcohol?"

Sonny looked out at the rolling waves and the children frolicking on the beach. An elderly couple strolled hand in hand down the curve of Seven Mile Beach. A newlywed couple, rings shiny and new, kissed under the same palm where Sonny had proposed to Dottie seventeen years earlier.

Sonny squeezed his eyes shut and swallowed hard. He adjusted his sunglasses. He remained silent for an inordinately long period of time. Jim had the distinct impression he was wrestling with himself. "She did."

"Well, then?"

Sonny kept looking out to sea. "I want a marguerita, Jim. Do you have a problem with that?"

Detecting the emotion in Sonny's voice, Jim knew what Sonny could not say. Jim knew then that taking him along to the nutritionist's appointment was Sonny's way of telling Jim that he was dying. By ordering the marguerita, Sonny was telling Jim that the diagnosis was fatal.

Sonny knew he was going to die and soon.

"I don't have a problem with it at all, Sonny."

Jim reached over and rubbed Sonny's shoulder affection-ately. Sonny put his hand on Jim's shoulder, though he didn't look at him. The moment was too emotional for either of them to speak.

They sat there on Sonny's favorite beach watching the infinite ocean run onto the shore, hearing children's laughter and lovers' promises to each other. There was life all around them and they absorbed it; sight, sound and smell.

We left Cayman the next day. Our flight was early in the morning, which was always Sonny's best time of day. For the period of our trip there, Sonny had slept late each day, spend-ing the mornings wrapped in a huge terry robe and shuffling across the saltilo tile floor in his house slippers.

This morning, he woke early and was dressed in crisp white linen shorts, sandals and a bright yellow and white shirt. His thick, wavy white hair was combed to perfection, and I'll always remember the cologne he wore. He greeted us with a bright smile. To me, it looked as if he was reborn. "I'm going to drive you to the airport myself," he said. Because Sonny was so weak, this was a huge undertaking.

"Captain Dewey can take us," Jim said, referring to Sonny's elderly handyman who often drove Sonny about the island when Sonny was too ill or tired to drive.

"No, he's busy today," Sonny lied.

I hugged Dottie far too long and failed at hiding my tears. A horrid sense of a world collapsing engulfed me. "Aren't you going to the airport with us?" I asked her, squeezing her hand.

"No," she whispered. "Sonny wants to take you alone."

I shivered. "Oh, Dottie." I knew then I would never see them together on this island again.

Bravely, Dottie went inside while we piled our bags into the Suburban. Painfully, Sonny climbed behind the wheel of the car and backed out.

We talked of everything and nothing on the way to the airport. Jim made plans to travel to New Orleans in a month to see Sonny again about a business deal. They promised to phone each other every morning, as they'd done for over fifteen years. They were both making promises they could never keep, but believed against all hope would come true.

When we said goodbye at the airport, I hugged Sonny carefully so as not to hurt him in any way, but with my heart, I told him that I would watch for him once he made it to the other side. He gave me a look I will never forget. I knew in that instant that Sonny would find a way to make contact with me even after death.

Once we were on the plane, I fell into a deep sadness. Jim let me have the window seat so that I could watch the island fall away from us as we were airborne. He babbled on about the next time we would come to the island to visit Sonny and Dottie. He was hoping.

Suddenly, as I looked at the crystal turquoise waters and reefs below, I saw the future in one of the clearest visions I've ever had. "We won't be back here again. Maybe ever. Sonny is going to die, Jim. He will never live to see Christmas. Before Christmas, we will be at his funeral."

Jim fell silent. Tears welled in his eyes. "I can't lose him. He's my best friend."

"I want you to be prepared, Jim. I know you love him, but he's going to leave this earth. But he's not going away."

This was almost too much for Jim to bear. Not that he didn't believe me. I think he wanted to believe me.

Over the next five weeks, Jim called Sonny's house in New Orleans, but we only got a recorder. I faxed Dottie. I called her cellular phone. I never got an answer or a return call.

I knew something was terribly wrong, but we didn't know what. Jim even called Sonny's office and the secretary told us he was at his ranch. Two weeks later, she said Sonny and Dottie went on a little trip. There was always a "story."

In the middle of the night of December 16, Jim awoke suddenly. He was shaking. He couldn't breathe.

I awoke as well, fearing he was having a bronchial or asthma attack. "What is it? Are you all right?" I put my hand on his bare back. He was icy cold.

"Can you feel it?" He stared around the room.

"What?" Chills coursed my spine.

Jim bolted out of bed; suddenly he was panting.

"Jim, are you sick? Maybe we should call the paramedics."

"You have to feel it!"

"I . . . I don't feel a thing, Jim. I'm not sick."

"What do you mean you can't feel it? There's something wrong. Something is wrong in the universe! It's here. It's all around!" He hugged himself.

Of all the people on this planet to never, ever use the word "universe" or even know what my concept of "spiritual" is, Jim is the one. It's one thing for me to make a prediction he can blow off and pretend he never heard. It's another for him to experience the reality of the unseen world.

Quickly, I looked at the clock. "It's three thirty-three."

"What does that mean?"

I knew it wasn't the time to go into a detailed explanation of the literary and mystical interpretations of the number three. "I was just checking the time."

"For what?"

"For later," I replied, feeling another wave of chills across my body. I looked at Jim. "Oh, dear. Something is wrong."

"That's what I've been trying to tell you."

"Please, come back to bed. You're frightening me. Take a deep breath. Relax. Everything is fine."

Jim slipped back into bed. "Something is wrong in the universe, I tell you."

"I believe you, Jim," I tried to comfort him.

The next morning the phone rang a little before eight o'clock. I answered it. It was Sonny's secretary. She told us that she was calling for Dottie. She explained that ever since we left Cayman in October, Sonny had been in the hospital. Dottie had stayed with him day and night for over seven weeks. They hadn't gone on vacation at all. Sonny had been fighting for his life and he lost. Sonny had died. The funeral was set for December 18.

I hung up the phone, shivering with eerie chills.

Jim sat at the table next to me and took my hand. His fingers were icy. He was in shock. "On the plane . . . you said Sonny would die before Christmas. How could you know that?"

"I think Sonny told me himself with his mind. He was a proud man, Jim. He wanted your friendship, not your pity. He used me to tell you the truth when he couldn't."

Nodding sadly, Jim said, "That makes sense." He looked up at me. "Last night. That was Sonny in the room with me, wasn't it?"

"I believe it was. I know how we can be certain."

"How?"

"When we go to the funeral and see Dottie, ask her what time he died."

The next day, just before the ceremony, Jim and I had a moment alone with Dottie. It was Jim's chance to ask about the details of Sonny's death.

"I was lying with him in the hospital bed holding him like I do every night. In the middle of the night, the nurse came in and said, 'Mrs. Hughes. Mr. Hughes has passed.' I couldn't believe it. He was lying in my arms. He was warm. He just wasn't breathing was all."

I put my arms around Dottie to comfort her.

"Dottie, I hate to ask, but I have to," Jim said. "Do you know what time he died?"

"Why, yes. The nurse said it was three-thirty exactly."

Jim's eyes met mine. His were awash in tears. "Dottie, he came to me that night. He came to our room. To our house. I woke up and told Catherine that there was a shift in the universe. I could feel it."

Dottie took Jim's hand. "Of course he came to you, Jim. You were like his brother."

"And he was mine."

In my life, I've been to many, many funerals. In fact, as a child I thought funerals were family reunions with a dead body as the main attraction. I was fourteen before I ever went to a family wedding. I thought everyone always cried when they were together and wore black and spoke in hushed tones. Death for me seemed the most natural part of living.

But of all the funerals I have been to before and after

Sonny's death, I have never quite felt the pervading sense of an entire world ending as I did at this one. It was as if the universe had crashed against this universe. Something happened that night when Sonny came to visit Jim and announce his rebirth into the spirit world. Something happened to me.

It was on that night I knew my destiny was to create this particular book of true accounts of the unseen world. I knew then that with all my being, I had to press on for the publication of *Wings of Destiny*. None of this was a new notion to me, only that the timing was at hand.

All my life I have been afraid to tell the visions I see, to share the things I know with the people who need to hear them the most. I have fought the spiritual side of myself for fear of being labeled a freak, geek or insane.

Sonny's death was the beginning of my own rebirth. I have an incredible connection to Sonny, all my own and precious to me for its own reasons. I was not privileged to know Sonny in health, during the good times and the fun times. I only knew him once he was aware he was dying.

As my father told me during his dying days, he was "between the worlds." These worlds and planes are visible to those who are attached to the earth only by virtue of their bodies. It is the living who must acknowledge the existence of the other world and the actual, physical "work" that our beloveds do for us on the other side.

Theirs is the work of unconditional love.

All they ask of us is simply to accept it.

Jim's First Encounter of the Angelic Kind

I've noticed over the span of my lifetime that men have no problem understanding you when you use the word "hunch." "Gut feeling" is another one they like. But venture into "intuition," "psychic dream" or "spiritual visitation" and the inexperienced get real nervous. They hem and haw, change the subject, switch on the television or walk out of the room. That's when you know you've got their attention. If they really and truly didn't believe you, they'd never make a comment. They wouldn't care.

At the point of this particular incident in our lives together, Jim was very much like the others of his gender. He was skeptical of my angel watching, but he was still believing, "just in case" I might be right.

Sonny had been dead over a year and though Jim missed him terribly, he had told himself that Sonny was in a better place. I told Jim I didn't quite feel that Sonny was all that far away from us and at times, I truly felt as if I could sense his presence. Granted, I didn't have any overt "signs" to prove my theory. It was just a "hunch."

Jim didn't understand that. If Sonny was actually still "around," then why was he not seeing him? I stated that perhaps Sonny had sent a sign, but Jim might not be looking.

Jim replied that no, he'd know a sign from Sonny because they had certain interests that had bonded them. One, in particular, was their mutual love of planes. They had both owned jets at one time. They had loved comparing notes, designing the interiors of their aircraft and trading special stories about the sale of this one, the acquisition of the next one.

Jim believed that as Sonny's best friend, Sonny should have been trying to send him a sign, if what I believed about the afterlife was true. In feeling this, perhaps Jim had sent a signal to Sonny to prove himself.

Well, Jim got one and in spades.

Jim's air flights back and forth to South America were routine to us by the time of this story. Because he flew so often, he meticulously checked and double-checked his departures, his seat assignments and arrival times.

On this particular day, Jim walked up to the Continental ticket counter and presented his ticket and passport. The attendant told him there had been a mistake and that Jim was not booked on the flight. Jim politely corrected him, stating he'd checked only the previous day and that everything was in order. He had a first-class window seat.

The attendant checked the booked flight to Quito and found that only seat 16E was available. If Jim wanted to get to Quito that day, he'd have to take the seat. Jim was incensed that he'd paid full fare for a first-class seat he didn't get. Still, he had to get to Quito for business two days hence. Grumbling, he took the last seat on the plane.

Jim was very angry about the situation. To him, it was the last straw in a terrible business week. In addition to his work in South American, he was still dealing with a power project on the island of Anguilla. He'd been on the phone for hours hunting down Rodney George of Watsilla Corporation, a Swiss power company with whom he'd done business in prior years. It was imperative Jim find Rodney, but no matter what he did or how many calls he made, even to Switzerland, no one knew how to find Rodney George.

Disheartened by the week's events more than simply angry, Jim boarded the plane. It was a hot day and to make matters worse, there were mechanical problems on the plane. The air-conditioning was not functioning properly and Jim was sweltering. However, they taxied to the runway and began the interminable wait in line. More mechanical problems cropped up, but the captain did not choose to deplane the passengers.

With nothing else to do, the two men sitting next to Jim decided to pull out their briefcases and get some work accomplished. Jim waited for them to reach under the seats for their work materials before bending down to retrieve his own. The man next to Jim opened his briefcase, and just as Jim bent slightly, he read the man's company letterhead: Watsilla Corporation.

A smile filled Jim's face as he thought to himself, how good is this? He turned to the man and asked, "I see by your letterhead that you work for Watsilla. Do you happen to know Rodney George?"

"Why, yes, I do," the man replied. "I've worked with Rodney on several power projects in the Caribbean."

"This is amazing! I have been trying to find Rodney for two months. It's imperative I get in touch with him."

"Just a minute," the man said, pulling out his palm-size computer scheduler. "Here's his number. Let's call him."

The plane sat on the runway for another hour, which was long enough for Jim to make contact with Rodney and set up a meeting. Jim no more than finished conducting the business he needed with the two men next to him, who both worked for Watsilla, when the captain announced that the flight was being cancelled altogether for the next day. They returned to the gate and deplaned.

Jim went to the ticket counter and spoke with the attendant. Because the flight had been cancelled, Jim was able to rebook his flight for the following day, complete with his original first-class window seat.

When Jim called me to come back to the airport and pick him up, he was ecstatic. It was his first bona fide encounter of the spiritual kind. He was both awed and amused. It was the sense of irony and twist of fate in the end telling Jim that Sonny was sending a message loud and clear.

What Jim didn't know was that there were to be many more encounters over the following months.

Jim's Second Angelic Encounter

O n one of his numerous trips to Anguilla, Jim had prepared as he always had: meticulously. Meetings with all the top island officials had been set for weeks. He had double-checked with the hotel to make certain each person's favorite foods were available, as well as their choices in wines. He left no stone unturned. He had even gone so far as to have backup dates and times in case governmental business should stall the proceedings for his business venture.

With weeks of preparation, Jim was confident that this last trip would be the one to finalize all that was necessary for his business. The trip was only to last for three days, so there was little time for anything other than back-to-back meetings, summits and prearranged business dinners.

Feeling confident, Jim flew off to the Caribbean. All went incredibly well the first day. Jim was jubilant. Things went better the second day. Jim was energized on the morning of the third and last day of his meetings.

With his last meeting scheduled with the Chief Minister, Jim had only to catch the afternoon launch to St. Martin and then the plane home to Houston that evening. He promised he would be home for dinner at eight.

When Jim walked into the Chief Minister's office, he was informed by the assistant secretary that the Minister had been called off the island on business. Unfortunately, he was not expected back for days. Possibly, not until the following week.

Knowing he had other business in Houston, Jim saw his carefully orchestrated plans crumble. Dejected and disheartened, he checked out of the hotel early and left for the launch. The trip from Anguilla to St. Martin was speedy as usual, but Jim's mood was dour. He was impatient now to simply get home to Houston and the family.

Fortunately, there was room on an earlier flight and he was airborne. He watched out the window as Anguilla disappeared from view, much like Jim's hopes for closing his business matters.

The plane was in the air no more than thirty minutes when they hit an incredible amount of turbulence. Jim braced himself. The pilot came on and informed everyone to stay strapped in. More turbulence. The jet began dropping like a stone.

Having once owned his own jet, Jim was far too familiar with the potential danger of wind shears and currents to be fooled by the pilot's anti-panic talk. Jim knew the truth. They were about to crash.

Suddenly, 100 plastic oxygen masks fell from their compartments overhead. Passengers screamed and moaned with fear and anxiety. Jim grabbed his mask and helped the woman next to him with hers. "Are we going to die?" she asked him.

"No. Don't worry. Everything will be fine," Jim answered and glanced out the window. Because he'd taken this same flight numerous times, Jim knew the landscape below like the back of his hand.

"See that down there?" He pointed to the earth. "That's Puerto Rico. The pilot is taking us in. Just put this mask on. It's only a precaution."

"Thank you," she whispered gratefully.

Jim tightened his seat belt and hugged the pillow the attendant had passed out only moments prior.

Sure enough, the pilot announced they were attempting an emergency landing in San Juan.

The landing was successful, but once they were off the plane, Jim was frazzled and just as nervous as the rest of the passengers. To make matters worse, they had all been told there was not a flight out of San Juan for eight more hours.

Of all the things that Jim despises in life, the worst is waiting in airports.

Normally Jim flies Continental Airlines worldwide. On this particular trip, he flew American Airlines because Continental did not fly to Anguilla. Due to the emergency landing, the airline had graciously allowed the passengers of Jim's flight to rest in the Admiralty Club. The gesture was a good move on the airline's part, Jim thought. His nerves were so rattled that a glass of wine and something to eat were definitely in order.

He found a pleasant couch on which to rest, and had set his mind at ease after making calls to home. There was nothing left to do, but wait and bemoan his inability to meet with the Chief Minister on his trip. For that, there was no cure.

"Is this seat taken?" a male voice asked Jim.

"No. Go right . . ." Jim looked up.

Looking down at him was none other than the Chief Minister of Anguilla.

Jim was on his feet in two seconds. "Mr. Chief Minister."

"Jim? What are you doing here?" They shook hands.

"I was waiting for you," he laughed.

"I'm sorry I missed our meeting. How did you know I was going to be here?" the Chief Minister asked.

"I didn't know you would be here. I was on my way to Houston. Our plane had mechanical difficulty and we nearly crash-landed." Jim scratched his head. "I was praying I would see you on this trip."

The minister nodded. "Looks as if your prayers were answered."

Jim laughed. "Yes, I think my angels were listening. But I think the next time, I need to warn them not to be so forceful!"

They sat down then and conducted their business until it was time for the Chief Minister to leave.

As Jim flew through the night to get home, he looked up at the sky and this time he knew exactly which angel was directing his compass and course. He knew his friend, Sonny, who had died just the year earlier, was orchestrating this encounter, just as he had the last flight to Anguilla.

The two of them had shared many good times of friendship and business on jets together. One of the things that Jim loved about Sonny was his perpetual sense of humor. That sense of humor had seen them both through financial and personal hard times.

These days, each time Jim gets on a plane he wonders if he'll be running into Sonny again and what kind of "miracles" Sonny will have waiting for him.

Dottie and Sonny on the Plane

A year after Jim's second airline encounter with Sonny, I spoke with Dottie at great length. In fact, even our phone conversation was an out-and-out demonstration of Sonny still working in our lives.

I hadn't spoken with Dottie for the longest time. Jim and I had been back and forth to South America; we were building a house, I was touring. The usual. I was neglectful of my friends due to prior commitments.

However, Dottie was never long out of my thoughts. I worried whether she was happy now that she'd relocated to her home in Georgia, but I knew there was much healing and grieving she had to accomplish and when she was ready, I would hear from her.

That summer I went to Atlanta on my book tour. I was there for four days and wherever I went, I thought of her incessantly. However, I was rushed from one media event to another, went to bookstores and then flew home.

The morning after coming home, I retrieved my messages
from my voicemail and, lo and behold, I heard Dottie's voice!
Thrilled, I phoned her immediately. I asked if she'd seen me
on television that week and if that was why she was calling.

"Why, no. I didn't even know you had a new book out. It
was just that I have had you on my mind for weeks and I
couldn't stop thinking about you. I thought I would call and
tell you I've remarried."

I was stunned, but happily. I related to Dottie how a year
previously, Jim had told me about a dream he'd had that night
about her. In the dream, Dottie told him all about a man she
was seeing and that she'd fallen in love with him. Jim said,
"I've never seen Dottie as happy as she was in my dream."

Of course, we both prayed this was true. We wanted only
the best for our dear friend. However, to hear Dottie describe
her new life with John was so much like Jim's dream that I
was blanketed by chills during most of the conversation.

Finally, I told her Jim's stories about his airplane encounters with what we believe was Sonny's intervention.

"I absolutely believe you, Catherine," Dottie said.

I asked her if she thought Sonny was still around.

Dottie stated that not only did she believe he was around,
but that she could smell sweet roses whenever he was present.

Now, this was something! We'd never smelled roses, but
she clearly had. She also stated that yes, Sonny would use an
airplane to help make his point. He had done as much with
her. She told me that when she was flying back from Cayman
on their airplane, she had smelled the familiar rose fragrance.
She turned to the other passenger and asked if he could smell
roses. He replied he could not.

She said, "I think Sonny's here."

He dismissed her statement as ridiculous.

"Oh, really," she said. "Lean your head back a bit and then tilt your nose to right here," she said, pointing to a space just above his face. "Tell me what you smell."

To disprove her claim, he did as she asked. Sniffing the air, he gasped, "It's roses!"

Dottie said she only smiled. That was her proof.

I told Dottie I loved that story, and that from then on, I would remember the story about roses. However, now that Sonny had appeared in various forms to everyone else, I was glad to know he'd contacted those he loved.

Dottie laughed and said, "Better watch out, Catherine. You're next."

"Don't be silly. I didn't know Sonny well enough or long enough for him to waste his time visiting me."

"He loved you all the same, Catherine. Just remember that."

Six months later I flew into New Orleans for a convention. New Orleans was where Sonny and Dottie had lived so many years and it was where Sonny was buried.

I rented a car at the airport so I could drive into the garden district and stay with my cousin Sonja, her husband, Bob and their brand-new baby girl, Lila.

Since I'd lived in New Orleans for three years back in the early 1970s, I knew my way around quite well. Or so I thought. I took Interstate 10 into the city and before I knew it, I was passing out of town, rather than finding the exit for the garden district. No problem, I thought. I turned around and headed back and retraced my steps. I got caught in a maze of underpasses and spaghetti bowls that made Houston's infamous 610 Loop look tame.

I did it again!

I couldn't believe how lost I got in my own former home. This time I was on the north side of town. Finally, I worked my way back to I-10. Going west, I spied the exit to Metairie Park. I thought, I know where I am now. I took the exit, came up under the underpass and stopped at the light.

My jaw dropped. Dead ahead was the very cemetery where Sonny was buried.

I broke out in peals of laughter. Sonny had me driving all over that town, just because he wanted me to stop by and say hello. I drove straight into the cemetery and waved to him all around the block. I blew him kisses and laughed even more. He was having a grand old time with me, that was for certain.

I got back on the freeway and sure enough, I found the right exit and was at my cousin's house within ten minutes. It was the easiest route I'd ever taken.

I was flying on an angel's wing.

A Valentine from Daddy

While putting up our Christmas tree this past year, I knocked the center stone out of my diamond ring. Jim and I searched every inch of the floor around the tree and what felt like every needle, trying to find that stone.

Each week, I went through the vacuum cleaner bag, sifting through the dust and dog hair for my diamond, but could not find it. I went through my closet, thinking perhaps the stone had come off in my sleeve. I even checked my purses, the bed linens, drawers, thinking perhaps I had not lost it while twisting the tree into the stand, but earlier that day.

When Christmas was over, we took the tree apart, sawing the limbs off one by one so we could double-check for the stone. Our neighbors even came over and looked through the pile of needles that had accumulated in the stand. It was worse than a needle in a haystack.

I gave up hope. Jim took the ring to Dallas on a business trip and had his jeweler put a pretty blue sapphire in the setting so I could still wear the ring. I told Jim that if by some miracle we ever did find the missing diamond, the only thing I wanted was a heart of diamonds. When I was in second grade, my father had given me a little locket with a blue zircon, my birthstone, on it. Being so young, I lost the locket while out playing one time and it had never been replaced. All these years, I've never had another heart-shaped necklace.

Jim agreed that would be very nice to do someday.

As January came and went and our careers geared up, I never gave the missing stone another thought. The insurance agent had told me that unless the ring was stolen, he couldn't do anything about it. It was not covered on my policy.

Valentine's Day for me is a very special day. As a child we made a big deal out of every holiday, but I loved Valentine's Day. My brothers and sister and I came home from our Valentine's party at school and pinned our classmates' valentines to the draperies in the dining room. That was the one winter night you could count on Mother to have a special roast beef meal complete with Thanksgiving-like trimmings. When I was very small, I remember the Glenn Miller 78s playing in the background as we helped set the table and stole smidges of icing from the heart-shaped cake, or checked on the red Jell-O heart shapes in the refrigerator.

My brother Ed was in the Boy Scouts, and he was assigned the job of building a roaring fire in the fireplace. Because we lived in northwestern Indiana, it was almost always snowing. I suppose in our own way, we were all hopeless romantics.

My father would come home from work bearing a heart-shaped red box of candies and a special box from the jeweler. Most times, I remember Mother getting a piece or two of her sterling flatware. Later, when I was in high school and college, there were pretty gold bracelets or lovely costume jewelry. We were by no means rich, but I always thought how exciting it was for us to watch and see what Father had selected for Mother for this most romantic evening.

When it came time for my father to die, he chose the one day he knew none of us would forget. Valentine's Day.

For more than a few hundred thousand reasons, I celebrate the joy of this special holiday.

This year when Valentine's Day rolled around, I had not only decorated the house for the holiday with hearts and teddy bears everywhere, but had bought valentine collars for our three golden retrievers, Beau, Bebe and Junior.

Jim and I planned to stay home this year since Junior is still being house trained, but in actuality, the night was pleasantly cool and we wanted to grill out and snuggle in.

The week before Valentine's Day, I was dressing for a meeting and happened to look down at an empty Boucheron perfume bottle I've kept since Jim gave it to me for Valentine's Day five years ago. Remembering that day, I was deep in thought and nearly missed the dazzling object at the apex of the perfume bottle. There, before my very eyes, was my missing stone! I gasped. Thoughts of the incredulity of this moment zinged across my mind.

For one, I hadn't lost the stone in my closet. And even if I had, I'd cleaned this closet three times since Christmas. I would have seen the stone before this. Two, I clearly remembered knocking the ring against the tree trunk while situating it in the stand. And three, who put the stone on that particular Valentine present? The UPS delivery man?

There was no explanation for this mystery except one. My father.

Somehow, my father had put my stone in my room where he knew I would find it.

I raced downstairs to Jim and showed him the stone and told him the story. Jim wasn't sure. He suggested that perhaps the cleaning girl had found it and put it there. Skeptically, I replied that she would have given it to me, perhaps expecting a reward or my praise at least. She might even have kept it. Jim wasn't quite ready to give my father credit.

Jim called his jeweler in Dallas and asked if we could trade the stone for a locket or heart-shaped necklace. Max agreed. Jim faxed to Max the appraisal of my ring, which I'd contracted through one of the most reputable jewelers in Houston. Once Max read the appraisal, he gave Jim a dollar amount and we sent the stone to Dallas.

On Valentine's Day, I excitedly waited for the Federal Express man to deliver my new necklace. Unbeknownst to me, the delivery had come. Jim chose just the right moment to give me the necklace that afternoon with our trio of puppies looking on.

Handing me a red leather box, Jim said, "This is from your father and me."

I burst into tears on the spot before I opened it, because I did believe my deceased father's spirit had something to do with my stone. Little did I know, the story of the stone was not over.

Jim had tears in his eyes as he related, "Max called me the day he got the stone and told me there had been some mistake. The appraisal we had faxed him stated that the stone was three-fourths of a carat, that it was a certain clarity and flawless. When Max got the stone, he said it was well over a carat, was brown in clarity and had two distinct flaws. They were of the same dollar value for the trade, but . . ."

"They aren't the same stone!" I said.

"Precisely," Jim replied. "Not only do I now believe your father's spirit put that stone in your closet, he magically made a totally different stone appear."

Spellbound, I stared at Jim. The moment was filled with a thousand emotions for both of us. What Jim didn't know was that earlier that week, I had an interview with CNN. I was asked by the journalist if there was anything in particular I wanted for Valentine's Day.

I said, "Yes, I would like a sign from my father that he's still around and that he loves me."

I got my sign. My wish was fulfilled, but more than this, I was given this story to show others that love is eternal.

Harbor Lights

*I*n March 2000, I was out in California on business, staying with my friend Georgia Durante in her wonderful 1938 stone house off Coldwater Canyon in the Valley. After months of writing and preparation my co-writers and producers, Doug Dearth and Brian Powell, and I had finally whipped our story into shape and were ready to pitch the big studios. And big they were— Columbia, Paramount, Disney and Spielberg's DreamWorks. I had to swallow hard every time I said those names aloud. The knocking of my knees was surely similar to the sound David heard when he approached Goliath.

I was energized on just about every human and spiritual level of my being. Not only was I ready for the challenge, but I believed that our story about Lillie, Zane and Teddy was more than just another tale to tell. This was the beginning of a new career and a new direction for me, as well as my chance to weave my spiritual message into an adventure story for kids. In my heart, I believed I was firmly walking my divine path. This project was intrinsic to fulfilling my destiny.

I got up the first morning and was saying my prayers and dressing when Brian called to check on me.

"You won't believe the dream I had last night," Brian said. "I saw your father."

I was dumbfounded. "My father came to visit you? In your dream?"

"Yes! Isn't that amazing?"

"Yeah, and not fair. Why didn't he come see me?" I pouted.

"I don't know, but I saw him. He was with us when we went into the studios to do our pitches."

"Really?"

"Yes. I saw you sitting on a sofa and he was sitting on the arm of the sofa on your right side."

My first thought was that this scenario was rather odd. I'd never pitched a studio head, but in my mind, I envisioned us sitting around a long conference table or on the other side of someone's desk, seated in chairs. A "sofa" didn't figure into my equation.

"So did he say anything?"

"Not really. But he kept smiling at us, approving."

At this point, I was a bit miffed that my father didn't pop up in my dreams. After all, he was my father!

Then the thought struck me that perhaps Brian wasn't seeing him at all. Maybe his night visitor was some ghost posing as my father. Things like that can happen.

Perhaps my attorney father had taught me well when he said, "Question everything."

"Tell me, Brian, what did he look like?"

"He's a big guy. About six foot with a barrel chest. Black hair, thinning on top and big blue eyes. Like yours."

My neck hairs prickled and I felt those goosebumps scooting across my back. "Holy cow, Brian! That's him!"

The key was "black" hair. Normally, when a person describes someone with dark hair, they say "brown" or "dark," but actual black hair is rare.

To make the story even more interesting, my father was born with red hair. When he was in college or law school, he developed diphtheria and all of his hair fell out. When it grew in, it was black.

Even stranger, when I was born I had coal-black hair. My brother Ed has red hair. My sister Nancy was blonde, like my mother was as a child. My brother Bob has mother's brown hair. But mine was black, like my father's second round of hair. This little mystery has never been explained to me.

"So, I really saw him?" Brian asked proudly.

"You most certainly did," I assured him.

"What a nice guy. I really liked him a lot."

Our meetings that week were superb. We were all energized and excited about the story and our ability to tweak it and make it better from one telling to the next. The experience of our time together taught us how synchronized in thought the three of us were. From our synergy, we were being shown that this was no ordinary work situation. Brian, Doug and I began to feel like family. We were finding each other after years of wandering in the desert or, at least, of sinking in a quagmire known as "paying one's dues." We felt as if we'd been let out of prison. We were having a blast making goals, planning our futures and exchanging ideas.

Interestingly, in each meeting we were never in an office,

never at a conference table. For some reason or other, at each studio such rooms were not large enough, "being used," or someone "forgot to reserve the conference room." In each instance, I was seated on a couch or sofa, just as Brian had seen in his dream.

Our meetings and other appointments were spread out over a two-week period and as fortune would have it, I was able to meet many of Georgia's friends, as well as getting to know her better.

Generally speaking, I am a firm believer along with Benjamin Franklin that "fish and visitors smell after three days." I don't like imposing on friends or family for long periods of time. However, one of my meetings kept getting changed and moved further and further out, necessitating an extension of my stay.

Though she was gracious and always giving, I was afraid my presence would wear on Georgia. Miraculously, it did not. Instead, we bonded in a way that will stand us in good stead, I pray, for the rest of our lives. I am overwhelmed with the realization that my first impression when we met was that I had found a "soul-sister." In those two weeks at her home, where with both our crazy and different schedules we could have easily gotten on each others' nerves, we did not. In fact, our daily habits and energies were in harmony.

Therefore, for two weeks every morning when I arose, I found myself humming.

Finally, on my last day at Georgia's house, just as we were about to leave for dinner at the Los Angeles Country Club with her neighbors, she asked me, "What is that song you've been humming for days now?"

I hadn't thought about the song, it was a mindless thing I was doing while cleaning my room or dressing. "Harbor Lights," I blurted and immediately slapped my hand over my mouth. I shook.

"What?" she asked. "You look like you've seen a ghost!"

"I have," I smiled. "That song . . . it was my father's favorite. He used to request it for my mother. When I was a kid, on the weekends we'd go to diners or bar and grills around the countryside of northern Indiana, places where they knew my dad and let us kids go in for a burger. He'd give us dimes and nickels to play the jukebox, and he'd always say, 'Make sure the one you play is "Harbor Lights"!'"

Now it was Georgia's turn to slip on the ashen look. "Come on," was all she said.

She turned on the security, locked the back door and we got into her car for the ride to the country club.

"What?" I asked.

"Listen," she smiled slyly. She punched a disk on the CD. The music filled the car.

"Harbor Lights?" I nearly screamed. "Nobody has 'Harbor Lights' on their CD!"

Georgia was laughing. "I know! Can you believe it?"

"When did you get this? Have you had it a long time?"

"It was a Christmas present. I have all the old Platters' hits on this CD. I love it."

"Christmas?" I mused. "That was just about the time we talked about my coming out here to get this project going."

"That's right. In fact, if you remember, you were planning to come before Christmas and then your trip was moved to the first of January."

I leaned back in my seat. "I know you don't believe me, but none of this is circumstance. This shows you what I mean by 'signs.' This is my father's way of saying he's still here. He's still watching over me. He still loves me. Can you see how *alive* he is?"

She shook her head. "I don't know, Catherine, you sure are making me look at things very differently than I ever have before."

"I think, but I'm not sure, that it's my job to make people see deeper. Think on more levels. Maybe that's why I'm here."

"Well, it's working," Georgia chuckled as we drove away from the house.

After our wonderful and fun dinner that night at the Los Angeles Country Club, Georgia and I drove back to her house, passing over the fabled Mulholland Drive, where I could look down and see all the glittering lights of Los Angeles. It was a clear night with the stars shining down on us so brightly, it was hard to discern which lights were man-made and which were God-made. I couldn't help thinking in that moment how heaven was reflected on earth. Just as it should be.

The cool night was perfection. We opened the sunroof to drink in the cypress and eucalyptus-scented air. We turned up the volume on the CD player, letting the words of "Harbor Lights" drift up to heaven.

I thought of my childhood when I dreamed of being in just this place, seeing Los Angeles like this. The city of angels. Even as a child, I had wanted to tell stories to film. Was I making this all happen for myself way back then? Or was this something God had planned for me and I'm simply his instrument?

I thought of my parents and how they were with each other when they were young. I thought of times in La Porte, watching sunsets on a Sunday night when my father would just take us for a drive in our car. I remember him always singing. He loved to sing. He sang with his buddies around the piano at friends' houses whenever he had the chance. I remember my mother's beautiful voice joining in with him. I remember her humming songs while she took the clothes out of the washing machine and put them in the dryer. I remember "Harbor Lights" playing on a radio in a 1950s station wagon.

I was filled with awe at the simple things in my life and the lives of all those people living in Los Angeles. I sensed their hopes and dreams spiraling to heaven on the wings of their prayers. I wondered how many of them realized how protected they are by their loved ones on the other side. I thought of how fortunate I was to be alive on this night.

With "Harbor Lights" playing as we whisked over the hills, as loud as I could yell, I shouted to the sky, "This is for you, Daddy! I love you!"

Someone to watch over Me

*G*eorgia Durante's fabulous Coldwater Canyon house has been featured in commercials and movies for an obvious reason: It exudes magic.

Its Old World peaked dark green gables, battered and carved double wood doors and stone facade ramble over meticulously landscaped grounds, canopied by majestic, heavy-limbed pines. It gives the impression of an enchanted, though rather large cottage, which one could only find in Germany's Black Forest or in a Grimm's fairy tale.

I'd seen photographs of Georgia's house on her Internet site. Besides being a model, stuntwoman and author, Georgia was clearly blessed with a talent for interior design. Each room was spacious, cheery and homey. Clicking on-line from room to room, I thought I knew all there was to know before my arrival. But no snapshot prepared me for the experience of visiting the 1938 structure in March 2000.

Because of my intuitive ties to my own past life in the

1920s and 30s, I am fascinated when I come into contact with furnishings or structures that remind me of that life. I discovered, however, that only the main living room and kitchen/laundry area were original. The rest of the house was added on by Georgia.

I took the guest room, which had been Georgia's daughter Toni's room when she was younger. The room was enormous with a high-pitched ceiling rising fifteen feet. A wall of glass was covered with dark stained Plantation wood shutters from floor to ceiling and overlooked the gardens. Antique furniture filled the room and thick dark hunter green carpeting covered the floor. I instantly felt right at home.

My bathroom was next door and across the hall from the sunroom porch where Georgia worked on the computer and at her desk, sixteen hours a day, I discovered.

After a light supper that evening and catching up with each other's news, we finally retired for the night. I'd brought both reading and writing with me, and read for a bit before feeling sleepy and turning out the light.

As usual, I began my prayers before falling into unconsciousness. After saying a prayer of gratitude for my safe trip to Los Angeles, I was right smack dab in the middle of a protection prayer for Georgia and her son and daughter when I was oddly compelled to say an "Our Father."

Upon finishing the prayer, I rushed to say another. I started repeating the prayer silently, then I began whispering it aloud. By this time I was not in the least sleepy, but wide awake.

The "Our Fathers" blended one into another. Time passed. Hours, in fact. A sense of need, though not fear, pushed me to mentally "wash" the interior of the house with a purple flaming light. I envisioned bands of blue and white colored lights around the outside of the house, around myself and around Georgia.

I told myself I was doing all this to make my next day a good day. I told myself that I felt the need to pray, because I was about to conduct very important meetings with my co-producers and studio executives in the morning.

My prayers evolved into focused visualizations of flaming, burning crosses which I placed in the name of our savior, Jesus Christ, on the roof of the house and in the front yard. In my mind, I used lamb's blood to cover the doorways and every window opening of the house.

I felt as if I was sent to protect this house, and its inhabitants, from the Angel of Death. Still, fear did not press upon me, only that nagging feeling of need.

These exercises, along with hundreds of "Our Fathers" being recited continually, lasted all night. I never slept a minute that night. In fact, it was a shock to me when the sun came streaming in the windows.

I sat up, expecting to be exhausted, and instead was quite refreshed.

I showered, washed my hair and got dressed for my meeting. It was that morning when Brian, my co-producer, called and told me about his dream of seeing my father's ghost. (See the story "Harbor Lights" for details.)

After coffee and breakfast, I told Georgia none of this as I left to drive to Los Angeles for my meetings.

That evening before dinner, Georgia asked me, "By the way, how did you sleep in that room last night?"

"Actually, I didn't sleep at all. I spent the entire night praying."

An odd look crossed her face. It was that look of recognition and substantiation. I realized she'd expected me not to sleep in that room.

Once again, my neck hairs prickled. "Why are you asking me this?"

"My son never liked sleeping in that room."

I swallowed. Hard. "Why?"

This time her smile was sheepish. "My house is haunted."

I rolled my eyes. "I think I know this."

Suddenly I saw him. "It's a little boy, right?"

"How did you know?"

"I can see him," I said without thinking. And I did. "He has dark hair and clothing from the 1930s, dark pants and a white shirt. About eight or nine years old." Just as I said the words, his vision faded from my view.

"We've always had funny things happen. Like the television going on or off when no one is around. Or lights flickering. Or things being misplaced only to show up again somewhere else. I've never felt frightened precisely, but . . ." Georgia rubbed her arms, chasing her own goosebumps away.

"But there's more, right?" I asked.

"Yes. When I was redecorating the guest house, I was taking the mirror down from the wall and behind the mirror was a perfectly clipped newspaper story about a little boy aged eight being murdered in 1938. When I read it, I knew it was the little boy ghost I'd sensed in the house. But to be perfectly honest, I couldn't be certain. Then later, when I was renting the guest house out, the two women who wanted to rent it were so excited about it that they were willing to pay $200 a month over my asking price. Strangely, the very next day, they called and wanted to cancel.

"I asked them why. The one woman explained that she'd had a dream the night before that she'd been nudged on the shoulder. She woke from her dream and saw a ghost of a little boy standing by her bed. He was dressed in 1930s clothing. He was saying 'Help me. Help me.'"

My senses went on alert as my mind kicked into overdrive. "That's it!"

"What's what?" Georgia asked.

"This boy ghost is why my father showed up in Brian's dream last night! This was why I prayed all night and couldn't stop. I was cleansing the house. Now all we have to do is help the little boy find my father. My father has come here to help the little boy to the other side. To heaven."

Georgia looked at me like I was crazy, but only for an instant. "Do you think so?"

"We'll know shortly. Besides, both of us were brought up Catholic. Remember how on All Souls Day, November 2, we would go to church and pray the souls in limbo or purgatory into heaven? Maybe we were really doing it then and we didn't even know it. What can it hurt?"

"Nothing. Let's try it."

"All right," I said. "Envision the little boy in your mind. Now envision my father." I described what my father looked like. "Now, let's tell the little boy to go to my father. To see him standing there holding out his hand to him. If the little boy goes with my father, he will turn him around and take him to the light. There in the light he will find his own parents, even his pets to greet him. He can go home now. To his real home, his celestial home. And he won't feel lonely anymore."

Georgia and I concentrated on this for several minutes.

"Now, we'll read from the Bible."

I picked up her Bible and thumbed through the pages, letting the verse come to me. Lo and behold it was the 23rd Psalm. "The Lord Is My Shepherd." It couldn't have been more pointedly perfect.

We said a prayer for the little boy and thanked whatever angels had brought us the information to help him.

Georgia and I talked of many things for several hours. I slept on the couch that night with the night light on and with the Bible open, dozing, then reading more verses to help the little boy find his way to heaven. I didn't sleep much that night, either, but it was worth it.

Over the next several days, Georgia and I both noticed the atmosphere of the beautiful house becoming lighter and lighter. More sunlight appeared to stream through the windows. The air was energized with a new life it didn't possess when I first walked into its interior.

Of course, we have no proof, no video, recordings or photographs that there ever was a ghost in the first place. Nor can we prove we did anything at all, other than pray a great deal for several days.

But, like all mysteries, we'll discover the answers one way or another, on the day we pass over to the other side.

SECTION
5
FIVE

Angel
Visitations

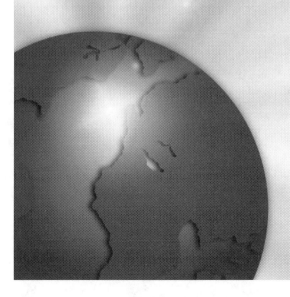

*T*hese stories are rare, but they are real. These are not visitations in dreams, such as Jacob or Joseph received as related in the Bible. These angels are actual appearances of angels in human form who appeared at a moment of crisis or near death, then just as suddenly as they appeared out of nowhere, they vanished.

Angel books abound on the retail bookshelves. I would venture to say there must be a billion words written about angels, and this book is certainly one of them. These stories are not to explain what angels are or are not. These are true accounts of actual sightings. Lives were changed or saved, because of this intervention from the angelic realm.

It is my belief that these incidents are more than miracles: they explain by their actions that angels exist.

"By their actions shall you know them."

Mary Ann's Angel

A s the author of this book, I have been blessed with stories that have seemed to fall out of the sky to me from friends. Upon explaining to my friends what I had set out to do, it has amazed me the kinds and sheer number of angelic experiences this world enjoys on a daily basis. But of all the stories I've heard, none is more moving, more lovingly angelic than the one told to me by Sammi Kirkpatrick about her sister, Mary Ann Guarino.

Mary Ann, like all of us, awaited the birth of her beautiful baby, Marilyn, with anticipation, love and the normal angst that comes with being a parent.

However, before Marilyn was six months old, Mary Ann noticed something disturbing about her lovely baby daughter. Marilyn didn't respond properly to loud noises. She didn't notice when her mother approached the crib. She didn't hear Mary Ann cooing to her as leaned over her. Marilyn responded to sight, but not to sound.

Terrified of the worst, Mary Ann took Marilyn to the doctor, who put the baby through a battery of tests. The angst that Mary Ann had felt wasn't normal pre-baby jitters. It was a dead-on premonition.

"I'm afraid Marilyn has a 95 percent hearing loss," the doctor said.

Mary Ann's heart nearly stopped. Of all the pains a mother wishes she could absorb, those of her child's traumas are the ones most welcome. What mother wouldn't want to suffer in her child's place? Mary Ann was no different.

Nightmares of Marilyn's future spiraled in Mary Ann's head day and night. She tried to will away the truth, but still the awfulness of it remained. Marilyn was doomed to a life with no sound.

The doctors told Mary Ann that Marilyn would have to wear two hearing aids to pick up even the loudest of sounds. She would have to go to special schools and learn to sign. Mary Ann knew she was up to the challenge God had given her as Marilyn's mother. She would take her to the best teachers, she would learn right along with her daughter. She would make the quality of her life no less than any normal child.

But of all the things that bothered Mary Ann the most, the thought of her beautiful tiny daughter wearing two hearing aids bothered her endlessly. Far too easily, she could envision other children making fun of her sweet Marilyn for wearing those hearing aids.

Mary Ann's shoulders were heavy with the burdens she was undertaking. Too heavy for a human to bear. Because God had given her such a precious child, she knew that God in turn would send her a sign that Marilyn would not have to bear scars of ridicule in addition to her loss of hearing.

One day, while Mary Ann was shopping at Sakowitz Department Store in her hometown of Houston, Texas, she saw the most beautiful blonde woman she'd ever seen walking toward her. She was tall, sleek, chic and dressed completely in white. What was most astounding about the woman was that she was walking two platinum white Afghan dogs on white leashes.

Mary Ann stopped dead in her tracks, doing what she normally never did. She stared. The woman walked by her, never making eye contact, just glided past her like a vision. Just as the woman passed by, Mary Ann's heart leaped in her chest.

"Why, she's got hearing aids. Two of them!"

Mary Ann started to go on about her business, but the sight of the woman was so astounding to her, that she did something else she didn't normally do. She turned around to stare at the woman again.

But the woman was gone. She'd vanished into thin air.

Shocked, Mary Ann raced to the nearest counter where one of the female clerks was straightening out a clump of silk scarves.

"Do you know who that woman was?" Mary Ann asked excitedly.

"What woman?"

"The one that looked like a movie star. The woman in white." Mary Ann looked around again, but still could find no trace of the woman who had just passed by her.

"I didn't see any woman in white."

"Well, of course you had to. How could you miss her? Walking those two white dogs. Afghans, I'm sure they were."

"Afghans? Dogs in Sakowitz?" The woman shook her head

tersely. "That's impossible. We don't allow pets in this store."

"You don't allow . . ."

Suddenly, Mary Ann's skin broke out in goosebumps. She shivered and backed slowly away from the counter. Her cheeks flamed as she touched them. For a moment she thought she was losing her mind.

"No," she said to herself. "I've just found my mind," she said with a gasp. "And the answer to my prayers."

She looked up at the woman with a knowing smile. "It wasn't a woman."

"But, lady, you just said . . ."

Tears welled in Mary Ann's eyes as she cut her off. "It was an angel. It was Marilyn's angel. My daughter is going to be fine."

Taken aback by the emotion in Mary Ann's voice, the clerk smiled back. "I'm sure she will be," she said and excused herself.

Mary Ann's knees were shaking as she left the store that day. Walking to her car, she thanked God a thousand times for giving her a miracle. She knew in her heart that she would never let the vision of that beautiful lady fade from her mind. It was her sign, and a sign to all mothers of deaf children, that our future is what we make of it. Mary Ann knew that day her daughter's future would be happy and filled with love.

At this writing in August 1999, Marilyn is twenty-seven years old. She graduated as valedictorian of her high school class. Today she has a full-time job with a Houston oil company. Best of all, Marilyn has grown into the loving woman Mary Ann had dreamed she would be. What is more, the entire family is happily and busily planning Marilyn's beautiful wedding in November.

All mothers wish their children to have love, to give love and to receive love. Mary Ann has lived to see her daughter have all of these and more. Mary Ann is a very special mother. After all, how many mothers have witnessed their child's guardian angel walking through their department store?

Ryan, the Truck and an Angel

From the day my son, Ryan, was born in 1972 until today, nearly his twenty-eighth birthday, I have been petrified. Even at an early age, I had confidence in this tiny mirror version of myself, but the world being what it was, it was Other Things and Other People that frightened me the most.

That's why I thought my life was over that warm October afternoon as I was writing at my computer at home and heard a frantic knock on the door. My office was adjacent to the front door, so the pounding sounded like thunder. We'd only lived in our new neighborhood less than a year, so it didn't surprise me when the woman on the other side of the door called, "Lady! Lady!"

The panic in her voice shot me out of my chair. I rushed to the door and opened it. "Come quick! Your boy's been hit by a truck!"

Terror froze the marrow in my bones. My deepest, most silent fears had become reality.

"Ryan . . ." My thoughts fused in a thousand dire images. It was impossible. He was in his room, I thought, playing with his Transformers. He was right where any eleven-year-old should be. Safe.

Then I remembered he'd said he was going out on his bike to visit neighbors and try to sell them the plywood Christmas yard decorations he drew, cut out with our jigsaw and then painted. He'd sold an entire "Snoopy" family to one neighbor. Now he was making a trio of snowmen.

Visions of sugarplums vanished, as in my mind's eye I saw Ryan's body now mangled. Crushed. Bleeding. Lifeless. Dead.

I failed to shut the door and took off running across our lawn, across the empty lot that separated our house from the corner. It was a short distance. Yet it was the longest span of earth I've ever crossed. I felt as if I were moving in slow motion. I was a good runner. Why wasn't I going faster? Why couldn't I see him yet?

I tried to scream his name, but lost my voice. I felt horrifically cold and numb. I couldn't feel my bare feet as they pounded over grass, then stones in the rough pavement. Suddenly, I remembered the day he was born. His first day of school. His last birthday. His smile. I knew my life would be over if he were dead.

Then I did what I was warned and taught never to do. I bargained with God. "Please God, take me. Not him. Take me. I'm ready. Let him be alive. Let him be alive."

As I rounded the corner, I saw the huge Suburban and the woman driver, a neighbor I'd waved to often, but had never formally met. She wasn't crying. Her face held a stunned, incredulous look.

"Where is he?" I finally screamed at the top of my lungs.

"Mom!" Ryan's voice mercifully cut through the panic in my head.

My eyes shot to him, sitting calmly on the curb. He had the same stunned, glazed look in his eyes as the woman driver.

"You're alive!" I burst into tears. I rushed to him and hugged him. My terror still not abating, I immediately inspected him for broken bones, internal injuries. Surely something was being overlooked. By all rights he should have been dead.

As I sat on the curb next to him, squeezing and poking his thin arms, my eyes glanced at the truck. There under the back tires was the remains of Ryan's bike, completely and utterly mangled and twisted beyond recognition. My instincts were right to look for injuries. How could anyone survive this?

I realized instantly that something was very strange about all this.

"What happened?" I asked the driver.

She was wringing her hands, her voice a croak against her dry throat lining. "He was riding his bike between the patio homes there, and those huge bushes always hinder my view of the street, but I never expected to see anyone riding a bike down those walking stones. Before I could even put my foot on the brake, his front tire was already across the sidewalk and into the street. I hit him head on."

I looked at Ryan. Not a scratch. "I . . . I don't understand."

"Mom, it was the weirdest thing. I saw her coming in the truck, but it was too late. I knew I was going to hit the Suburban and then . . . well, it was as if a huge hand just picked me up and put me here on the curb. I didn't hit the truck at all. I sorta just flew over here."

The woman nodded. "He's so right. He didn't hit the car, but he was airborne. I saw him! I know this makes no sense. I heard his bike being crunched under my tires. I closed my eyes thinking he'd deflected to the side. When I opened them, he was just sitting right there as you see him. Pretty as you please."

By this time the police had arrived, sirens blasting. The policeman asked Ryan and the driver the same questions and got the same answers. Their story did not deviate in the least.

The policeman scratched his head as he looked at Ryan's bike. "This is impossible! There is no way that bike could be twisted like that and your son not be dead. No way."

"Sure there is," Ryan said. "I was saved by my guardian angel."

The policeman was dumbfounded.

I smiled and winked at Ryan. He and I had been down this road before. We knew where to look for angels and when to expect them. And they always showed up on time.

"That's right," I said to the policeman. "He was saved by an angel."

Ski Angel

Over the years, I have developed some wonderful friendships with my booksellers and book buyers. Jerry Courville is one of those special people; upon meeting, we struck up an instant rapport. I've told her many times I felt an angelic sensation whenever I was around her. She is always smiling, forever more organized than I and no matter how taxing her work, she has time to spend with me and all her customers, simultaneously.

However, it wasn't until several years after we'd met and worked together on my book signings and for events in the community that she shared this amazing, blessed story with me.

Years ago, when Jerry's children were young, the family used to travel to Colorado to go skiing. The children were delighted to be on the slopes and they took to the sport as most young children do—with speed, abandon and quickly learned skill.

Jerry, on the other hand, was well into adulthood when she decided to learn to ski. Her fears were more well-honed than her mastery of the slopes.

On one particular outing, the family was having a ball. The children were up and down the slopes two times to Jerry's one. The morning was wonderful and invigorating. They lunched on the slopes and prepared for a run or two before calling it quits.

Just after lunchtime, a winter squall came over the mountaintops, draping the peaks in snow and wind. At first, Jerry didn't see there was a problem. The children and her husband were well within sight of her, though she tended to ski at a slower pace. She could hear the children's laughter and see their bright ski suits as she rounded bend after bend.

The storm picked up momentum. The wind howled, bringing more snow with it. The light flurries transformed into a thick, impenetrable veil of white. Suddenly, Jerry couldn't see her children or her husband. Sounds muffled. Sunlight dimmed into darkness. The mountain slope now looked like the dying embers of day, not midday as it was.

Jerry's fears surged. She forced herself to ski faster, but she could barely see her ski tips, much less where she was going.

From out of nowhere, she heard a voice. "Jerry, go back to the warming hut."

This was not her husband's voice. She'd didn't recognize the man's voice at all.

She looked around and then heard her name again. "Jerry," he called.

She looked overhead and saw a man riding on the ski lift above her. He was dressed in a bright red ski jumpsuit. He had blonde hair, blue eyes and was extremely handsome. Just looking at him, she felt her fears melt away. She smiled at him, waved and kept on skiing into the storm.

Amazingly, when she'd looked up, she could see the man clearly, but when she looked ahead of her, she was nearly blinded by the whiteout. Groping forward on her skis, unsure about anything, she heard the man's voice again.

"Jerry, go back to the warming hut."

She looked above her, and sure enough, the man was coming around on the ski lift again. He waved and gave her a quelling look.

A chill went down her spine, warning her of danger. This time Jerry didn't fight her intuitions or his warning.

It was impossible to see where she was going, but looking around, she could see the lights of the warming hut not fifty feet away, in the opposite direction. Carefully, keeping her eyes on the lights spilling out the windows of the warming hut, Jerry made her way to safety.

After putting up her skis and poles, Jerry found her family inside the warming hut, very much worried about her.

"Where were you, Mom? We were scared something had happened to you."

She hugged them. "I was trying to find you, but I was blinded by the storm. If it hadn't been for the nice man on the ski lift, telling me to come here, I wouldn't have known what to do."

"What man?" Jerry's husband asked.

"The nice young man who told me to come back to the warming hut."

"And where was he?"

"On the ski lift," she replied. "In fact, he told me twice to come here. I wonder how he knew you were all here?"

Jerry's husband scratched his head, trying to make sense of what she was saying. "What ski lift?" he asked.

"The one we rode up on, of course."

"But Jerry, we've only been separated for fifteen minutes. The ski lift doesn't even come around that fast. Plus, if you'll look, the ski lift is shut down. One of the guys on ski patrol said they shut it down at lunchtime, because they knew the storm was coming and they didn't want anyone lost on the mountain. It's been shut down for over two hours."

"It what?" Jerry looked outside. The lift was dead still, the chairs dangling from the wire like feathers on a leather string in the wind.

"How could you have talked to anyone on a ski lift that wasn't running in the first place?"

"Maybe he was a ski patrol person," Jerry said with a lump rising in her throat.

"Not likely . . ." her husband's words froze on his tongue. "Just exactly where were you when you saw this man?"

Pointing out the window, Jerry said, "Almost straight across from here and up a bit. Not but a few feet from that tall clump of trees."

"Jerry, there's nothing over there except a seventy-foot drop off a cliff. Didn't you see the orange mesh barricade around that area?"

"Barricade? I couldn't see my own feet! How would I see some orange mesh?"

Suddenly, the impact of what they were all saying hit them.

Jerry's hands flew to her face. Her eyes widened. She felt a flood of chills wash over her. "The man on the lift wasn't real. He was an angel."

"Yes. Sent to save your life!"

Jerry burst into tears and hugged her family close. It was at that moment Jerry said she realized not only how blessed she was, but that she had been saved from the jaws of death for a reason.

After Jerry told me this story, I couldn't help thinking how empowering it would be for those of us who find ourselves questioning our life's purpose, wondering why God wants us to be here, what's the reason for all the tragedy that we endure. If each one of us had ever been visited by an angel like Jerry's ski angel, just maybe we wouldn't question so much anymore. Maybe we would understand that we are doing exactly what it is we were sent here to do. Loving our families. Loving our friends. Being true to our God-nature.

Like most people, I ponder those few who are blessed with apparitions in time of need. How fortunate they are to see the divine. Then I wonder, maybe we are all seeing the divine every day in a million tiny ways, but too many of us are blinded by the snow in front of us and unable to see and hear what is really happening.

God bless you, Jerry, for sharing this enlightening story with me.

Highway 59 Angel

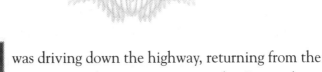

I was driving down the highway, returning from the airport on a clear, sunny summer day. It was thirty minutes until rush hour, so the traffic was still moving swiftly. The Loop 610 in Houston is one of those monstrosities of modern cities that encircles the city, but which if you don't know your exits, you can ride forever. Whenever I think of this freeway, I think of that song from the late 1960s about poor Charlie on the MTA, who rode the subway night and day, never getting off. It's an eternity thing.

After living in Houston for over twenty years, fortunately, I do know my way around. Approaching the Galleria area from the South Loop 610 toward my home is as familiar as my own backyard.

I was coming up to the exit to Highway 59, which I do not take, but rather I drive ahead several miles and take the Woodway exit.

All three left-hand lanes were beginning to stack up with approaching traffic. I remember thinking to myself there seemed to be an inordinately large number of late-model luxury cars on the freeway at this time of day. In my idle mind, I was wondering if they were going shopping, on their way to late lunches, were they busy? These are the kinds of thoughts I have, always pondering the next novel. The next story.

The right-hand exit ramp to Highway 59 South was braking to a standstill. Rush hour was moving in, but fast.

Suddenly, a four-door blue Mercedes zoomed forward in the left-hand lane next to me and crossed directly in front of me, without his turn signal on, in order to jog into the far right-hand exit ramp. This was about the most illegal, dangerous maneuver I'd ever encountered.

In that split second between life and death, I had the choice to veer to the right, and at fifty miles an hour would have hit the bright black and yellow striped barricade, or I could shoot off into the left-hand lane and crash into the oncoming flow of cars there. There was no time to check a rearview mirror or side mirror.

The Mercedes was directly in front of me. When he realized he was about to ram into the barricade, he slammed on his brakes.

There's no question in my mind, the man should have died. The real question was whether he was going to take me with him.

I didn't think. I reacted.

I swerved into the left-hand lane, knowing I was going to sideswipe the car or cars I was certain had come alongside me by now. My adrenaline went into overdrive. I felt my heart racing as the moment of death fell on me. I cringed.

There was no impact.

Shocked that I had not collided with another car, I glanced around me. The Mercedes was far behind me, its grill smashed against the barricade.

But to the left of me, where there was incredible potential danger because I had not looked to see whom I would be hitting, it was a clear path! Not a car in sight. In fact, mine was the only car in the lane.

This can't be! There were a half dozen cars in this lane only a split second ago! I thought.

I swallowed hard as I looked into the rearview mirror.

Chugging along at no more than thirty-five miles an hour, if that, was a huge old clunker of a car. It looked exactly like the awful pea-green 1957 Dodge my father had bought for us kids when we were in high school. I think he paid less than $100 for it. For one year, it got us to and from school two miles away, but that was all. Then it died.

The eerie thing was that I'd never seen another car like that in all these years since that time. The appearance of the car itself was a "sign."

I remember clutching the steering wheel so tightly that my hands went numb. My mouth was dry and I felt like ice.

A black man was driving the car. He lifted his hand off the steering wheel to give me that slight wave that motorists do when they know they've been of assistance, or have been so kind as to "let you in" when you've been edging your car out of that parking space instead of graciously letting them pass.

I expelled a huge sigh of relief. I was alive and I had this man to thank for it. I was so terrified, I remember smiling back at the man in the mirror, but my upper lip was stuck to my teeth and I could do no more than blink my eyes at him.

I glanced ahead of me for a brief second, taking in my destination, seeing that the highway was still clear.

"Thank you, God," I said aloud. I peeled my fingers off the steering wheel.

Then I glanced back into the rearview mirror, hoping to wave properly to my "savior." He was gone!

I turned to check every single lane on 610. He had disappeared.

Now, except for the Highway 59 exit there are no other exits off 610 at that point. One must drive on to the Westheimer exit, which was clearly in front of me. Behind me and three lanes over, there was no sign of that familiar-looking Dodge.

My heart started racing again. Chills sprinkled themselves over my entire body. "This isn't happening! I've had an actual encounter with an angel!"

Again, I checked all the lanes beside me, behind me, in front of me. I moved over to the next lane to better view the lane I'd been in. There was no question about it, the Dodge had vanished into thin air.

I couldn't help smiling to myself on the rest of the trip home. I had a real guardian angel looking out for me.

I should have died that day. It wasn't the first time I'd been placed in a situation when I knew I was going to die, but that experience reiterated to me that for some reason, God and my angels want me alive.

They believe I have purposes in life yet to be fulfilled. In my darkest hours when I'm scrambling for hope, for a sign to keep banging my head against this wall called life, I remember that angel in the car which looked far too much like the car my father had bought for us (which is a divine sign in itself). And I know that I'm here for a reason. I still haven't figured out what that reason is, but as long as God knows, that's good enough for me.

SECTION
6
SIX

Divine
Nudges

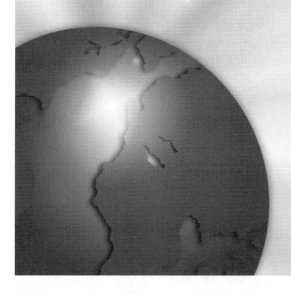

Seldom have I ever met a person who has not experienced a "divine nudge." This is more than a dream that comes true or a precognitive thought or awareness. A divine nudge occurs when you've been traveling down the road of your life, smugly thinking that you've done a pretty good job. You're feeling a bit complacent in your everyday work, family and social relationships. Your ego tells you that you have the world by the tail.

Then whammo! Along comes a spiritual awakening the likes of which would make St. Paul's conversion look like a Sunday afternoon picnic.

A decade ago, I met, over the telephone, a former roustabout biker who had lived on the edge of the law, both God's law and man's. Short of murder, he'd done it all. He told me the story of how he was the leader of his gang. He was running drugs, abusing women and children both sexually and physically. He prided himself on being Satan's son.

One day, he was riding his motorcycle down a divided highway in east Texas. Suddenly, a blinding white light flashed across the sky.

His motorcycle went out of control. At his breakneck speed of over seventy miles an hour, he shot across the median, across the path of oncoming traffic, over a gully and into a grove of trees.

He hit a tree and mangled his motorcycle. His helmet was split in two. Dazed, he stood off to the side of the wreckage staring at the debris. Incredibly, he had not a scratch.

Suddenly, a booming voice thundered from the heavens. This voice was so overwhelming when it called his name that he sank to his knees from the vibration of it. He trembled with fear.

The Voice told him that he was God's son, not the son of Satan, and that from that day forward, he was to be allowed to walk the earth by God's hand. He was to become a preacher to the bikers and God would speak through him. He would never again utter a single word in his life that God didn't put there.

This man told me that he felt his blood turn to ice, then heat up to a boiling point. He thought he would explode. He felt all the anger he'd encapsulated inside his cell structure, for all his former lifetimes and this current lifetime, seep out of him.

He burst into sobs as he watched his life, and several past lives, flash in front of him. He saw all of his mistakes. He saw all the pain he'd inflicted on people from their point of view. It was as if he was going through the pain, heartache and sadness himself.

It was then, he said, that he realized we are all one. One heart. One soul in God.

The Voice told him that for the rest of his life, he was to tell people this story. He was to tell people that he'd been saved by God for one reason only: to give testimony that God exists, that he is totally loving and forgiving. If God could forgive this man, then he needed to forgive himself and be the light for others.

When I spoke with this man, it was ten years later. His following was large and increasing by the day. He read his Bible every night and breathed love into every motivation for his every action. He didn't preach. He didn't tout one religion over the other, though he had a personal preference. He simply reiterated that all of us are one with God. There is no room for intolerance, hate, jealousy or racism.

He was as close to a "holy man" as ever I'd met one.

I call this man's experience "hand of God." It was a divine nudge to the max!

In my own life, I've had several "divine nudges." Times when no matter how hard I've tried to keep the status quo, God had other plans for me. On the outside, they may not have seemed holy, but they were. I've had to end a complete way of life, a career that I loved, in order to pursue another aspect of my divine path.

Some people may look at those times as "failings," but they weren't. Good came out of all my "derailments." For some of us, divorce is part of our mission. In the process of being laid off work or fired because of a co-worker's jealousy or spitefulness, a better position always comes along.

That divorce might have been difficult for me, but I might have saved a life in the process.

It's extremely painful to lose a friend, but I've also discovered after fifty years of living, that I've never lost a friend. They might have become lost to me for awhile, but I've never stopped loving them. Some had to move on to do other things than give me support or I support them. Sometimes it's our turn to move on or move over. Perhaps we were holding them back from being all they could be.

"Things always have a way of working themselves out." I can't tell you how patronizing I used to think those words sounded. That's all fine and good, but while I was waiting around for things to work out, my bills needed to be paid, my books needed to be completed and my heart needed mending. When you're flat on your back emotionally, it's difficult not to lose patience with yourself.

Just when you think you can't take any more, I've discovered this is when the divine nudge comes in. From out of the blue you meet a new friend, find a new job, fall in love, cure your own illness, find a new house, the car you've needed appears or the perfect mentor reveals himself or herself.

"When the student is ready, the master appears." This is another saying that I've found is intrinsic to "divine nudges."

Many has been the time when I've prayed and prayed for an answer, then let the prayer go, given it over to God and within hours, the right person has walked into my life to change its very course.

It's happened so many times to me by now that I sometimes think I'd better make darn certain that when I snap my fingers, I'm absolutely specific about what I want. Magic like this is not to be taken lightly!

These are also the stories of soul mates who were finally brought together by divine intervention. Not only are there stories of marriage partners meeting through unusual circumstances, but of career partnerships being put in line with one another. My story of how I met my publicist and coauthor for

The Evolving Woman: Intimate Confessions of Surviving Mr. Wrong, sounds bizarre even to myself, but it happened to me. Every word of it is true.

More fascinating are the recounting of my father's near-death experience and his last dying days. Those five years of my father's life when he was "suspended between the worlds," as he stated, were the most spiritual of my life. My life changed forever after that. My perspective of the slightest action I take in my everyday life has completely altered.

Not once but three times, I have slipped back in time to what I believe is a past life. I have read and reread Dr. Moody's books and though he states that he has found no proof to disprove the existence of past lives and reincarnation, he has found no proof of them either. For him, hypnotic trances or deep meditations that bring a past life "scenario" to the conscious mind are simply devices the mind uses to correct a behavior situation in the current life, to cure a disease or phobia.

What I experienced was more than this. I was not in a trance. I was awake. I occupied one space, but in two different time zones.

I could never equivocally or scientifically state that I have proof of reincarnation. Nor am I a theologist or metaphysician. If anything, I am simply a chronicler. A journalist, if you will, recounting as exactly and precisely as I can the strange occurrences that have happened to me or to my loved ones as they have described the phenomena they have witnessed to me.

Dorothy's Angel Message

AUTHOR'S NOTE: *The following story was written in my mother's voice and from her point of view. It is a unique story, as all hers are to me. Therefore, I felt it best that she be the one telling it.*

*O*n Friday morning, October 22, 1954, our family was saying our breakfast prayer for my father who had been terribly ill. Two weeks prior, Frank and I had flown to New Orleans and gone to the Oshner Clinic where my father was scheduled to undergo exploratory surgery.

I had been worried about my father's health since his and my mother's visit to Indiana in March. Oddly, he had complained of pain in his calves, but Mother and I had thought it was simply cramps or muscle fatigue from his constant horseback riding on his cattle ranch. Mother wrote through the summer that even though in pain, my father continued to ride almost daily until the end of September. Finally, the pain had become so severe that they went to New Orleans for a diagnosis.

After the surgery, which turned up little to cause alarm, Frank had a court case to try and we knew we had to get back to Indiana.

All our thoughts were on my father as the children finished their prayer. I looked up and saw a mail car drive up our driveway to deliver a special delivery letter.

"Who is it from?" Frank asked.

Ripping the envelope open, I said, "It's from my mother."

I sat down at the table and read the letter aloud to my family.

"Mother says she's taking Daddy home from the hospital," I said, looking at Frank.

I knew he must have read the concern in my face, because he asked, "Why aren't you happy? She says he's better. It's the answer to our prayers. What could be wrong?"

Instantly, I put the letter down. It was as if it were burning in my hands. "Something has changed since she wrote this letter."

"But it's special delivery . . . it can't be but two days old."

I felt chills course down my spine. Dread spread through the marrow of my bones. I was having a premonition. I knew the feeling well now. I hugged myself. "Frank, I want you to go to the bank and get me five hundred dollars."

"What on earth for?"

"I have to fly to New Orleans. Now. There's no time." I jumped up from the table. I didn't realize there were tears running down my ashen face. "Daddy's dying."

"What?" Frank's eyes flew to the letter. "It can't be . . . the letter said he's going home tomorrow. Everything is fine." He looked back at me and saw me shiver. He put his arms around me to comfort me. "Never mind. I know that when you're like this . . ." He looked at the children, who were staring at us with fear-filled faces.

"I'll get the money. You always know best," Frank said, and immediately went to the front door to get his hat and coat.

I dashed into Cathy's room and began pulling her clothes and Nancy's pajamas out of drawers and laying them on the bed. Frank came to the doorway, I suppose to check on me one last time. "I'm off to the . . . what in the world are you doing?" he asked.

Yanking the girls' sock drawer open, I said, "I'm packing for the children and for you, of course."

"Why?"

"I have to get everything ready for you to drive them down to Florida for Daddy's funeral." I cranked my head around to see Frank shrug his shoulders, but move a bit faster out the door and to the car. I knew he could feel my sense of a race against time.

I continued packing all morning. I had all of Frank's clothes laundered and packed, everything the children would need and my own suitcase was filled and locked, ready to go.

At noon, my Aunt Irene called from Mobile, Alabama, to tell me that Daddy was dying. My brother, Jack, was driving Mother from Crestview to New Orleans at that very moment.

"Aunt Irene, I already knew this. I'm packed and have made a reservation on the first flight out of Chicago. However, it doesn't leave until midnight."

"You know? Who called you?"

I wanted to tell her that an angel called me. Or maybe I

was reading my father's thoughts. Or maybe God himself called me. "No one called. I just knew."

"You guessed, you mean."

"No, Aunt Irene, I knew. I'll be there as soon as possible. I'll be flying through the night, but I will get there. I won't let him leave before I get there."

Frank drove me to Midway Airport, which was over an hour and half from our home. O'Hare Airport did not exist at this time and so, it was the closest airport to us.

I was frantic on the trip over. I prayed so hard I thought my mind would explode. I knew that Frank was praying, too.

It was pouring rain when I got out of the car and checked in. The process alone seemed to take an eternity and I knew I didn't have an eternity to waste. I kept wanting to scream at people, "Hurry! Hurry! My father is dying!" But they wouldn't understand.

Frank's patience was better than mine, I thought. He kissed me as I left the gate and he watched while I climbed the metal rollaway steps to the airplane. But, when I looked back to wave goodbye to him, he was turning to walk away. He didn't look back.

"Something is wrong," I mumbled to myself. Again, dread spread through me like a rush of cold wind. I knew Frank better than I knew myself. There had to be something wrong, because he had always waited until I was on the plane or bus or train or even in a friend's car. It was his way.

My nerves were already frayed, but at that moment I felt incredibly alone. My father was dying and Frank had not stayed to wave good-bye to me. I hadn't realized how much I'd needed to see him there, but he was gone.

The flight seemed interminable. My prayers banged through my brain over and over, endeavoring to give me hope, but even they could not overcome what I knew to be the truth. Death rode the wing of that plane that night.

When I landed, the taxi driver was in no hurry to get me to the hospital. I was about to explode with fear and emotional pain. "Please," I said, moving forward on the seat enough for him to hear me better. "You must hurry. You must drive faster."

"It's the speed limit," the driver said.

My eyes stung with hot tears, but I swallowed them. "You don't understand. My father is dying. I have to get there before he leaves."

The driver shoved his foot down on the pedal and raced through the city streets, just as daylight peeked over the horizon.

"Thank you," I breathed for what seemed the first time all day and night.

I raced into the hospital and immediately found Mother and Jack. We embraced quickly. "Is he still alive?"

"Yes, but barely," Jack replied.

A nurse came up to me just then. "Would you like to see your father?" she asked.

"Yes," I said.

She took me to a door where I could see my father lying in an iron lung. My blood froze in my veins as the shock of seeing my father like that registered in my mind.

"Do you want to speak to him?" the nurse asked.

I turned back to look, but the vision of my father lying there, hopeless, helpless, swam in my tear-filled eyes. "No, my father knows I'm here. But, he would not want me to see him like this."

"Are you sure?" the nurse asked.

The fireball in my throat nearly kept me from speaking, but I managed to reply, "Now that I'm here, he will die."

The nurse's eyes flew wide open at my words, but I didn't care what she thought. All I could think about was how much I was going to miss him.

Five minutes later my father died.

The doctors asked us to sign papers to allow them to perform an autopsy. Mother said no, but Jack and I convinced her that we had to agree to it. I told the doctors that I was certain he died of lung cancer. I had quit smoking the previous December and had tried to convince him in March that he needed to quit smoking as well. I told him that I believed smoking caused lung cancer. As usual, he pooh-poohed the idea. (This was a decade before the medical community began researching the connection between cigarettes and lung cancer.)

The doctors looked at me as if I were nuts. "We have proof that he has no lung cancer. We have X rays, which we took only thirty-six hours ago, that show perfect lungs."

"It was lung cancer, I tell you. He told us he had pain in his calves. I think the two are correlated," I said defiantly, not having a shred of knowledge about the subject. All I knew was what my intuition and my angels were saying to me. And that was good enough for me.

"Fine. We'll assign three medical students to search our medical records to look for any such case."

It took months before Mother received a letter from the medical team saying that they had found one case in *Lancet*, the British medical journal, in which a person had died of lung cancer where there were no symptoms at all . . . except for weak calves that hurt.

My father's sister, Lola, had ridden to New Orleans with Mother and Jack. So, the four of us rode back to Crestview that Saturday. I had called Frank before we left the hospital and told him the news. He put the three children in the car, along with the luggage I had packed, and drove non-stop from northern Indiana to northern Florida in eighteen hours. It was the middle of the night when they all arrived.

The next morning, Frank sat up on the side of the bed and I saw that an awful rash had broken out on his back. I could tell he was in quite a bit of pain. I called the doctor I'd known for years and he told me to bring Frank to his office immediately.

"You've got shingles, Frank."

I knew this was an incredibly painful condition affecting the nervous system and was often triggered by stress.

The doctor gave him a shot and a prescription. The shingles cleared up within a few days. That doctor died shortly after that, but a lot of people, even today, would like to know what his "miracle cure" for shingles had been.

Frank told me the shingles had started Friday night as he was driving me through the rain to Midway Airport.

"But Frank, you should have told me you were in such pain."

"Why would I do that? Your father was dying and I knew, when I saw you packing those suitcases for the kids, that I'd be driving to Florida within a few hours. There was no time to be sick."

"I'm amazed," I said. "You never said a word. . . ?"

"No, you are the one who amazes me," he replied.

The Professor and Me

I was born to be a writer. I understand that some writers are made, but I was quick on the uptake. I knew what I wanted to be.

My mother was quite ill during my childhood. Having two brothers and a sister all younger than me, I entertained them by telling stories since my father refused to buy an "idiot box," otherwise known as television. I didn't write my stories down, since this was pre-kindergarten and my early learning-to-read years, but by the time I was six, I used to grab the Sunday *Chicago Tribune* and shoot to the comics. Brenda Starr was the most intelligent woman I could imagine. Her journalism took her to foreign countries, paid her enough to afford a fabulous hair stylist and equally incredible lingerie, and her boyfriend, Basil St. John, was always stuck in some jungle, leaving her free to pursue her career. How good was that?

By the time I reached college I'd had a lifetime of parents, family and teachers supporting my dream of becoming a journalist. I was bright-eyed, swallowing my education without chewing, and naive as any seventeen-year-old could be. I should have seen it coming, but I didn't.

On the recommendation of the head of the English department, I was chosen to participate in a creative writing seminar intended for second-semester seniors and taught by a traveling Harvard professor who would be on campus for six months. I was the only freshman in the group.

After a month of lectures and small assignments, we were instructed to write our first short story. The stories would be read aloud and then critiqued by the rest of the class. I had no clue I was the Christian. They were the lions.

The night before I was to read, the professor telephoned me to come to his office "for a chat."

This quintessential professor, well over six foot six, tweed jacket with leather patches on the elbows, horn-rimmed glasses and booming voice, commanded me to enter and sit down. My behind hadn't hit the chair when he slammed the folder containing my short story down on the desk with such force, it skidded across and landed in my lap.

"Frankly, Miss Lanigan, your writing stinks."

Shock kept me from bursting into tears. I saved that for later. "What's wrong with it?" I asked, my dry lips sticking to my teeth.

"You have absolutely no idea about plot structure or characterization. How you were ever recommended for this class is beyond me. You have no business being here. One thing's for sure, you'll never earn a dime as a writer."

"There's not anything redemptive?"

"I'll give you that your description is nice," he said dismissively.

"Nice?" I felt like Catherine in *Washington Square* at the part where her father has just paid off her lover and she hears the carriage wheels on the cobblestones and her father says, "Don't worry, Catherine, at least your embroidery is nice."

Visions of Brenda Starr's overly stamped passport faded fast. I'd never considered other options in my life. I'd only had one dream. It was a mission. It was my life. Wringing my hands, I fought tears (badly) and asked, "What will I do?"

"I don't know. But," he said raising his forefinger triumphantly in the air, "you are a fortunate young woman, because I have caught you at the crossroads of your life. Your parents are spending a lot of money on your education. You wouldn't want to waste that money and your time on something to which you're not suited."

"No."

"I suggest you change your major. Get out of journalism."

"And do what?" I was aghast at the thought.

"You could be a nurse."

Comebacks have always eluded me. I didn't even know I was doing it at the time, but I looked him in the eye and said, "Geez, I could be a teacher."

It went over his head.

"Miss Lanigan, I'm mindful of the fact that you have declared your bid for summa cum laude. To do that, you can't take anything less than a 'B' in this class. [And I'd have to have straight "As" throughout the rest of my courses.] You can't even do that without a great deal of assistance from me. So, I'll make a bargain with you. I'll be your crutches. I will get you through my class and give you a 'B', if you promise never to write anything ever again."

In my mind's eye, Brenda Starr was gone. All I saw was a gaping black tunnel as my future. I felt dead inside. Being a devout Catholic, I had been taught to revere authority under any and all circumstances. Including logic.

I didn't know I was looking into the face of the devil, but I was. I knew he was asking for my soul, but I was very inexperienced in devil-deals. I wanted my writing. I wanted that summa cum laude.

"Okay," I said weakly.

I took my short story with me and went back to my dorm, grabbed a metal trash can and matches and went to the roof. It was night. I burned my story, and as the ashes spiraled up, I promised God that I would never believe in childish dreams again. I would be smart. I would use logic. If I couldn't see it, taste it, chew it and spit it out, I wouldn't believe in anything again.

For fourteen years, I didn't write. Instead, I read everything I could get my hands on. If I couldn't write it myself, I'd read what others had the talent and courage to do.

In the summer of 1979, I was in San Antonio with my family the weekend after Judge Woods had been assassinated by the Hell's Angels. Every journalist, television producer and film crew was in town. Sitting under an umbrella table around the pool was a group of writers, and I did something I'd never had the assertiveness to do. I went up to them and said, "I just want you to know that I think what you do is the most important work in the world. Searching for truth. I always wanted to be a writer," I gushed.

One of the writers, cigar in his mouth, looked at me and said, "If you wanted to be a writer, you'd be writing."

"Oh, that's okay. I have it on good authority that I have no talent as a writer."

"Who told you that?" he asked.

I related my tale about the professor. Finally, he said, "Why, I'm ashamed of you. You haven't even tried. Here's my card. If you ever write anything, give me a call."

I'm ashamed of you.

Of all my mother's key guilt-layering phrases, that was the one that spurred me to action. When I went home, I bought a stack of loose-leaf lined paper and a pack of pens and started writing a novel about World War I. Since I didn't own a typewriter, I later borrowed one from a friend, typed the 400 pages I had and sent them to the writer. He called me a month later and said, "I read your manuscript and it was damn good. I sent it to my agent and she's going to call you in half an hour."

Thirty minutes later, Kathy Robbins called me from New York and said, "Catherine, you are startlingly talented."

Shock prevailed for the second time in my life. She asked me questions about whether I saw the book as a "softcover" or "hardcover." Maybe we should go "trade." Industry terms came rattling at me like gunfire. Finally, I stopped her and asked, "Does this mean you liked it?"

"Yes! I want to sign you with my agency today. I'll send the contracts out. I think I can sell this by Christmas."

She did. In fact, she had two publishing companies bidding for that book. September 1999 marks twenty years since that time and I've published twenty novels.

I met a psychologist once who explained to me about the professor. "Don't you see what happened? His response was violent and angry. To coerce you into a bargain like that means that he was jealous. He saw something he didn't have. He saw talent."

"I don't know about that, but I learned that writers make something out of nothing. We make dreams into reality. That's our nature, our mission. We were born to it."

I will never give up my dream again. Never.

Cherry's Soul Mate

AUTHOR'S NOTE: *The following story is written in my friend Cherry Hickson's voice, retelling this story from her point of view.*

I was born and raised the first five years of my life in College Station, Texas. My father was a veterinary student at Texas A&M after World War II. If you've ever heard anything about A&M, you would hear about its school spirit. I was raised singing the Texas Aggie fight songs. When other children were being sung lullabies, I was singing "Saw Varsity's Horns Off!"

When we finally left College Station for my father to begin his lifelong occupation in the Mississippi Delta, we never went back, but I knew those fight songs all my life.

At the age of twenty-five, I divorced my abusive husband after six and a half years of torment. However, even in the pain was hope. I now had three of the most beautiful boys God had ever blessed a woman with. My ex-husband "disappeared" for nearly eight years and, during that time, the boys and I were on our own.

I began working, of course, and would come home to three babies, each of whom was an independent spirit demanding individual attention and love. They also needed to eat, take a bath and go to bed with prayers. The needs I knew they had, and my inability to meet them all, filled me with pain.

My romantic life was nonexistent during the first four years after my divorce. There wasn't time, and there certainly wasn't money. There was also my need to be loved and try as I may, my sons could not fill that void. I remember many times lying on the staircase after I had put my boys to bed and literally being racked with physical pain for someone to just hold me, to care. I wanted nothing more.

As my boys grew, we moved back "down South" to be closer to my parents. I knew they needed more love than I could give them by myself, and my parents on weekends and holidays were the perfect answer to that prayer. It also gave me time to do things for myself. At the time I felt that a lot of people looked at me negatively for that, thought I was self-ish and not a good mother. Or maybe those were my thoughts about myself. Even now I don't know. However, I began dating. I also became number one in the country for the company I worked for. When my company transferred me to Knoxville, Tennessee, I promised my sons they would never again live in an apartment.

I had no money, but somehow I "wheeled and dealed" and bought a beautiful four-bedroom, three-bath home with a fireplace for my boys. We were all so very blessed and happy!

When I came back to the South with my sons, I made some friends who told me about an astrologer in Memphis.

They told me she was a true astrologer and that she was tremendous. It was at this time that I met Geneva. (See "Cherry Follows the Stars.")

Even though I had my chart read by Geneva every year and she was right to the date about things that would happen to me, I still remained somewhat skeptical until her next prediction about me came true. And the next. And the next.

So many times, she would say to me, "Now, Cherry, just have fun. This man coming into your life is here for a reason, but he's not your soul mate. You are meant to learn things from this current beau, but that is all. Just have fun!"

I bet I couldn't count on my hands the number of men's charts I'd had Geneva read, hoping that this next one was my soul mate. I'd make call after call to her, only to have my heart break again. Through the years Geneva helped me to understand that I wasn't crazy. Some things we are destined to experience, and from that comes our learning.

In 1982 she recorded my annual chart in which she said I would meet my soul mate in a year and a half. She told me that he would have dark hair. Again, that was so unusual, I let it drop from my mind. That same year, I met once with a clairvoyant and a psychic, who confirmed that I would meet my soul mate very soon and that his name would be David.

Well, I didn't know any David and I wasn't attracted to anyone but blonds, so I just let that go as well.

During that year and a half, I made many life changes. I changed jobs twice (which was not like me in the least) and moved to Dallas, Texas. I met my dark-haired David exactly one and a half years after Geneva told me I would.

I loved him immediately. My sons loved him as well, and

David adopted each one as they turned eighteen. He has been a true father to all three. He is eight years younger than I, and he knew that I could not have any more children when we married. He had none of his own, either. But that didn't stop David one bit. When I asked him if he was sure about me, he said, "To always have my soul mate? You're worth it."

Twists of fate are always fascinating to me. When it was time for David to move his multimillion-dollar company, he chose College Station, Texas. What's more, David had graduated from Texas A&M, just like my father. When David built his first office, he bought the exact piece of land where I had lived the first five years of my life!

In July 1999, I became a grandmother for the sixth time. Before the millennium, my seventh grandchild will be born and all of us live in our hometown, College Station.

I don't know about others, but destiny has more than played a hand in my life and those of my sons. We are all living proof that when God is steering the ship, you will always sail aright.

Saving a Life

I was forty-three years old when I moved back to Indiana from Texas to care for my ailing mother after my father died and, in all honesty, to find myself again. Sometimes we have to go back to our roots to find out that the grass is green no matter where we go, as long as we're providing the nourishing for others.

I didn't know this when I went home. I only knew my life as I'd known it was no more. I felt rootless. Unneeded. My publisher had cut back and I was without a publishing contract. I had tons of stories to tell, but no one wanted to hear them.

Because I have the energy of three midwestern tornados and a couple dozen Texas-size hurricanes blowing my creativity into warp speed on any given day, to just loll around a house watching game shows is definitely not my style. My sister, Nancy, owned and still owns a retail corporate basket business. She was shorthanded and, fortunately for me, she needed help.

By this time, the family joke was that I'd been in the retail business since my first lemonade stand at the age of six. I lived and breathed customers. I loved working "the floor," meeting people, helping them choose gifts that would make them and the recipient happy. My job at Celebrations-to-Go saved my emotional and, probably, physical life. I was busy ten hours a day, six days a week. At Christmas, we all worked eighteen hours a day, including my seventy-two-year-old mother. The mother-daughter-daughter bonding we enjoyed was and is stronger than superglue.

However, as exhilarating and flat-out fun as these days were for all of us, moving the store, building a new business and creating magic for everyone who walked through the front door, I still felt empty inside.

I wasn't writing. I wasn't being true to myself. I questioned everything. I wondered why—besides my being there for my family and they being there for me—I was back in Indiana when Ryan was in Texas and I missed him so much? Sometimes I missed him so much, my belly would scream. I missed my girl-friends. I missed the air and dirt of Texas. I loved Indiana, but now I felt how my father must have truly felt when he was dying and would tell me he was "between the worlds." I was between worlds, except mine were physical worlds.

I struggled at night trying to come up with the most per-fect novel that would tweak the interest of a publisher. I'd fired my agent for sins I thought were unforgivable. I had no connection to publishing anymore. I was adrift.

Frankly, I felt like Jimmy Stewart in *It's a Wonderful Life* when he's ready to jump off the bridge into the icy water. As I drove around La Porte, I realized there were no bridges to jump off of. I took that as a sign. Suicide was out. Nope, I had to keep going. I had to "get happy" somehow.

One autumn day, as we were preparing for the Christmas season's retail goods to arrive, I was working the floor, putting out a new display of crystal bowls. A beautiful, young blond woman walked in the front door, looked around and then at me.

"You're Cathy Lanigan, aren't you?"

"Yes," I said smiling curiously. This wasn't a reader of mine, I realized, because they always call me "Catherine." This was someone from my childhood, but she was too young for me to have known her as a child. I racked my brain. As so often happens with my brain, I came up with nothing.

She smiled. Angelically, I might add. "I heard around town that you were working here. I didn't come here to buy anything today. I just wanted to see you and thank you for saving my life."

"What?"

"Thank you for saving my life."

"I'm sorry," I replied, shaking my head. "I've never saved anyone's life."

"You saved mine. I'm Jane Nicholson. I was the baby who drank the turpentine when you were baby-sitting for me. You found me in time, and knew what to do instantly. My mother still talks about it to this day. She says I was blessed because Cathy Lanigan saved my life. She still marvels that, when you were only thirteen years old, you knew to flush out my mouth and make me throw up. You called your parents and they took me to the emergency room and after it was over, you called my parents. Mother says I was already back home by the time they arrived. They said you were as calm as could be."

With her every word, the past flooded back to me. I was barely thirteen when I had worked for the Nicholson family.

Jane was barely crawling. Julie, her mother, was an artist and had an easel and paints set up in the basement. I had been playing with Jane on the rug in the playroom, when it was time to start her bottle. This was the day of glass bottles and pans on the stove with a couple inches of water to warm the baby's milk, rather than a microwave.

I was a speed demon up and down stairs and I couldn't have been gone more than sixty seconds to take the bottle out of the refrigerator, plunk it in the water in the pan and turn on the electric stove and then hightail it down the stairs.

The second I hit the floor, I saw Jane was gone. She'd crawled off the rug and all the way into the adjoining room, picked up a glass jar of turpentine and had it to her lips. When I shouted her name, she dropped the jar and it broke.

Jane's screaming is part of what might have saved her life, as well. I instantly picked her up, turned her upside down and slapped her back. Whatever had been in her mouth and throat was now on the floor. I raced her upstairs and washed her mouth out with water and soap. I called my mother while keeping the baby upside down.

Once at the hospital, they told my parents that Jane had not ingested any turpentine and I'd gotten it out of her mouth fast enough so there was not the slightest burn or poisoning.

In all my life, to that point, I'd never prayed so hard. I called down every angel in heaven to help this baby and they came rushing to my aid.

Jane was right. She could have so easily died.

To this day, I wish that jar of turpentine had not broken. I'll always wonder how much she really did drink. Was it that she didn't drink but a tiny bit? Or did she drink enough to kill her and the angels saved her?

"I didn't save your life, Jane," I said.

I will never forget the wise look in Jane's eyes when she peered back at me. "I know. I know."

I hugged her that day as she left. "You have no idea how much your coming here has meant to me," I said.

"Maybe I'm just returning the favor, huh?"

I winked at her. She knew. I knew. The angels had sent Jane to save my life that day.

What makes this story even more amazing is that the very next day, I received a call from my friend Charlotte, who was in Los Angeles having lunch with a friend of hers. She'd told him about my dilemma of not having an agent. He told her about a woman he knew and trusted by the name of Kimberley Cameron.

Read the following story of "Max and Mom" for the continuation of this amazing, two-day, angelic intervention into my life.

Max and Mom

*T*his is the second half of a two-day angelic intervention in my life. As I said in the previous story, "Saving a Life," I had felt adrift in my life because I needed a publishing contract. I worked on a story about a young mother who kidnaps her son and runs away from her abusive husband. I called the book *Star of Hope*. In Houston, there is a Christian family shelter called The Star of Hope Mission, for which I'd done some public relations over the years hoping to raise awareness of the mission itself, if not to raise dollars.

My story was about Susan Kidd, who changes her name to "Star," and her son Robin, who changes his name to "Max." It was finished and ready to be seen by editors. The problem was that I needed an agent who would take it to the right people.

During these years, publishing on all levels was going through a major shakeout. Mergers of houses were commonplace. Conglomerates ate up smaller publishing houses and fired the editors with whom I'd once worked. Later I discovered that once I'd moved, lots of publishers had lost track of me, as well.

I poured my heart out to my friend Charlotte, who then took it upon herself to find me someone I could trust.

For those who are unfamiliar with publishing, not all agents are trustworthy. By and large, the majority are incredibly hardworking people with families to support and their own reputations to consider. They are not the sharks. They are great people and I admire them, tremendously. However, as I stated, this was a time of transition and some people were desperate. Desperate people do desperate things. At the very least, in my case, it was even more of a case of what they didn't do that bothered me the most.

They didn't return phone calls. Didn't push for a sale. Didn't show my work. Didn't have film contacts. Didn't. Didn't. Didn't. All that time an agent spends on someone else's career, translates into my phone bills not being paid.

That afternoon when I returned home from work, Charlotte called and said, "You absolutely won't believe what happened today."

"Try me."

"I went to lunch at Bistro Gardens on Rodeo Drive with a good friend of mine. I was lamenting about your situation of not finding the proper agent for your work. I told him your recent problems with agents and he concurred that these things happen. Anyway, I found myself telling him the story about Susan and Robbie and how they change their names to Star and Max.

"I told him that the way the mother and son bond, in the pages I've read, just got to me. Anyway, my friend said,

'Charlotte, I know who would be a good agent for Catherine. Her name is Kimberley Cameron. She's honest and has an office right here in Los Angeles. When I get home, I'll call you with her number.'"

Charlotte then told me that they'd walked out to the parking lot together and were waiting for the valet to bring around her car, when a Jeep four-wheel-drive drove up and this beautiful young woman got out.

"My friend sucked in his breath and told me he couldn't believe his eyes. Here was Kimberley Cameron, standing right in front of us."

After being introduced, Charlotte quickly explained that she had a writer friend in dire need of an agent, could she call Kimberley the next day? Kimberley graciously gave Charlotte her card and they parted.

"But Cath," Charlotte said, "that's not the spooky part about this meeting. Just then, the valet drove up with my car, I paid him, got in and happened to look at the license plate of Kimberley's car. Cath, it spelled out 'Max and Mom'! Do you think this is a sign?"

"It's more than a sign, Charlotte. I guess Kimberley will be my new agent."

Kimberley later read my work and was the agent who sold *Becoming* to Dorchester Publishing, along with an historical romance, later titled *Seduced*. Through Kimberley, I embarked upon nearly a six-year career with MIRA Books.

Glorious Angel

I t was a child's worst nightmare.

I got the call right after work. My sister, Nancy, said, "Mom *and* Daddy had heart attacks. Daddy was dead for twenty minutes before they brought him back. They're in ICU in Flagstaff. Get on a plane and I'll meet you in Phoenix. We'll fly together from there."

I was more than in shock as I made my flight reservations and drove to the airport. All my life, I've been aware of the precariousness of life. How one's fate turns on a dime, and that every breath we breathe is precious. But to lose both parents in an instant was devastating.

I met Nancy in Phoenix, and from there we took a late night flight on a puddle-jumper to Flagstaff through a thunderstorm. I prayed the entire way, for Mother and Daddy and for us, that we'd make it in time.

When we arrived, we discovered that Mother had only had altitude sickness, had been released and was waiting for us at the ICU nurse's station. I doubt I've ever hugged my mother so tightly. She was in a panic over Daddy's condition, but she was alive. I was thankful.

Nancy and I went to see Daddy right away. He was groggy, but incredibly coherent, which gave me great relief since my father was the most brilliant man I've ever met. For anything to have happened to his mind would have been a tragedy. He'd always had a wry, sharp wit. Blessedly, his sense of humor was intact.

"I don't see why you should be surprised by all this, Cath. How many times have I said I wanted all four of you kids to see the Grand Canyon? Your mother says the boys are on their way, too."

"A massive heart attack is a bit dramatic, don't you think?" I asked.

He squeezed my hand, tears came to his eyes and he said, "I love you. I came back to tell you that."

"Came back?" I shook my head, not understanding.

He pulled me closer. "From the other side. I was there. First it was dark. Then I saw this brilliant white light. It was very peaceful."

He winced. I could tell that speaking caused him great pain.

"Then why didn't you stay over there?"

He looked at me as if I were crazy. "I came back for you kids and your mother. I couldn't leave her alone. Besides, they had all that damn humming over there. You know how I hate humming."

"You mean like music?"

"No, it was humming. I distinctly thought to myself that there should be words to the music, but there were none. In fact, it wasn't like music. It was like a rushing, sing-song sound."

"Like a river flowing?"

"Yes, more like that."

At the time of Daddy's near-death experience, very little was published about this phenomenon. Later, I began reading anything and everything I could get my hands on about people in similar circumstances. I read that the rushing sound, or "humming," was a flow of energy that others had described when they were close to or in the presence of the God-source.

Right then, however, I was a bit weak in the knees hearing all this. My mother was nodding, as if she knew what he was talking about. But then Mother had sat at many a deathbed; her aunts, cousins and grandparents had all explained similar sightings and situations. She was from the Deep South, where the family kept a deathbed vigil. Hospitals were for the living. Dying was done at home. Because of this, my mother had heard stories of heaven looking beautiful and green. Angels were common in her repertoire.

"And you came back for us?" I asked, holding his hand.

"Yes. They said people are put on earth for only one reason. The lesson of love. I guess I'm not finished with my lesson yet."

Though my father was brilliant, it was true, he was not the most demonstrative of men when it came to emotions. He was raised in a very strict Catholic family by my grandmother, who, bless her, was elderly when I was born. As a child, I thought all too often her heart was made of stone. She was an ice queen and she clearly didn't like any of the four of us kids in the least.

Looking back, I realize how difficult it must have been for her being elderly, surrounded by my energetic self, multiplied by my equally active siblings. We were a handful, as Mother used to say.

My sister and I remained in Flagstaff for a week. We spoke with the doctors, who explained the chances were slim my father would recover enough to come down off the mountain. The drop in altitude would kill him, they said. My sister had three children and a husband at home and a retail business to run, and I had a job, family and writing career that beckoned. She and I made plans with our two brothers to take shifts staying with Mother while Daddy died.

Because we were only allowed to see our father for a half hour in the morning and a half hour in the evening, our days were free. Nancy and I decided to finally see the Grand Canyon.

Even for this writer, there are no words to describe this natural wonder. Nancy had a master's in geology. She was in her element explaining every rock formation to me. As we stood at the south rim of the canyon, the most bizarre thing happened to me.

I traveled back in time.

Suddenly it was 1903, the air was heavier, the sunbeams on the canyon walls were more golden, as if the world were viewed through a sepia-toned filter. I realized that back then, the ozone hadn't thinned and split open. I felt the pinch of high-buttoned shoes, the flap of a grosgrain ribbon from my straw hat against my shoulder. I could still hear my sister's voice as she listed the Mesozoic age, the Jurassic period, etc. I "heard" a horse whinny, then felt its warm breath against my back. Carriage wheels crunched against rock.

Then, just as suddenly, I was back.

(Read "Reincarnation Proof" for a more detailed account of this incident.)

Nancy turned to me and said, "Are you going to have a heart attack, too? You're white as a sheet!"

"I'll tell you about it over some lunch."

Walking into the enormous log and timber styled lodge and restaurant, I couldn't help noticing the bronze plaque at the front door stating the lodge had been built with timber from Oregon in 1903. The same year I felt I'd just "experienced."

I told Nancy what happened to me and, mercifully, she didn't scoff. Instead, we both contemplated the enormity of time, nearly losing our father and the distinct, sad possibility that he would die any day.

While gazing out the room-sized plate glass window at the canyon, my mind's eye began "playing tricks on me," as Mother called such phenomena when I was a child.

Looking toward the cliffs on the opposite side of the canyon, in my mind's eye I saw the vision of an Indian princess, dressed completely in white or light tan leather clothing, fall off the cliff to her death. I remember the sensation of hearing a thud when her body hit the ground. Then from the canyon floor, I envisioned a white dove soaring upward to the sky. I could hear her voice, and she told me her name was White Dove.

Then, just as clearly, a vision of a tall, elegant, dark-haired woman dressed in a turn-of-the-century brown riding habit appeared next to our table. She was so real to me, I remember blinking, but she didn't fade away.

She didn't speak, but communicated telepathically. It was as if I could read her mind. I knew somehow she'd been to the Grand Canyon back in 1903. I knew she and her husband, the faint image of a man who briefly flashed before my mind, had been involved with the building of the lodge. The woman was very sad because she'd wanted to be a journalist in her lifetime and instead, once married, was too busy with her social life and travel with her husband to write. She was from San Francisco and told me she survived the earthquake of 1906. Finally, she told me she wanted me to write her story and that I was to call it *Wings of Destiny*.

Again, the vision of the Indian princess and the White Dove wafted across my mind. Wings of the dove, and wings of destiny, became intertwined in my mind.

Obviously, I must have had a strange look on my face, because Nancy began asking me what I was seeing out there in the canyon. I related every detail about my vision as it unrolled. Nancy was more than fascinated.

When we returned to the hospital that night, each taking our turn to see Daddy, Nancy couldn't wait to tell Mother about my vision, or whatever it was. Mother simply nodded her head and, before Nancy finished the tale, blurted out, "You must mean Aunt Barbara."

"What Aunt Barbara?" I asked.

"Aunt Barbara and her husband from San Francisco. He sent Barbara to Paris twice a year to buy her spring and fall wardrobes. They lived through the earthquake of 1906. I don't know much else about her, except that she was on my mother's side of the family. Kratz was her maiden name."

I sucked in my breath. "I got the impression that her last name began with a 'K.' I thought it was Kendrick."

"Kratz," Mother assured me.

Nancy and I exchanged a stunned glance.

Mother shrugged her shoulders, "You were seeing Aunt Barbara." She acted as if this kind of thing were an everyday occurrence.

"Mom, this means I was seeing a ghost," I replied incredulously. This had been a whopper of a day for me. As if traveling back in time wasn't enough, now I was being visited by a deceased family member. The first time I'd seen a ghost, my grandmother Ethel Manning, I was only thirteen and it was a week after her death. It was simple in the ensuing years to pass it off as a dream, a flight of my imagination. However, now I was in my late thirties. This was not a childhood fantasy. I knew what I saw. What I didn't understand was why Barbara, and this book she was demanding I write, were of any importance.

The weeks passed, Daddy improved and a month and a half after his massive coronary, we brought him down from the mountain. With an oxygen tank strapped to his wheelchair, he flew back to Chicago and home to Indiana.

Over the next five years, Barbara came to "visit" me too many times, because each time she appeared Daddy suffered another heart attack, another stroke, another seizure. He died again. He came back again. His experiences with the "other side," or heaven, began to take on a clarity and purpose. Many times we spoke about what he was seeing and experiencing. Always, the story was the same.

"They" sent him back to learn the lesson of love. I remember once in his hospital room he looked at me and said, "Would you tell that woman on the ceiling to get down from there. She must be freezing."

He spoke the request as if asking for a glass of water. It was then I realized that he was seeing the next dimension, as clearly as he existed in this space and time.

"Why do you think she's cold?" I asked.

He looked at the ceiling. "Because it's so blindingly white. All that snow."

"I don't think it's snow, Daddy. I think it's light. It's the white light of heaven everyone describes. Do you know who she is?"

"No, but she's young and very beautiful." He looked at me. "They're all young on the other side. Not more than thirty or so. Odd."

"I don't think it's odd," I replied. "It makes sense. If there is only time and gravity on earth, then why would the spirit age anywhere but here."

This was only one of many such exchanges we shared. More years passed, he lived to see two more grandchildren born and three more of my novels published.

During this time I worked voraciously on *Wings of Destiny*, struggling to incorporate the otherworldly experiences my father related and the truths he was discovering. The story grew to over 1,200 pages at one point. My agent banged against every door he knew in publishing, but we could not get any takers. No one wanted to venture into this spiritual/visionary arena I was describing. Editors claimed that ghosts and spirits could not drive a plot. I refused to give up. I kept working on the book.

Barbara's visits became more than frequent. She was not only with me all the time, but my girlfriends began "seeing" her as well. One of my favorite Barbara visitations was at Thai Pepper Restaurant here in Houston. My friends Stacy and Vicki arrived at the same time I did. We walked up to the hostess, who inquired, "You'll be three for lunch today?"

Vicki's eyes grew wide, she laughed and said, "Make it four."

"Four?" I asked.

"Yes," Vicki replied and nodded to my left.

Sure enough, I glanced over and frankly, I don't know how the hostess could have missed Barbara, she was such a clear presence.

Stacy smiled. "I like your outfit," she said to Barbara, who smiled back.

We followed the hostess to our table and sure enough, Barbara sat down on the empty chair, as if she intended to order right along with us. For a solid ten minutes she remained with us. We all exchanged comments with her, though she never spoke. Vicki kept asking why she had chosen this moment to appear, but Barbara's reply was always to look at me.

The next day, I got another call from home that Daddy was in the hospital again. It was then I realized the connection. Barbara wasn't hanging around simply to inspire me to write *Wings of Destiny*. Her appearances were a harbinger of my father's inevitable death.

I was on a plane the next day bound for Chicago, then a bus to Indiana. Mother was exhausted taking care of Daddy, and I feared for her health as well.

Finally, Daddy went to the hospital to die. It had been five years since Flagstaff. His dying of congestive heart failure, in which the body drowns in its own fluid, was torturously painful, but he adamantly refused all medications. No pain pills, no IV, no tubes. Not even a Tylenol. Just a bed and nurse, so that Mother wouldn't strain herself trying roll him over or get him up.

Again, I flew to see him. I was sitting in the room with him, leafing through a magazine. Mother sat in a chair next to his bedside. Daddy was talking about the weather and the Bulls' game the day before. The sorrow in the air was thick as smoke. We all pretended not to see it.

I asked him, specifically, why he wasn't taking pain medication.

"I don't want anything to cloud my brain. I want to have clarity of thought." He spread his arms. "You see this room? Me? I am dying. This is my world. But there are two worlds. I am suspended between the worlds. I see things you don't see."

"Like that woman on the ceiling the last time?"

"Yes. She and others."

Suddenly, he stopped, as if the effort to speak was too much for him.

"You should rest now, Frank," Mother said.

He nodded.

I agreed and picked up a magazine to read. I had only turned two pages when Daddy sat bolt upright. "Cath, there's a human being sitting on top of your head."

I stared at him, glanced to the side and saw Barbara. I could hear her voice. She was telling me what she wanted me to say to him. The time had finally come.

I put the magazine down, nodded and gathered up my courage. I'd never talked about Barbara to anyone, fearing their derision, except my girlfriends, who had been chosen by Barbara to see her as well.

I realized at this moment, I was here for my father. "I know. It's a woman."

Mother gasped. "You *know?*"

"Yes!" Daddy said. "She looks a lot like you. Big eyes."

"But hers are brown, right?"

"Yes."

"Now, she's standing beside me and she's wearing a brown riding habit, brown boots and is slapping her riding crop against her thigh. Her name is Barbara. She came to me when you were in Flagstaff. She's been around for five years. She's impatient."

"Yes, but how can you know all this?" he asked warily. "I've been telling your mother I have seen this woman. Mother doesn't believe me. She thinks I've lost my mind."

"No, Daddy, you haven't lost your mind."

Mother was trembling. "Your father screams out at night. It's all a bunch of nonsense."

There were tears in my father's eyes. "I was afraid," he said.

I could sense his fear and this shocked me. My father was a war hero. He'd been down to death and back again, several times, and he'd never said he was afraid. This was something altogether different.

Chills shot down my spine. "Tell me, Daddy. What could make you afraid?"

"These people, I could see them, very clearly." He clutched at his hospital gown at the area just above his heart. I remember thinking it significant about the area he grabbed, though I don't yet know what it means. "These spirits wanted to come into my body. One of them did once."

I was stunned. In the past years of my foray into the metaphysical and information about near-death experiences, I'd read articles about people claiming that ghosts entered their bodies. I'd seen the movie *Ghost* in which Patrick Swayze's character entered the body of Whoopi Goldberg's character's. But, to think that the most intelligent man I knew was stating such incidents were not fantasy, but very much real, was a shocker.

"They went into you? That means their thoughts could become your thoughts?"

"That's what made me afraid. I never knew it was possible. I was afraid I would be missing somehow."

"But would that mean you were dead and they took you over?"

"I don't know," he said, looking at me hopefully.

"I've read about this kind of thing, but it was always in a positive vein. Like an angel takes over a drug addict's soul and turns their life around. That kind of thing."

Then I asked, "How did you get them out?"

"I didn't. They told me that my body was too decrepit. I was too diseased."

"So, they travel on to find another body?"

"Yes," he replied thoughtfully. "I would assume so."

Of all the paranormal incidents in my life and those of my kin, this was truly the single, most frightening event of all.

If what my father said was true, that ghosts/spirits can enter our bodies once our will is weakened, then there must be some validity to "walk-ins." Does this now lay more responsibility on human beings to be resolute in their efforts to "keep pure the body temple"?

This then would give credibility to accounts I'd read or seen on television of auto accident victims who walked away from near death, only to completely change their lives; many of whom turned to lives of charity and community contribution. Perhaps it's not that the soul had been awakened, made an about-face and begun ministering to their fellow man. Maybe these new personalities were an entirely different soul altogether.

Is this what is meant by the saying "the angels walk the earth"?

"So none of them overtook you?"

Now, my father's tears flowed profusely. "Only one, a small boy for a day or so."

At that moment, the air in the room became supercharged. I remember thinking I needed to concentrate on my breathing or I'd float away myself.

Unbelievably, I saw the essence of a little boy standing between my mother and my father's bed.

I swallowed hard. "Daddy, there's a young boy beside you. He's letting me know that he's the one who came to you before. He's about two years old. He's dressed in black short pants with suspenders, white shirt, brown oxfords, knee-high socks. His clothing is of another period in time, like it's the 1920s. He has black hair. He said his name is Andrew and that he's your brother."

"That's impossible!" Mother said. "Your father's brother had red hair and his name was not Andrew."

Daddy reached over and took Mother's hand. "I never told you . . . I had another brother who died at the age of two. He had dark hair and his name was Harold Andrew."

Mother gasped. I was covered in chills. I didn't know whether to burst into tears or faint. I was light-headed and everything about this encounter was surreal. It was as if somehow I'd been transported to this place where my father "lived" in between the worlds. His visions were as clear to me as my mother sitting in the chair with her needlepoint in her lap.

"Then I'm not crazy," my father said.

"Not in the least. I'm beginning to think that the rest of us are crazy not to see what you see."

Daddy's eyes were filled with gratitude. "I couldn't take it, thinking I'd lost my mind. I've willed myself back to life so many times."

"I know you have. Why do you keep doing that? This is all so painful for you."

"Don't you see? I want my children and my grandchildren to know the power of the human will can do anything. Even conquer death. They can do anything with their lives if they desire it, will it to happen.

"I purposefully have not taken any drugs or painkillers, because if any of you children thought I'd gone crazy at the end, that I was rambling, that I was making up these visions, then all my suffering would have been in vain. You see that, don't you, Cath? I've been living for them."

"Yes, Daddy, I see it." Now I was crying, too.

He looked at me expectantly. "Do you know why Barbara and Harold Andrew are here?"

"Yes. They're here to help you over to the other side."

He dried his eyes, nodding. "That's what I thought."

Daddy got better after that for nearly a week. At least it was long enough for all of us to think he'd pulled another "comeback."

Just before I flew back to Houston, my father told me, "When I go, I'll leave you a very special sign."

As I left, I couldn't imagine what that sign could be. Four days passed.

On Valentine's Day 1992, my father took his last breath. He'd left a sign all right. Valentine's Day, the one day of the year meant for love. My father told us that when he'd gone to the other side, he was told all human beings come to this earth to learn one lesson: love. By dying on Valentine's Day, he was saying that he'd learned his lesson.

Those last five years with my father were some of the most memorable of my life. I wouldn't trade a second of the phenomenal experiences we shared, suspended between the worlds.

As I said in my father's eulogy, "The angels must have been glorious when they came for him."

Barbara left that day, too. I haven't heard from her or seen her since. I have a feeling I will see her again someday . . . when it's my turn to see Daddy again.

Reincarnation Proof

W hen it comes to reincarnation, a lot of people just plain don't believe it. They need proof. They fear the proof, even if they saw it firsthand. The rest believe they'll be damned in some manner for believing in reincarnation.

I rather take the stance that reincarnation is like microwaves were fifty years ago. Just because you can't see the microwaves doesn't mean that someday we won't be cooking with microwave ovens. For me, reincarnation is about the most common-sense, religious/spiritual belief anyone could come up with.

The Bible says, "You reap what you sow." If a person chooses to be destructive, mean and evil in one life and he or she seems to make it through life always on the winning side, it makes sense to me that first, perhaps they "earned" that abundance in a previous life of charity and second, justice will find them on the losing side in their next life.

Life is a series of lessons. Since we know there is no such thing as linear time—Einstein showed us that—then life is an explosion of lives happening all at the same time, just in different places, circumstances and time periods.

I suppose you could say the people are the same, they just wear different costumes. The key cohesive factor in all these life experiences is love. We are all here to learn the lesson of love, in one way or another.

Sometimes it's self-love: to love ourselves enough not to deny our inner spiritual and divine connection to God. God loves us, so why not love ourselves? We can't be all that bad. Relationships with our families, friends, co-workers, nation, even our enemies, are what make our lives.

Understanding all the above will help you to understand the following two incidents that happened to me.

I slipped in time. I traveled back to past time, without losing focus of the present dimension in which I stood. I was shaking, but I was standing. I was not meditating. I was not praying. I was not fasting, on drugs, drinking or even taking a non-aspirin substitute. I was not sick or hungry. Both times this amazing event happened to me, I was perfectly normal and sane. I was not in a tumultuous emotional state whatsoever. In fact, both times I slipped back in time were lovely, sunny days. If anything, both times I'd felt as if all troubles or trauma were something of the past. I was happy. Content.

Because of this tranquil frame of mind, I find these incidents even more fascinating. Perhaps there is something to the saying, "Let go and let God."

The Grand Canyon

My sister, Nancy, and I had flown to Flagstaff, Arizona, to see my father after his first heart attack. (See "Glorious Angel" for a more detailed explanation of his near-death experience.)

Several days after visiting Daddy and knowing he was resting as comfortably as could be expected, we decided to drive up to the Grand Canyon. None of us had ever seen it, and it was Daddy's wish that we would view his favorite natural wonder.

For a writer to not be able to describe something is humiliating, and shakes the roots of my writing skills. The Grand Canyon is beyond description. It is an experience of visual wonder. Its timelessness pervades the soul, minimalizing one's existence to that speck of sand we know we are when we encounter the magnitude of the universal heavens on a clear night.

Such was my mind-set when Nancy and I stood on the south rim of the canyon, gazing at the morning sun illuminating the varied colorations of rock cliffs. Nancy, who was well-versed in geology—she had a master's in rocks—rattled on and on about the Jurassic period layer, the Mesozoic period and more. I was trying to memorize what she knew as she explained why each layer was a different color rock, but instead something bizarre began to happen.

In an instant, the air around me became heavier. The sunbeams on the canyon walls were infused with a golden light, as if the world were viewed through a sepia-toned filter. I could still hear Nancy's voice, but she sounded as distant as if she had moved away.

The knowledge hit me like a thunderbolt. I had slipped back in time.

I knew the year was 1903. I don't know how I knew it, but it was as if the mind of the girl I now was contained a different form of reference. The time of day was the same, about 11:30. I knew the day was the same, Tuesday. But the year was not the same.

I was fascinated by the difference in the air quality and at the time, I didn't think to question it. I kept my eyes trained on the rock across from me, still examining the alteration in the density of the air. I didn't dare move and break this spell I was in. I also didn't want to slip so far back that I wouldn't return to the present. I can't say that I was afraid, but I was cautious.

I wiggled my toes, and that was when I realized that my shoes were boots. They were tightly laced up my ankles and my ankles hurt from the lacings. I didn't think to untie them, I felt that I was used to wearing tight lacings and that for some reason, I preferred my shoes laced in this manner.

It was then I realized, this girl was myself. Inside her head, I knew how things should be at that point in time. I knew that I was on a vacation, that I did not live there. I knew that I wanted to turn, go to the wagon and get a camera that we had brought along. The camera equipment was quite extensive, but I knew that taking photographs was the primary reason for our visit that day. I knew Nancy was my friend, not my sister, and that her real name in that other time was something more French sounding, like Nanette or Lucette.

My mind was flitting from age to age, personality to personality. It was very strange and frightening, but I did feel that I had been this person before. I didn't feel as if I "fell into her," like a lost soul in time being plunked into someone's body. I felt comfortable. I felt like me. Basically, I was nearly the same height and size. My hair was dark, my eyes blue, though I was rather young, in my teens, I believed.

Then I felt a wind across my cheek. I could "feel" a hat on my head. It was a straw hat, I knew, with a narrow brim. There were grosgrain ribbons hanging down my back and they flapped in the wind and hit my shoulder blades.

Still, I did not turn or dare to blink. I trained my hearing on the sound of my sister's voice.

Then I distinctly heard the whinny of a horse, as if I were standing in front of a horse-drawn buggy, wagon or carriage of some sort, though I did not turn to inspect it.

I touched my clothing. I could feel a thin cotton or linen skirt. It was white, or at least I had the impression that it was white. My white cotton blouse was tucked into the waistband of my skirt. I didn't feel that my clothing was anything special or expensive. It was rather ordinary, probably what most young women wore on a warm day at the turn of the century.

Again, I heard the horse whinny. Then the coach or wagon must have rolled back, because I heard the crunch of stones or shells beneath the wheels. The sound was rather loud and it was enough so I missed a few of the words my sister was still saying.

"Nancy," I said without looking over at her. I didn't dare break my concentration.

"What?"

"Do me a favor?"

"Sure," she replied.

"Reach out and take my hand," I requested.

"Are you okay? You look rather pale," she replied.

"Just take my hand."

Nancy reached over and took my hand. I could feel a glove of some sort on my hand, the kind that has no fingers. When Nancy's hand touched mine, she was wearing a glove as well. Somehow Nancy's hand had slipped through that veil or time barrier or next-dimension wall and had moved into the time where I was, though she herself was still very much in the present.

I squeezed her hand. In an instant, I was back.

I didn't feel light-headed in the least, though Nancy claimed I was white as a sheet. I remember saying that maybe my blood sugar was low, but the truth was, I was confused. What had happened to me?

I believed I had slipped in time, but how do you tell someone, "Oh, I crossed a time barrier. You know, that thing scientists have been trying to do for a half million years or more." Wasn't this the next step to meeting an alien? And I sure as heck didn't want little green men sliding into my Grand Canyon tour.

I was dumbfounded, amazed and shocked.

I didn't ask for this to happen to me. I remember sitting down to lunch, looking at Nancy and explaining my experience. She didn't bat an eye.

"I believe you."

"What? How could you? I don't believe me!" I said. "The thing is, it wasn't but a blip of time. Maybe not even two whole minutes, but it seemed a lifetime. And what was that with how the air was so dense. I could almost taste dust in my mouth, it was so thick."

Nancy was nonplussed. "Cath, I saw your face. Something happened to you. There's no question in my mind. And as for the air, it makes sense to me. Nearly one-hundred years ago, our ozone layer was intact. The sunlight alone must have looked different than it does today. Perhaps that was what your experience was there to teach you."

"That I need to become an environmentalist?"

"Perhaps."

Nancy sometimes is too wise for words. She's always had a habit of taking a zillion pages I write, and nailing the kernel of truth in two words. If I'm the prosaic, she is the poet.

"This from a rock person," I said.

"Maybe this happened to you so that you could tell people about it. It could be it's time we took responsibility for the air we breathe. For one-hundred years we've been polluting the heck out of the water, earth and air. Your slip in time shows that what we've done has had a dramatic effect."

"But could we repair the ozone?"

Nancy smiled. "If God saw fit to have you slip in time to tell everyone about the air, don't you think he'll give someone, a scientist or inventor somewhere, the idea how to fix it?"

I returned her smile. "I understand inspiration. It happens to me all the time. Besides, I think you're right. It would be a silly waste of God's time to slip me in and out of time barriers, if he wasn't trying to make a profound point.

"I'm not sure if he wants me to clean up the air or if he simply wants to drive home the message that all times are one, or maybe I'm supposed to realize that there truly are past lives. That we all continue on, age after age."

Nancy shrugged her shoulders. "I think you got a package deal."

I felt like slapping my palm against my forehead. "It's all of the above. Layer on layer. Truth upon truth."

Nancy agreed. "I also think that the more you ponder on your experience, you'll see more messages."

At that point the waiter came and took our order. We gazed at the Grand Canyon out the giant plate glass window.

"It's just awesome. All of it. The canyon. Slipping in time. Daddy's recovery. What an incredible time in our lives," I said to Nancy.

"Well, look at it this way. You can cross time travel off your list. You won't have to do that again!"

I remember laughing with relief.

I had no idea that six years later my time travel would be much more profound.

The Arizona Biltmore Hotel

I t was springtime 1992, and I had traveled to Scottsdale with a friend who had business there. I'd spent weeks working long hours on a new novel, which though always fun and exhilarating, still takes plain hard work. I was looking forward to being in Scottsdale and relaxing poolside with a novel.

On our second day there, I was totally relaxed after spending a day in a chaise lounge and a night under the clear, starry Arizona skies. This was rejuvenation.

On Sunday, we decided to have brunch at the Arizona Biltmore Hotel. I'd heard about the hotel, but frankly, knew little about it. Had I known it had been built by Frank Lloyd Wright, one of my all-time favorite architects, I probably would have suggested we book a night there.

The hotel was situated at the base of Camelback Mountain and had been built in the late 1930s, and opened in the early 1940s. It was a mecca for all the hot movie stars at the time.

Clark Gable, Gary Cooper and more came to golf and enjoy the clean Arizona air, much the same as I was doing.

We strolled through the lobby, crammed with authentic Frank Lloyd Wright designed and commissioned furniture. I was nearly drooling over the period Tiffany lamps, the mission tables, the sleek chairs and the heavily upholstered sofas. It was like a walk back in time.

We explored it all. I bought souvenirs for my son and my girlfriends in the gift shop, slipped into several of the ballrooms and stopped for coffee in the patio coffeehouse. Finally, we walked through an arbor and to the back of the hotel where the pool with the original cabana houses stood. I loved seeing some of the original metal lawn chairs still in use, as well as a couple vintage lounges just for the fun of it.

It was early Sunday morning and, therefore, not a soul was about. We had the pool area to ourselves. We chatted for a while, commenting on the beautiful plantings. I was amazed at the profusion of colorful snapdragons and pansies. It was all so beautiful.

Then, we rounded a curving path that led past tall, meticulously manicured hedges to the tennis courts. Again, there was no one around. Even the pro shop was not open, which disappointed my friend who wanted to purchase a new tennis racquet. We went up to the metal fence and I gazed onto the empty courts.

For the second time in my life, I slipped in time.

I grabbed onto the metal fencing with my hands. This time, I was not with my loving sister, Nancy. This time, I was with an out-and-out skeptic about such things. I didn't dare say anything.

"Cath, are you all right? You look pale."

"Pale?" I felt my breath catch in my lungs. I kept staring at the tennis courts.

"Translucent. Transparent. Pale. What's the matter?"

I couldn't help thinking I was fading away into another time zone.

At this point, my experience became even more surreal than the previous "slip" six years earlier. Suddenly, I heard the voices of two men who were laughing, and then they appeared. Ghosts, specters of the past, they were dressed in tennis outfits clearly from the late thirties or early forties.

They wore long white slacks, not shorts. Their sweaters were V-necked, edged in black. Their racquets were nothing like the lightweight aluminum racquets we used. They were made of wood, with different stringing. Even the tennis balls looked different. They were white with black stitching.

One of the men turned around to face me. I felt my heart stop. I gasped aloud.

"Come on! Come play with us," he said.

I realized the ghost was my companion in this life. As the ghost he was much older, perhaps twenty years older, and quite obese.

Just as before, my clothing altered. In the past dimension, I was wearing a similar V-necked white sweater, edged in black. I wore a tennis skirt that was nearly to my knees, edged in black. I remember thinking that the fabric was sharkskin. I wore a scarf around my face to tie my long hair back so that it wouldn't get in my eyes. My shoes were light as feathers and my anklets were rather thin stockings, as compared to the thick, bulky tennis socks I used in my current life.

I was very concerned about the ghost's health. I wanted him to quit playing. I wanted him to rest. I even said aloud, "The doctor said you shouldn't."

The ghost laughed at me, dismissing my concerns. He was having a wonderful time.

This time, I took more liberties with my "repositioning in time" and looked down. The tall, manicured hedges I had just passed only moments ago were now short, tiny new plantings. The tops of the hedges rose only to my mid-calf.

I clung to the fence with a firmer grip. Truly, this was not happening to me.

Then the ghost moved slightly to the side and his tennis partner ghost was revealed to me.

I stared at the older man. I didn't know him yet, we had not been introduced. But in that moment, his eyes met mine. He had dark brown eyes and he was older than myself at the time as well. I heard my lover ghost tell me that this man was a movie producer and that he was interested in my latest screenplay.

I was shocked. I had always, always thought that if I was ever anything in a previous life, if such things were real, I knew I had to be a writer.

I kept staring at the man and never in my life, this one or that one, have I ever seen such incredible lust in a man's eyes. It was one of those kinds of looks that I could only imagine happen in fiction, not in real life. But then, this wasn't real life. This was a dream. A time-travel dream.

The man kept staring at me. He didn't smile, but he sent me telepathic messages, all of which carried one bottom line. He wanted me. I knew it was more than sexual need. This was a meeting of souls across time.

It scared the heck out of me.

"Catherine, what's the matter with you?"

My companion's hand clamped around my arm. "What?" I turned and looked at him.

I was back in the present.

"You're sweating and it's not fifty degrees out here. Your skin is clammy. You're as white as a sheet. Are you sick? Is it the flu or something?"

"Or something," I said, looking around to see if anyone had seen me. Then I thought to myself, see me do what? Transform? Transmute? What was I doing? How could this happen twice?

The worst part was that my companion didn't even like Peter Pan or ET. How could I explain something like this?

"I'm fine," I replied.

"Maybe we should get something to eat," he said.

"We just finished breakfast," I replied. "I was just looking at how lovely the tennis courts were. I was wondering what they must have been like when this hotel was first built. I was imagining the movie stars who used to come here," I lied.

"Like who? Lon Chaney?" He took my arm protectively. "Come on, let's get some juice."

"Okay," I said giving in. In fact, I just wanted to forget my experience. The fact that this had happened once before to me didn't make matters better. It made them worse. I questioned my sanity, as I always do when paranormal situations creep up on me. It's a natural reaction.

We turned and passed a two-story wing of hotel rooms to our left from the tennis courts. I glanced up to the corner room, second floor—and it happened again.

I was back there. On that day in the early forties, I surmised. I was in the hotel room with my ghostly tennis lover. There was a blond wood chest or bar against a wall and on top was every manner of whiskey and Scotch in the world. We were drinking Scotch on the rocks, no water, not even a splash, in heavy crystal glasses. I never drank Scotch in my present life. It was too strong for my taste. The fact of the matter, I was inexplicably repulsed by it.

I was wrapped in a towel with a towel on my head, just after bathing. He was coming out of the shower in a terry-cloth robe, drying his hair. There was a huge Cuban cigar in the ashtray, still burning. He was full of energy and life and I loved him very much.

I was cold to him. We had been arguing. I was angry, because he had promised to leave his wife and would not. I had the impression this argument had gone on for years. I was tired of fighting a fight I could not win.

Suddenly, he dropped to the floor. There was not an instant to save him. He was dead.

I felt a wave of agonizing pain and loss, the breaking of the eternal heart.

Then, just as suddenly, I was back in the present.

"What are you doing?" my companion asked.

"Nothing," I quickly replied, wondering if I was dreaming this whole past/present thing entirely.

"Why did you stop like that?" he asked, raising his eyes to the same corner window. "What's up there? Did you see someone you know?"

I couldn't believe how on-target he was with his questions. It was as if he intuitively knew what was happening, but could not bring himself to admit it.

"I was just wondering how long those rooms have been here."

"They're part of the original structure."

"In the early forties, they were part of the hotel?"

"That's right," he replied, taking my hand. "Come on, I want to show you this favorite little place of mine."

We walked under the arbor and back into the hotel. To the right of the back entrance was a small alcove with a small fireplace, perfect for cuddling or contemplation.

"When I lived in Scottsdale, I would come here to think. I don't know what it is about this little area, but it speaks to me," he explained as we sat on another original sofa, flanked by two original Wright lamps. The window was huge, offering a view of pretty gardens.

Just as before, I was slipping again.

Gazing out the window, I could see the specters of the past. Beautifully dressed women in long gowns and men in tuxedos were dancing on a terrace to a large band seated under a garden arbor.

"What happened to the dance terrace?" I asked aloud, without a censoring thought in my head.

"What?"

Training my eyes on the scene from the past, I replied, "People used to dance out here in long gowns and tuxedos."

"Yes, they did when the hotel was new. But there's no way you could know that, is there?"

"No."

"Tell me the truth," he asked good-naturedly. "You read up on the history of the hotel before we left Houston."

"No. How could I have time to do that, when I've been writing about Chicago? I've never even heard of the hotel. When I came to Arizona before, I was in Flagstaff with my father in the hospital. I've only seen the Phoenix airport, like I told you. Sedona, I know. Scottsdale is completely new to me."

Finally, the dance scene faded. I was completely back in the present. "You didn't answer my question. When did they remove the terrace?"

"A long time ago. I'm not certain exactly when. But it was attached to the dining room here. They opened the doors and after supper there was always dancing. There's a hallway with all kinds of photos of when the hotel was under construction and its opening years, if you like."

My jaw dropped. Validation? Just the thought of finding historical evidence to back up my "visions" or "slips" or whatever they were, was too good to be true.

"Let's do it," I said and we rose.

Just as we walked out of the alcove, the thought struck me that this little place was also quite dear to me in that "other life." I had also come here to contemplate my life. I gazed back at the fireplace, and for a flash, I saw myself seated on that sofa dressed in a dinner gown, blue satin I think it was. I was inordinately sad. I wasn't certain if this was a scene before or after the death of my lover, but I could feel the woman's heart breaking.

I was overwhelmed with emotion. I wanted so much to go to her, put my arms around her and console her. The least I could do was bless her. Whoever she was.

In the history hall, I called it, there were, and probably still are, fantastic black and white photographs of movie stars and hotel golf pros, staff, managers and Scottsdale residents arm in arm enjoying the hotel grounds.

Examining the photos, I did not see anyone who looked like me in any manner, whatsoever. I suppose I took far too long looking at the smiling faces staring back at me from a time forgotten, because my companion complained that he wanted to go for a jog before lunch.

I decided I could come back later, after lunch, and finish my investigation. Just as I was about to walk away, a particular photograph caught my eye.

I stood stockstill. Goosebumps shot down my spine. Staring back at me was the face of the man who had died in my past life vision/dream.

I gasped, but tried not to call any more attention to the moment than necessary. For one thing, my companion was already thinking I was coming down with the flu. If I'd told him the truth about what was happening, he would have thought I was nuts. He scoffed at mental telepathy. Time travel would have put his narrow-mindedness over the brink. He couldn't handle it.

Secondly, I was getting more than a bit nervous about moving from one dimension to the other as it was. I feared that if I concentrated on that photograph, I'd find myself back there again. That would be four times in one day. What if it was possible for someone to travel back or forward in time and never return?

All I knew was that the woman I was then had been crushingly unhappy in that life. I didn't want to be her. I wouldn't have known how to handle her grief any better than she had.

As ill luck would have it, there was no description or plaque with information about who the people in the photograph were. I was sorely disappointed. To have a name I could track down would have helped enormously.

We went for our jog, ate lunch and after stopping at the reception desk, we received a message about a particular meeting for my companion back in Houston. We had to cut our stay short by a day. We packed hurriedly to catch the next flight back to Houston.

This incident took place over eight years ago. I have not been back to Scottsdale since that time and, as a result, have not visited the Arizona Biltmore Hotel.

What is curious to me, even today, as I retell this story, is that those moments of seeing into the past are as vivid to me now as they were then. I believe that truths stick with us. When we have a certain dream that changes our life somehow, an angelic dream, it stays with us decade after decade.

I suppose I'll never really know if I was gifted with an insight to the past, or if I actually "moved" back there somehow. Physicists will discover the axioms of time and space more accurately in the future. That explanation will give the skeptics the "facts" they desperately need to provide them comfort.

For me, I only know my own truth. That's what life is all about, isn't it? Finding our own truth.

Even though I never traveled back in time again, I did have one more incident that validated this particular time travel incident. Read "Forever Yours" for that story.

Forever Yours

A year after the incident at the Arizona Biltmore Hotel, cracks in the foundation of my relationship with my companion had become fissures. The largest schism between us was our differences in spirituality.

He was a die-hard humanist, he said. He'd long ago tossed away his religious beliefs and, though I claimed he threw the baby out with the bathwater, he spent the better part of his time arguing with me and pointing out the fallacy of my faith in God.

The underpinnings of my tolerance burst free. I decided we would be best parted. However, there was a strong bond between us and emotionally, neither of us was ready to let go. We decided to give it one more try.

My idea of once again around the block included his acceptance of my spiritual and religious way of life. I was not so concerned with trying to convert him, but rather only wanted to be myself.

He agreed and wanted to prove his earnestness. Again he reiterated that he did not believe in past lives or life after death, despite my stories about my father's dying experiences. Nor, did he believe in a great and lovely place where our souls go between this and our next life, whatever and wherever that is to be. He said humans were maggot food.

Frankly, such thinking to me is so depressing and life then becomes so pointless, I wonder that any of these people see any merit in living whatsoever. If it's just a ride for nothing, then where do they get their hope? Why would they even want to be nice to anyone? What point would there be to loving their families or caring about friends? And how can they possibly not be committing suicide in droves? Just what in the world are they doing here?

"Prove to me the soul lives on," he challenged, "and I'll believe you. I'll become your greatest disciple."

I knew in that moment, I had one shot to make my point. No argument or debate was going to do the trick. I needed a demonstration. "I have a meditation you can try. In it, you will regress to our most recent past life together. If you don't see anything, experience anything, then I will never mention past lives to you again. I'll keep my mouth shut, though I won't stop believing. Plenty of couples have made it through with mixed religions under one roof. Ours would be no different. On the other hand, if you do see something, you will tell me about it and we will go on from there. Agreed?"

"Absolutely. But tell me," he said, "how do you know about this regression thing?"

"I read a book by Kenneth L. Ring years ago, when my father had his first near-death experience. In the back of the book, there is a meditation to go back through your past lives, which will have the most influence on the situations in this present life. It helped me to understand why I've done some of the things I have. Why certain people came into my life and then left again. It helped me to understand the cause and effect of my own actions, and the actions of others on me. It makes a lot of sense when you look at it that way."

"Never let it be said I was chicken," he quipped. "Now how do we do this?"

I explained that he only needed to relax and keep an open mind. In fact, I didn't think it was possible for him to open his mind. Therefore, I prayed to every one of my angels and guides and repeated the "Our Father" about six times to myself as we started. The conclusion to this demonstration, whichever way it went, was going to determine the path of my life, as well as his. Talk about crossroads time. This was it in spades.

He stretched out on the sofa. I repeated a relaxation litany commonly used in all meditations. This process took about ten minutes, relaxing the face muscles, down the shoulders to the arms, the torso and down to the toes.

Then I asked him to imagine rising above his body and floating all the way to the stratosphere. Going through the different colors of the spectrum from a cloud of the color red, to orange, yellow, green, blue, indigo and finally white, I had him imagine himself looking down on earth from an angel's eye view.

Then he was to float back to earth, coming back in our most recent past life together.

Slowly, as his feet hit the earth, I asked him to look only at his feet. Then to describe the kind of shoes he was wearing.

"Spats," he said clearly.

I was stunned. Of all the people on earth to actually find himself in the middle of a past-life regression, this was not the man. I choked. I was so elated, I nearly forgot how to proceed. If nothing else happened that day, I had my validation. I thanked God. I could ask for no more.

But I did get more. A lot more.

"I'm walking down a sidewalk. It's brick, not concrete."

"Where are you?" I asked.

"San Francisco," he said, his eyes still shut, but from the flutters of his eyelids, I could tell he was seeing something.

"Do you know what year it is?"

"Maybe 1920. It's just after World War I."

"Where are you going?"

"To my theatre. I'm the owner. I produce vaudeville acts and little plays. Nothing highbrow. Just entertainment. I'm rich. I'm going up to my office, but I stop on the stairs."

"Why?"

"I'm listening to a woman singing. She has the most beautiful voice I've ever heard. It's you."

"Me?"

"Yes, I'm your employer."

At this point, my hands were shaking. I'd turned cold all over. Often I've been told I have an exceptional speaking voice, and in my younger years, I could sing rather well. I've thought before that if my life had turned out differently, I might have wanted to be a singer. Not a rock band singer, but a chanteuse, singing ballads and torchy, bleeding love songs.

"We know each other then," I finally said.

"I love you. Just as I do now. But there's a problem. I'm very unhappy."

"Why?"

"Because I'm married and I can't get a divorce. I have two children and my wife wants another child."

"Are we lovers?"

"Not yet, but I know we will be."

I was becoming quite uncomfortable at this point. I'd never thought of myself as a homewrecker, but perhaps I was once.

"Move ahead a few years," I asked him. "Tell me what you see."

"I've moved my family to Los Angeles. I'm producing movies now."

"Am I with you?"

"You're a screenwriter. You and I break up a lot. But that's because I won't leave my wife. I am so desperately unhappy. I've never known people could hurt this much inside."

Tears slipped out from under his eyes as he went on.

"We're at the Arizona Biltmore Hotel. I'm watching you drive up. My God, what a lot of luggage you have. All matching alligator suitcases. You have enough clothes to stay a month."

I stopped him. "You say I drove up?"

"Yes, in the car I bought for you."

Chills covered my forearms. Repeatedly in my teens, I had nightmares about dying in a car accident. I saw the car go over a cliff, and I was quite clear about the kind of car. In my dreams and later in a past-life regression, I clearly saw a yellow Stutz Bearcat convertible with whitewall tires and a tan interior. The thing I remember most about the nightmares, was hanging onto the mother-of-pearl steering wheel.

I had never told anyone about these dreams. No man. No girlfriend knew about those dreams. They were my most private fears.

My tongue stuck to the roof of my mouth as I asked, "What is the color of the car?"

"Yellow. It has light beige or tan leather seats. It's a convertible, I'll tell you that. It cost me a small fortune, but I thought it would make you happy, especially since I couldn't marry you."

"What else about the car?"

"It's a 1933 Stutz Bearcat."

I froze. In my wildest imaginings, I had never, ever thought I would find this much proof for past lives and, especially, for our past life together. He and I were more connected than I'd thought. My next question nearly didn't make it out of my mouth, I was so terrified of the answer. "What kind of steering wheel is it? Leather-wrapped?"

"No. It's mother-of-pearl."

Bingo.

I felt the blood drain out of me. I almost didn't want to go on, but I'd come too far. I had to know the rest. Because I had never told him the details of my slip in time back at the Arizona Biltmore Hotel, I wanted to know what he saw.

"Move ahead a few hours. What are we doing?"

"Playing tennis. You're pretty terrific. A natural-born tennis player. Not like in this life," he laughed aloud.

I was shocked that he was so adept at his ability to view the past and still comment on the present. This was his first regression. In fact, he didn't believe in such things.

"What do we do after tennis?

"We're in our room now. I've just showered. You're sitting on the bed. You just washed your hair. I think you're beautiful and I say so. You tell me that the reason you brought all your clothes is because you want to move in with me. You are demanding I file for divorce. Or . . . you'll leave me."

"What is your reaction?"

"This time I know you mean it. You'll really leave. I've pushed you too far. I'm afraid. Terribly, terribly afraid. Then . . . oh, no. I'm dying. My heart. My arm hurts. God, the pain! Oh, God. Oh, God." He was suffering through it all. I didn't want him to suffer.

"Come away from the scene." I reached out to touch his hand. "Float up to the sky and tell me what you feel."

"I'm so happy to be out of that body. I was fat and drank and smoked too much. I promise myself in my next life, I'll never mistreat my body again. I'm so happy to be free."

I instructed him to come back to the present, slowly to enter his body, remember everything he saw and experienced and wake up.

When he opened his eyes, he was stunned. "It was so real what I saw. I felt everything that man was going through."

"He was you. In a past life."

He paused for a long moment, taking in this experience. I could see the wheels of his thought process turning. The ramifications of all this bombarded his carefully structured belief system. A fuse had been struck inside him and he was about to explode. He had been given the truth.

And he couldn't handle it. It was too much for him. It was too foreign. To believe in past lives means that we are all accountable for our deeds and misdeeds. The sins of the past haunt us today. Our sins of omission as much as our sins of commission influence, not only ourselves and our victims, but we carry the retribution to the next life. Those sins or misdeeds determine our necessary return.

Because my dying father had told me we are here to learn the lesson of love, I saw this man before me rejecting my love again. Just as he'd done in our previous life. I knew in that instant, that though my theory of past lives had been sub-stantiated, I was still going to lose him.

"You want me to leave, don't you?" I asked.

I will never forget the pain in his eyes. "Yes."

We parted that day. I've only seen or heard from him once or twice since then. He still professes that humans are all "maggot food."

I can understand how devastating it is to learn that every tenet in life you hold dear is false. Several times, desperate times, I've been so disillusioned about my life that I have done just that. Thrown everything out, started over and said to God, "prove to me you're still here." I've asked for a sign.

The difference is, I get them. Over and over, God, angels, my family and friends now in spirit, reveal themselves to me more than once or twice daily.

As long as I keep my angel watch, I know they will always appear.

The Wallet

I walked out of my manicurist's office without my wallet one day. I'd left it in the chair I'd occupied. It is a large French wallet given to me by a friend in Quito, Ecuador. Because Jim and I traveled so much back and forth to South America, nearly every piece of identification was in that wallet, including my passport. There was little money in it, only twenty dollars, hardly enough to tempt someone to steal it.

The second I got home, I realized it was missing. I telephoned the manicurist and asked her to look in the chair where I had been sitting, which she did. She came back on the line and said it was gone. I requested she look around the room to see if someone had moved it. Again she obliged. Again she came back to the phone and stated the wallet was clearly gone.

In a panic, I decided not to believe her. I drove back to the shop to see for myself.

It is amazing to me how tiny details of things miss our eyes as they are happening, but when we are in that altered state of anger, fear or panic, the smallest clues to our puzzle begin to present themselves.

I remembered a woman coming in off the street and asking for a nail repair. She was not a regular customer. She was a tall, large blond woman, who seemed to have a chip on her shoulder when she entered the room. It was as if her vibes were disordered. Everyone had looked up when she came in, as if an ill wind had blown through the shop. I remembered that she shot me a disparaging, dismissive look at the time. One of those "if looks could kill" glances. I had bristled at the psychic attack, and now, I remembered wondering at the time what she had against me. I'd never laid eyes on the woman in my life.

That woman had occupied my chair upon my departure. I was certain she had stolen my wallet.

That night, I was scheduled to baby-sit for my granddaughter for the first time so my son could go to the movie with his wife. Once I got to their house, I told them the story about the missing wallet. I asked them to pray with me.

"I want that woman to be so riddled with guilt and shame over her actions that she can't stand having that wallet around. I want her to imagine that wallet even being hot to the touch. I want her to be so upset with her actions, she tosses the wallet out of the car on her way home."

Ryan and Christy weren't quite sure if this was how I should have gone about my prayer, but they indulged me.

"Sometimes, God needs a little boost. That's what we're here for," I explained. "All I want is my wallet back. It will take months to replace my identification items and passport, and I have to fly back to South America in five days. I don't have time to waste. God will hurry things along, you'll see," I told them.

Caylin slept soundly that evening, which gave me time to think, pray and watch a movie. Ryan and Christy came home, hugged me good-bye, and I drove back to my house.

That night I asked my angels to help me out. Then I gave the mission over to them and got some sleep.

The very next day around ten in the morning, I received a phone call from a Hispanic man who told me he had found my wallet and wanted to return it.

I was overjoyed. I asked about the passport and driver's license. "They are here," he said.

I asked him if there was any money in the wallet. "Yes, twenty dollars."

I was incredulous. The woman hadn't even taken the money.

My rescuer gave me his address and I loaded Beau and Bebe into my Tahoe. Off we went to the man's apartment. All the way there, I was laughing and singing and thanking my angels and God for finding my wallet.

When I got to the man's apartment, he gave me the wallet for me to inspect. I couldn't believe he'd found it. Then the story took an even more bizarre twist.

At that time, we were living a block from the Galleria. We were half a block from the Marriott Hotel. This man had worked in the kitchens there for twenty years. He had worked his way up from busboy to a position on the night wait staff in the main dining room. He was proud of his work and his life in the United States. He had awards for excellence hanging on his apartment walls, right next to his Mexican silver crucifix.

Unbelievably, the man found my wallet in the middle of Westheimer street right in front of the Marriott. This was only half a block from our townhouse! He had come out of the hotel late that night, walked to the streetlight and saw the wallet.

I told him that this was so strange to me since my manicurist shop, where I'd lost the wallet, was over six miles away.

"It's not strange. The angels brought your wallet back," he said.

Chills raked my skin. I knew he was right. "Most definitely they did," I replied. I offered him the twenty dollars in the wallet, but he didn't want it. I urged him to take it.

"I will give it to my church," he said.

We shook hands and I left. I thought at the time I would never see him again.

The next morning when I was walking my dogs, I heard a car horn honk at me. I turned around and the same man waved merrily to me. "Hello, Catherine! How are you and the doggies?"

I waved happily back, and again chills coursed my spine. I kept thinking I would call him again once I was back, to thank him for returning my wallet intact.

I went back to South America with my wallet, passport and papers securely tucked away in my bag.

When I returned that fall, I called the man at the number he'd given me as his apartment number. One of those computer operators came on the line and said that the number I had dialed was not a working number.

I stared at the receiver and smiled. Of course it was not working. Where he was, they didn't need telephones.

Soul-Mating

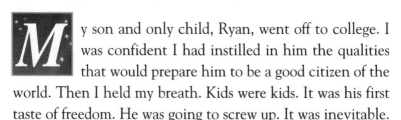

My son and only child, Ryan, went off to college. I was confident I had instilled in him the qualities that would prepare him to be a good citizen of the world. Then I held my breath. Kids were kids. It was his first taste of freedom. He was going to screw up. It was inevitable.

I had no time for "empty nest syndrome." I was preparing my lines for the moment when I would get those kinds of calls that we children of the 1960s and 70s gave our parents. "Hi'ya, Ma! I'm in jail." "But it was *just* beer! They said it was legal on campus!" Stuff like that.

Two weeks after my son went away, he came home, laundry bag in hand. His, his roommate's and that of a couple dorm mates. Since they were all Ryan's friends from high school and I'd been doing their laundry at times for four years, this was not unusual.

When I asked Ryan how he found college, other than filthy judging from the amount of dirty clothes he had, he said, "Well, you know, Mom, there are some really, really weird people on campus."

I imagined perverts, druggies, gangsta-type seniors, HIV-positive coeds pursuing their MRS. I asked, "Like how weird?"

"Like nutzoid. Mike and Carl and I went over to Darcey's room [Mike's girlfriend from home] to meet her roommate and some other freshmen girls. We were all crammed in this room and talking. Sharing old times from high school."

"But you only graduated three months ago."

"Yeah, like I said, Mom, old times." He continued. "There was this one girl there and she was just bizarro. We were all talking about stuff we did, who was going with whom and all that, and right in the middle of our conversation, this girl starts singing! Bursts into song. Not soft, but loud. Like kinda drowning out what we were trying to say. It was weird."

"The songs were weird?"

"No, *she* was weird. She wouldn't give it a rest, either. She would just keep humming to herself, even while we were talking."

"Where was she from?"

"Houston. But not from our school. Nobody knew her. She was assigned to her room. She didn't even know her roommate, Mom!"

"Imagine that!" I said, remembering my own college experience (wasn't that just last week?), when all our roommates were strangers.

"What kind of person wouldn't handpick their roommate?"

At this point I was feeling uneasy. Ryan was acting a bit too dictatorial. He sheepishly avoided my eye contact.

"Ryan, by any chance did you make fun of that girl?"

Silence.

My skin crawled with goosebumps and, suddenly, I envisioned myself in that room with those kids. I knew them all, except the singing girl. I also knew the razor-keen, caustic sense of humor my son possessed. He could give Robin Williams a run for his money. Suddenly, I felt the singing girl. Felt her pain, embarrassment and yes, her loneliness.

There were tears in my eyes as I hugged myself. "Ryan, you've always been too picky about people. I think you said something to hurt this girl. Something that maybe didn't seem like much to you, but to her was biting and dreadful. The minute you get back to campus, I want you to find that girl and you apologize to her."

"Aw, Ma . . ."

"I mean it, Ryan. This is very important. I sense that she's a very sensitive person. You don't have to become blood brothers with her, just apologize."

"Okay, Mom. I'll do it."

Ryan went back to school on Sunday night and immediately looked up the girl. He called me late Monday night and said, "Mom, you know the singing girl? She's gone! Her roommate told me that she left campus. Dropped out! Went back to Houston and enrolled at University of Houston."

I started crying.

"It's all my fault, Mom. I just know I hurt her, like you said."

"Let this be a lesson to you, Ryan, and from now on, always treat other people the way you would like to be treated."

His voice was smothered in guilt. "I promise."

The year passed and Ryan came home from college older and wiser. That summer, he worked long and incredibly hard hours in our swimming pool and spa business.

He and the crew delivered a spa to one of our customers who telephoned my husband later that day and said, "My daughter Christy saw a young man delivering our spa and she would like to go out with him, but she's too shy to ask. Could you tell me who the tall, blond boy is?"

"My son," my husband answered. "I'll be happy to pass along the message."

Ryan was puzzled. "I never saw a girl there. Though I do remember someone watching through the curtains at the bedroom window. Maybe that was her."

Ryan called Christy and made a date for the following Saturday night. He met Christy's parents and chatted with them, explaining where he was taking their daughter on their date and at what time they could expect them to return. Anne and Alan seemed pleased with the arrangement.

When they got to Ryan's car and were about to pull away from the curb, Ryan turned to Christy and said, "You were the singing girl in Darcy's room."

"Yes, Ryan. I was."

"I'm so sorry for how I treated you."

"I know you are, Ryan," Christy said.

When Ryan came home that night and told me the story, we both had tears in our eyes. I was flooded with that incredible feeling I get when I know my life has been divinely touched.

I looked at my son and said, "Ryan, you're going to marry that girl someday."

"I know, Mom." And he did, several years later.

Of all the joys in my life, knowing that my son found his soul mate is the greatest of them all.

Postscript

ngel Watch, I have discovered upon its completion, has evolved into an autobiography, albeit from an angel's-eye perspective. To my knowledge, no one has written a spiritual autobiography, so again, I find my destiny being one of creating new genres, new ways of stripping away preconceived notions and the manner in which we struggle as humans to categorize ourselves and our lives.

Because I have not told all my stories here and because I have only begun my spiritual quest, my evolution, there will be new stories to come. I am already compiling more of these stories in my next book, *Angel Watch, Cloud Two*.

If you have enjoyed these stories, I would like to hear from you. Perhaps you have a special story to tell, or would like to contribute your own special angelic intervention incident to my next book. If so, you can mail your story to me at:

Catherine Lanigan
5644 Westheimer Road
PMB #110
Houston, Texas 77056

If you would like a copy of my newsletter and an *Angel Watch* autographed bookmark, please enclose a stamped, self-addressed legal size envelope (best size for the bookmarks) with your letter or story. I open and read every letter I get, and I respond to everyone.

Or if you are only sending your story, you can fax it to 713-622-4105.

Or you can e-mail me at *cath_lake@prodigy.net* or you can visit my web site at *www.clanigan.com.*

God bless all of you on your journey over, under, around and through your divine path. Remember, the angels are watching, but it's more important that *you* keep angel watch.

Bibliography

Alper, Matthew. *The God Part of the Brain*. New York: Rogue Press, 2000.

Bell, Art, and Brad Steiger. *The Source*. New Orleans: Paper Chase Press, 1999.

Brinkley, Dannion. *Saved by the Light*. New York: Harper, 1995.

Bro, Harmon Hartzell. *A Seer Out of Season: The Life of Edgar Cayce*. New York: Signet, 1990.

Cayce, Hugh Lynn. *The Edgar Cayce Collection: Edgar Cayce on Dreams; Edgar Cayce on Healing; Edgar Cayce on Diet and Health; Edgar Cayce on ESP*. New York: Bonanza Books, 1986.

Cerminara, Gina. *Many Mansions: The Edgar Cayce Story*. New York: Signet, 1950.

Faraday, Anne. *Dream Power: Learn to Use the Vital Self-Knowledge That Lies Stored in Your Dreams*. New York: Berkley, 1972.

Fiore, Edith. *You Have Been Here Before: A Psychologist Looks at Past Lives*. New York: Ballantine, 1978.

Furst, Jeffery, ed. *Edgar Cayce's Story of Jesus*. New York: Berkley, 1976.

Goldberg, Bruce. *Past Lives, Future Lives*. New York: Ballantine, 1982.

Goldman, Malcum. *Angels: An Endangered Species*. New York: Simon and Schuster, 1990.

Graham, Billy. *Angels*. Dallas: Word Publishing, 1975.

Harris, Errol E. *The Reality of Time*. Albany, New York: State University of New York Press, 1988.

Hegel, G. W. F., Transl. J. Baillie. *Phenomenology of Mind*. London: G. Allen and Unwin, reprint 1966.

Heidegger, Martin. *Holzwege*. Frankfurt, Germany: Frankfurt-am-Main, 1952.

Hillman, James. *The Soul's Code*. New York: Warner Books, 1997.

Holmes, Ernest. *The Science of Mind*. New York: Dodd, Mead and Company, 1938.

Houston, Jean. *The Search for the Beloved*. New York: St. Martin's Press, 1987.

Janes, Julian. *The Origin of Consciousness in the Breakdown of the Bicameral Mind*. Boston: Houghton Mifflin Company, 1976.

Kenyon, Tom. *Brain States*. Naples, Florida: United States Publishing, 1994.

McDannell, Colleen, and Bernhard Lang. *Heaven: A History*. New York: Vintage, 1990.

Moody, Raymond A. Jr. *Coming Back: A Psychiatrist Explores Past-Life Journeys*. New York: Bantam, 1991.

___. *Life after Life*. New York: Bantam. Mockingbird Books, 1976.

Morse, Melvin. *Closer to the Light: Learning from Children's Near Death Experiences.* New York: Random House, 1990.

Peale, Norman Vincent. *Positive Imaging.* New York: Fawcett, 1982.

Peck, M. Scott. *In Heaven as On Earth.* New York: Hyperion, 1996.

___. *People of the Lie: The Hope for Healing Human Evil.* New York: Hyperion, 1989.

Ponder, Catherine. *The Dynamic Laws of Prosperity.* Marina Del Rey, California: DeVorss and Company, 1962.

Prophet, Elizabeth Clare. *Violet Flame to Heal Body, Mind and Soul.* Corwin Springs, MT: Summit University Press, 1997.

Rawlings, Maurice. *Beyond Death's Door.* New York: Bantam Books, 1978.

Reed, Henry. *Edgar Cayce on Mysteries of the Mind.* New York: Warner, 1989.

Ring, Kenneth. *Heading Toward Omega.* New York: Morrow, 1990.

___. *The Omega Project.* New York: Morrow, 1992.

Schlotterbeck, Karl. *Living Your Past Lives: The Psychology of Past Life Regression.* New York: Ballantine, 1989.

Sheldrake, Rupert. *A New Science of Life: The Hypothesis of Formative Causation.* Boston: Houghton Mifflin Company, 1981.

Steiger, Brad. *Guardian Angels and Spirit Guides.* New York: Signet, 1995.

Steiger, Brad, and Francie Steiger. *The Star People.* New York: Berkley, 1981.

Strean, Herbert, and Lucy Freeman. *The Severed Soul.* New York: St. Martin's Press, 1990.

Teilhard de Chardin, P., trans. B. Wall, Introduction by Julian Huxley. *The Phenomenon of Man*. New York: Harper and Row, 1959.

Twitchell, Paul. *The Eck-Vidya*. Minneapolis: Eckankar, 1972.

___. *Eckankar: The Key to Secret Worlds*. Crystal, Minnesota: Illuminated Way Publishing, 1969.

Van Praagh, James. *Reaching to Heaven*. New York: Dutton, 1999.

___. *Talking to Heaven*. New York: Signet, 1999.

Weiss, Brian L. *Many Lives, Many Masters*. New York: Fireside, 1988.

Wilson, Colin. *C. G. Jung: Lord of the Underworld*. Wellingsborough, England: Thorsons Publishing Group, 1984.

Zukav, Gary. *The Seat of the Soul*. New York: Fireside, 1990.